Moving with the
Face of the Devil

Moving with the
Face of the Devil

ART AND POLITICS IN URBAN WEST AFRICA

John W. Nunley

UNIVERSITY OF ILLINOIS PRESS

URBANA AND CHICAGO

This book is made possible in part by a grant
from the Ruttenberg Arts Foundation.

This book is printed on acid-free paper.

LIBRARY OF CONGRESS CATALOGING-IN-PUBLICATION DATA

Nunley, John W. (John Wallace), 1945-
  Moving with the face of the devil.

  Bibliography: p.
  Includes index.
  1. Secret societies—Sierra Leone—Freetown.
2. Masks—Sierra Leone—Freetown. 3. Arts and society—
Sierra Leone—Freetown. 4. Freetown (Sierra Leone)—
Social life and customs. I. Title.
GN655.S5N85 1987   306′.1′09664   85-16455
ISBN 0-252-01015-9

For my son,
Boyd Farris Nunley

Contents

Illustrations

Preface

The cultural complexity of Freetown is a boon to the student of cultural change, yet this phenomenon is itself nearly impossible to convey through the printed word. While driving on main streets of the city or walking through its neighborhoods, I routinely encountered masquerades. Some evenings I saw as many as three or four groups dancing, singing, and parading with their masqueraders, who in the local Krio language are called *devils*. This term, which undoubtedly originated with the missionaries, has lost its pejorative meaning and today denotes respect for the spiritual essence of the mask costumes. They say in Freetown that it is impossible to move with all the devils, but I eventually came to know which masquerade societies existed and were prominent in each neighborhood.

Mountain Cut is a neighborhood I knew well. It is literally carved from hard-rock cliffs at the foot of steeply rising hills that lead to Fourah Bay College. An old part of Freetown, it maintains the oldest of the city's mosques, while supporting the contemporary Firestone Ode-lay Society at 101 Red Pump. Its fine old Creole houses stand side by side with newly built concrete-walled apartments and the ubiquitous *pan-bodi ose* (a Krio term that denotes corrugated-metal-walled houses supported by wood-stick frames), suggesting the paradoxical meeting of old and new. Vacant lots, crown land, mountain streams, record shops, and an old cemetery cradled the Ode-lay societies while also sparking the appearance of the first Yoruba Hunting and Egungun ancestral societies, with their gods of iron (Ogun) and thunder (Shango), which the freed slaves brought from Nigeria. Mercedes Benzes, Peugeots, lorries, Japanese-made taxis, and wooden carts propelled by human power ply the streets of Mountain Cut and create traffic problems for both commuters and processional masqueraders. Vehicles give way to the ritual of mask spirits, as the spirits' attendants sprinkle medicines on their masqueraders to make them invincible. No one may obstruct the devil processions.

Procession permits are issued to masqueraders, who report at the Central Police Station to request forms and copies of regulations. Some societies, through political connections, are granted permits; other groups, which sometimes did not back a particular candidate in a past election, are refused. After careful screening, masked devils occasionally lose control and cause public disturbances. Police report the capture and imprisonment of masqueraders in the jail of the Central Police Station, and newspapers report the incarceration of the masked performers. In public outcry citizens ask how a spirit can be imprisoned; for, if in fact it is a spirit, it is invisible. In the past, Bloody Mary and Firestone Ode-lay groups have charged the law enforcers with illegal seizure and entry. Perplexing questions arise that call for resolution. Can a devil be apprehended for dancing without a permit? Are such entities subject to civil law? Is there a collision between the traditional rules of order and those imposed by a developing nation-state?

The cinemas of Freetown packed in audiences in 1978 to view films like *The Omen* and *The Life of Butch Lee* as well as Indian and Chinese adventure films. The filmed presentation of music, costume, accelerated violence, motion, and glistening color attracts audiences of the Ode-lay societies. Society officers show prints of Buddha, Bodhisattavas, and other lotus-sitting spirits to costume builders (artists) to be used as models for their creations. Conversations leading to such transactions take place in the secrecy of artists' homes in Mountain Cut. Kola nut, Captain Morgan rum, and perhaps some traditional medicines are given to these creators, who in turn offer such items to the spirits of the log that is to be cut and to the spirits of the commissioning society.

An artist's work is viewed with interest, as he fashions his creations, while fortifying himself with kola and occasionally drinks of tote-a-pack rum. When brothers of the commissioning societies come to inspect the costumes, they talk about the beauty of fierceness in the artist's work. Talk spills over into past masked performances that were superb, "Ah, the way the devil danced!" Fights between societies, the outlandish behavior of those crosstown unruly "brothers" of Education who carried knives in their textbooks, and other incidents are recalled. To throw stones is permissible, but to kill is an unforgivable act that far exceeds the aesthetic of fierceness. Nightly discussions center on politics and the grand patrons of important secret societies. Firestone recalls having made the reputation of one very powerful parliamentary assistant; Paddle Society proudly asserts its rejection of the same person from membership. While the artist works, members often sing society songs above the hum of the sewing machine used to make cloth parts of the costumes.

During evening rains everyone remains inside. Dark, history-rich Free-town pulsates with the creative act of readying itself for the next season's celebrations of masked spirits. Record shop hi-fis complement the creative work inside. Thoughts inevitably turn toward women. *Woman tote man* is a phrase used by men to acknowledge the strength of women. *"E dey get di swit yai."* *"Freetown woman, e bado!"* Those lovely ladies with hot flashing smiles always break your heart. With their hunger for money and fancy cloth, what is a man to do?

The entire city is involved with Hunting, Egungun, and Ode-lay groups. Some society members are Free Masons as well, and all are Christians, Muslims, or Freethinkers. Apart from these cultural diversities, African secret societies are the primal components of the city's social organization. Except for the Free Masons, the locus of urban cultic arts flows in the aesthetic lifeblood of African tradition. For the outside observer it is difficult to distinguish these cultural patterns and, moreover, to present them within a synchronic framework. The material cuts across academic disciplines and challenges literary presentation.

Apart from the problems of description are historical problems as well. What are the origins of these societies? Under what conditions and in what time periods did they evolve? To what degree have their art and musical forms changed since the beginning? How have they been affected by the developing urban environment? Has the function of the Freetown societies changed with respect to their effectiveness in politics? These questions prompted the writing of this book. If they could be answered, they would reveal the origin, development, and significance of the urban Ode-lay society.

In exploring the dramatic rise of the Ode-lay societies, this book introduces their art, lifestyle, organization, and social function. In this context, terms such as *traditional, contemporary, fine arts,* and *crafts* are of little use. African art historians, collectors, and dealers have, for apparent reasons, made such distinctions. These classifications reveal more about our own artistic biases, which are based on the criteria of authenticity and antiquity, than about their subject. The criterion of authenticity is often confused with age; that is, the older the piece is, the greater is its authenticity. However, these conceptions built into our aesthetic do not apply to African art.

To project our values on this art is a natural response, given the rule that societies focus on aspects of foreign cultures that are similar to their own. As a result of this selection process, the "sculpture" of Africa has been written about and collected. Other art mediums, such as cloth, mud, ceramics, raffia, and body decoration, have until recently received scant attention, because the Western practice has been to arrange these media hierarchically with sculpture near the top. Ode-lay members do not establish these artistic categories; much less do they analyze their art.

The problems of classifying African art in terms of *old* and *new* are alleviated somewhat with the introduction of the notion of transformation. Art objects that are modified in material, use pattern, and style are said to be in a state of transformation. This concept assumes a baseline for art forms, i.e., a time and space where the arts are static or pristine. Once this baseline is established, the art historian compares it with a contemporary art, with respect to a given set of characteristics, to determine the degree of transformation. Anthropologists have pointed out that, while materials may change, styles, underlying aesthetic, and functions remain the same. Thus, while the appearance of an object may change vis-à-vis its "traditional" predecessor, its structure and intent remain the same. This interpretation of the transformation concept has enlivened the study of African art. We should note that the application of the term *transformation* stems from that old aesthetic bias toward the antique and the traditional. The labeling of a piece of African art as *transformational* gives it credibility; for, although the appearance and materials have changed, the use pattern and aesthetic remain traditional. Consequently we are back where we started, and we can state with some authority that transformation art has integrity because it testifies to the persistence of a traditional African culture in the face of industrialization and, concomitantly, urbanization.

We must remember that the transformation-of-arts concept is, after all, the result of a projection of Western values nurtured by the philosophy of nineteenth-century Romanticism as viewed by such well-known personalities as Eugene Delacroix. In North Africa, Delacroix kept careful account of Bedouins in his Moroccan sketchbooks. His drawings of man and nature from the northern part of this exotic continent matched the naturalists' interest in flora and fauna, especially in rare specimens. Romanticism was habitually disposed toward the exotic, the past, and nature. With the contention that man and nature were in struggle, Romantics helped develop the concept of the endangered species—the helpless animal caught in the futile struggle against the forces of man. African art, also, has been treated as an endangered species; and in the attempt to save it, we have introduced the concept of transformation, as if to say that, although the art product has changed, its underlying structure has remained intact. Thus the species or art has survived.

Transformation also implies evolution. Species, as well as art, change by this process; and the degree to which they are modified is the extent of their evolution. By looking at African art in this way or, for that matter, at any aspect of "primitive" culture, we hope to retrace man's cultural evolution. This is no different from Watteau's great painting *Embarkation for Cythera,* in which lovers in the foreground look toward the background in longing search for the primal past. This also calls to mind Rousseau's concept of the Noble Savage. Our motive in the search for African art must be considered within these nineteenth-century philosophical currents.

How are we to remove these cultural projections and with clear and open vision study the arts of African peoples? This is a difficult if not impossible task, given that a study by one society of another must by some means validate the observing society. Societies and cultures are self-serving, for they must compete in an environment with finite resources. Thus studies outside a particular society must be supportive of the society that does the observing. Societies also seek homeostasis. One way of accomplishing this is to reaffirm old social values or to espouse new ones with the aid of outside observation of another society. But how do we accomplish this with little distortion of our view of the observed culture? If we do not maintain some safeguards, we are liable to miss important lessons. Though questions of history and transformation are important to us, we must search out what is important to members of a society and what makes art appealing for them. In this regard we introduce the terms *gestalt* and *analytic* to describe two modes of perception.[1]

A book can only provide a serial readout, an analytical portrayal of the multisensual phenomenon presented by the art-producing societies of Freetown. Eyes, ears, nose, hands, and the interaction of individuals bear witness to the aesthetic display of the city's festivals. These "events of the senses" are here translated into the imagery of words. Even the cubist writings of James Joyce and the cubist paintings of Pablo Picasso cannot overcome this sensory deprivation. It is telling that Carl Jung should have once complained of utter boredom on his first reading of Joyce's *Ulysses*. Not until he became annoyed with the author did he "get into" the book. Through a confrontation with Joyce, Jung participated in an artistic experience. Becoming an active participant with the imagined author activated Jung and brought him into a wider aesthetic experience than that offered by the mere placement of words on a page.[2] In brief, more of the psychiatrist's experience was utilized.

In my experience of many African cultural presentations, including the Ode-lay, more than words and an imagined interplay are offered. That Ode-lay art should be concerned with ancestors, deities, sacrifices, drama, uncertainty, dance, costume, sculpture, and dress is extremely important. What the event provides is a mixture that involves all the senses. To be drawn into a phenomenon with all the senses is to be completely involved in the perception of the gestalt. One is no longer merely an observer; one is part of the event.

This total identification of participant with event has also been a consideration of Western artists who have given us the happening, the installation, and environmental art. The Western artist has long recognized the blandness that accompanies the analysis of artistic expression, breaking it down into discrete categories, such as sculpture, music, painting, and drama. An Ode-lay participant realizes that a successful performance does not hinge entirely upon the stylistic and aesthetic merit of carving or costume, but upon an interplay of materials, timing, and individual interactions. All these factors must combine in such a way as to bring off a good show.

An Ode-lay cult presentation follows a ritual sequence, but the tone and intensity of an event are determined existentially, depending upon the interplay of the actors. Here is an important distinction between Western and African artistic phenomena. The interplay of the actors makes the art presentations in African cults spontaneous and vulnerable to change. Scenarios are followed, yet any Westerner who has attended cult presentations must have been struck, at some time, by their seemingly unorganized nature. Social conflicts appear to interfere with the progress of the ceremony, yet their resolution leads to a heightened aesthetic intensity. The aesthetic of Ode-lay is not in the analysis of particular features of particular "art" objects; rather, it is in the gestalt feeling of self-esteem heightened by one's commitment to and identification with a cultural event. Thus, the bigger the event, the bigger the feeling. One might well imagine the implications of this process at the national level. Where politics in the urban setting are expressed by Ode-lay presentations, an extremely volatile medium is available for individuals to use in the assertion of power. This relationship between art and politics will be explored in the subsequent pages of this book.

In African art history there are no major studies of urban cults like the Ode-lay. Interestingly, one of the best examples of the urban cult is presented in the Jean Rouch film *Les Maîtres Fous*. The film's characters include unskilled and skilled labor, traders, clerics, army personnel, and bureaucrats from Accra Ghana. These individuals live in an environment where interdependency is the means of survival. Apartments, private dwellings, low-cost housing, and shantytowns house the residents of Accra. Rouch's subjects do not have direct ties with the land; they are, in every sense of the word, urban dwellers.[3]

The religion of these men, Houaka, is a syncretic cult that emphasizes spirit possession. The actors of the cult travel to a sacred grove outside the city to engage in a series of ceremonies for the initiation of new members. They worship the god of technology and the forces of the colonial regime. During these ceremonies, cult members, who are mostly of Zaberma origin, become possessed by spirits such as the "General" and the "Governor," through self-mutilation, sacrifices, dance, and intergroup conflict, all of which heighten the intensity of the ritual. The art historian may ask, Where is the art of the Houaka cult? As a student of north Ghanaian art, I was struck by the similarity between the "art" forms of that region and those of the Houaka.[4] The mud shrine representing the governor, the egg and dog sacrifices, and the circle-dancing betray an African origin and, specifically, a north Ghanaian origin. The appearance of the Union Jack and carved guns is nontraditional, but their use is African. The cult is made manifest without masks, but this does not deny its Africanness. The simultaneity of personal conflict, motion, sacrifices, and possession are characteristics of the Houaka ritual that are shared by the Ode-lay as well as other African expressive associations.

Additional studies that marshal the arts in the urban setting might include the arts of the Yoruba, Benin, or the Ashanti, which have been studied by Cole, Ben Amos, Thompson, and others.[5] These arts are generally the property of the state and the prerogative of the king. Therefore, they stand apart from grassroots art, which is the subject of this work: art that is not "owned" by the state. To be certain, these societies and their rituals have been influenced by the political elite. The successful manipulation of the network of Freetown secret societies brought about a grassroots movement in 1978 in which the people, through a referendum, voted for a one-party state.[6] The ethical question of political exploitation of a tradition does not enter here. What is important is that for the first time the peoples of Sierra Leone, including the Freetown and rural areas, had been unified. This had been accomplished through a "peoples" culture that is manifested by the Hunting, Egungun, and Ode-lay societies.

During World War II the active harbor of Freetown served as a background for Graham Greene's novel, *The Heart of the Matter*. In the novel Greene described the forces that would shape the Ode-lay societies. In the story a police officer patrolled the central part of the city around the now abandoned railway tracks, which are still seen along East Brook Street. The area housed the teenage vandals so feared and hated by the British. One of the sections was controlled by a group of young men who are today known as Rainbow, an Ode-lay group with shrines and masqueraders. When Greene lived in Freetown, the present leader of Rainbow was a young boy. Many such boys, whom Greene described, have entered the trades; some have even aspired to high political office. Their encounters with the British taught them how to escape the hand of authority while looting and stealing on land or sea. Such survival techniques are today employed by Ode-lay groups despite local authority.

Rainbow, Civili, and Shangai Joe Ode-lay groups practice their illegal professions, and for this the city fathers and the electorate deplore them. Yet these same hooligans, as they have been labeled by the press, support members of parliament, who in turn afford them special privileges. The electoral body enjoys the vastly reduced prices of the black-market goods provided by the Ode-lay associations. Thus, the Ode-lay groups are feared and discouraged as well as respected and encouraged. Today they represent a significant force that any government must consider.

That force is acknowledged in this early passage from Greene's book:

> Walking along a light railway line Scobie made in the direction of the markets. At the corner of a warehouse he came on two policemen.

> "Anything to report?" [he asked.]
> "No, sah" [they replied].
> "Been along this way?"
> "Oh yes, sah, we just come from there."

> He knew that they were lying: they would never go alone to that end of the wharf, the playground of the human rats, unless they had a white officer to guard them. The rats were cowards but dangerous—boys of sixteen or so, armed with razors or bits of broken bottle, they swarmed in groups around the warehouses, pilfering if they found an easily-opened case, settling like flies around any drunken sailor who stumbled their way, occasionally slashing a policeman who had made himself unpopular with one of their innumerable relatives. Gates couldn't keep them off the wharf: they swam around from Kru Town or the fishing beaches.[7]

What Greene described while working for the British government was accurate and consistent with press reports of the time. What he could not see, however, was that beneath this urban-gang exterior was a strong African tradition that is based upon the religion and aesthetics of a people who came to Freetown from Nigeria in the early nineteenth century. When the British liberated the Africans from slave ships captured on the high seas after 1807, they set in motion a great cultural extension of Yoruba origin that would one day give shape to the secret societies of Freetown. Although the members of these groups embraced modernity, Christianity, Islam, and other forces in the developing Third World, they did so within a sociocultural cradle that is profoundly African. This study attempts to explore and express this relationship. It is my hope that through personal narrative, documents, illustrations, and transcriptions from native informants, the reader may experience the seething world of these societies and come to an understanding of the nature of their multisensual art.

Acknowledgments

I would like to thank Laray Denzer, who directed me to research in Freetown, and Robert Hess and Jan Rocek, who were actively involved in research programs at the University of Illinois at Chicago when my research proposal was submitted. Special appreciation to the Fulbright Hays Post Doctoral Research Program for funding the project, and to Fourah Bay College African Studies Program with which I was affiliated during my stay in Sierra Leone. With regard to the production of this book I especially thank Frank O. Williams for his support and encouragement throughout and Rita Zelewsky, whose untiring attention to successive manuscripts brought the book into focus. Frank and Rita took the time to teach me about the publishing and writing profession.

When I arrived in Freetown, I was met by Alusine Yilla, who through David Skinner became my field assistant. Alusine's understanding of the project, his patience with me, and his persistence kept us on schedule. Ambassador John A. Linehan and Claythan McClain Ross of the American Embassy at that time were very helpful in the research as well in assisting my wife and me in settling in Freetown. Individually I express my gratitude to the people of Freetown's masquerade societies, including Ibrahim Kamara, Nancy Koroma, G. T. Coker, Abdul Ajani Mukhtarr, Eustace Yaskey, John Goba, Mr. Okin, Baba McCauley, Dr. Fyle, John Thompson, Mr. Orbanks, Mr. Decker, and politicians Bobby Allen and Alfred Akibo Betts. I would also like to cite specific secret societies without whose cooperation and assistance this book would not have been. These groups include Bloody Mary, Firestone, Awodie Oje, Navy Oje, Autta Gelede, Lord Have Mercy, Juju Wata, Egunugu, Seaside Firestone, Paddle, Back to Power, Civilian Rule, Rainbow, Freetown Bundu Society, Zorrow Unity, and O. K. Murray Hunting Society. Appreciation also to the Lands and Survey Office and the Freetown police for maps and for allowing me to attend permit meetings for masquerades.

I would like to thank scholars and other persons interested in Africa for their support. These include René A. Bravmann and Stevie Bravmann, whose close friendship since graduate school and whose professional nurturing took me to Africa; Simon Ottenberg, who has helped in many pages of the manuscript; and Robert Farris Thompson, whose enthusiasm and spiritual guidance helped as well. Others I wish to thank are Mark and Andy Rosenberg, Janet Berlo, Frederick Lamp, Charles Bird, Mr. and Mrs. Nooter, Jeanne Cannizzo, Jola Ogunlusi, John Pemberton III, Hans Schaal (for lengthy discussions about art and philosophy), Michael Banton, Dr. and Mrs. Phillips, John Povey, Charles Miller III, Marilyn Houlberg, Henry and Margaret Drewal, Irmfriede Hogan, Donald Cosentino, Robin Poynor, Sidney Kasfir, Charles and Evelyn Wilson, Ann Goodfellow, Mary Douglas, Jeanne A. Havemeyer, and Mike Reed.

To Graham Greene whose *Heart of the Matter* conveyed the love I, too, have for Freetown and to his ability to describe countries of the so-called Third World in his other novels. Of recreational importance was the Omar Khayam Nightclub, which allowed me to disengage when necessary.

For my parents, Dorothy Georgia and John Lee Nunley, who taught me a love of music overseas.

I should thank the Joyce Foundation for a summer grant to pursue archival research in London, and the institutions there that made my work easy. These include the British Newspaper Library, the Public Record Office, the Church Missionary Society Archives, the Methodist Missionary Society Archives, and the School of Oriental and African Studies. Thanks go to Lois Flaxbart for typing the final manuscript and to James Burke, director of the Saint Louis Art Museum for encouraging the completion of this project.

I owe a special gratitude to David C. Ruttenberg and the Ruttenberg Arts Foundation of Chicago for the generous subsidy for illustrations in this publication. A special debt to Linda Horsley-Nunley, who created illustrations of masqueraders where photography was not permitted and who was patient when I was not at her side when needed; to Ryntha Johnson for her map-making contribution, and to Historical Pictures Service, Chicago, for supplying illustrations.

Moving with the
Face of the Devil

1

The Great Experiment

Freetown in the Early Years

The founding of Sierra Leone was marked by hardship, intrigue, failure, and success. Like the settlers in the New World, the liberated Africans who came to Freetown resisted the dominant political system, whether crown, Sierra Leone Company, or church. An ongoing competition between a central political system and that of a traditional African social organization, with its emphasis on group participation, was to endure from the establishment of the colony to the present. The role played by African culture, with its masquerades, religion, music, and medicine, was central to the unfolding of this political dialectic.

From 1771 to 1774 Henry Smeathman, who was sent as a botanist to collect specimens for Sir Joseph Banks of Kew Gardens, explored the area around the mouth of the Sierra Leone River. Struck by the beauty and agricultural possibilities of the land, he proposed in 1783 an ideal settlement to be composed of freed slaves and organized on the principle of democratic liberalism distilled from the then fashionable philosophy of rationalism.[1] Like French architect Charles Ledoux, Smeathman believed man could order his universe, including his settlement patterns and architecture. Thus, a colony near the mouth of the Sierra Leone River, with Freetown as its ideal city, would serve as an experimental model of rationalist thought. Before Smeathman's death, he organized a small group of poor blacks of London and, with the backing of British philanthropists, established the colony.

In London at about this time, several cases concerning the freedom of blacks were heard in the courts. When victimized blacks heard about the Sierra Leone project, they went to Granville Sharp, a strong abolitionist, for advice concerning settlement of the colony.[2] Sharp was to give the colony a radical and exciting form of government. To implement his system he had to secure a large grant from the British treasury. He called the experiment "The Province of Freedom."[3] Two of the immediate aims of the planners were (1) to provide a place for resettlement of London's poor blacks and (2) to provide a place for the release of liberated slaves upon free soil. With three ships and a total of 456 passengers, over 100 of them white, the naval sloop *Nautilus* led the 1787 expedition under Captain Thompson.

Thompson purchased a twenty-mile-square piece of land from the local Temne chief. The plot was located at the foot of the northern extension of the Sierra Leone Mountains. Previously this location had been used as a watering station by European slavers. The new settlement was called Granville Town. The colonists immediately faced hardship in the form of sickness and attacks by the Temne, who felt threatened by European settlement. Forty-eight of the surviving residents, under the leadership of Alexander Falconbridge, established another settlement about two miles to the east of the first town under the newly chartered Sierra Leone Company.[4]

Another scheme in the wake of rationalist thought materialized in 1791. To increase the likelihood of survival of the colony more people were recruited for settlement. A group of black Loyalists who had fought with the British in the American Revolution became involved. In return for their loyalty to the crown, they had been given land in Nova Scotia, a rocky, cold, and desolate place that was nearly impossible to farm. Thomas Peters, a representative of the Nova Scotians, came to Britain to protest the extremely adverse farming conditions in the colony. In addition, many Loyalists had been unable to secure land and were forced to work as farm laborers, a status that was, in their eyes, not far removed from slavery. In January 1792, three months after Peters's return from London, Lieutenant John Clarkson of the Royal Navy, on behalf of the Sierra Leone Company, transported 1,200 Negroes from Nova Scotia to Sierra Leone. This group formed a new settlement called Freetown.[5] (See map 1.)

From the outset the new occupants were mistrustful of the company's policy, and Clarkson constantly complained of the council's inability to act in the face of their suspicion. The colonists complained that the company had given only five acres to each person instead of the twenty originally promised. To make matters worse, in 1794 the French sailed into the harbor and burned the town. To offset the high cost of reconstruction, imported goods, and insurance premiums due to the French wars, the company introduced a land tax. This further alienated the settlers.[6] Adding to the frustration of the settlers, in 1796 the British imported Africans, called Maroons, from Jamaica to enforce company

MAP 1   Sierra Leone   Credit: Ryntha Johnson

policy in matters of taxation and form of governance.[7] Despite the internal conflicts and hardships of survival, the colony was secured. By 1808, the year the British declared the abolition of slavery, Freetown could claim the firm establishment of Christianity, a government, and many commercial enterprises. (See figure 1.)

The city was established along three main east-west roads that were intersected by nine smaller north-south streets. The grid reflected the rationalist thinking of the time. The first settlers' housing was constructed of mud-wattle and thatched roofs. Later this construction gave way to the more permanent side-board housing with raised stone foundations, the so-called Creole house.

FIGURE 1   A nineteenth-century view of Freetown Harbor. Photo credit: Historical
Pictures Service, Chicago

Until 1808 the Nova Scotian settlers continued their fight against the
central administration of the company. Through their churches, commercial activities, and political involvement, they managed to hold their
own. From the company's vantage, such resistance meant failure; but
from the point of view of the settlers, a truly independent Freetown was
in the making.

Two important acts of the British parliament were to affect the development of Sierra Leone. One was the passage of legislation to dissolve
the Sierra Leone Charter, which made the territory a crown colony. The
other served notice on the Atlantic slave trade. This meant something
had to be done with the Africans liberated by British warships on the
high seas. Freetown was chosen as the site for their liberation.

By the end of the slave trade, more than fifty thousand Africans were
liberated at Freetown.[8] Many of these former slaves had been victims of
the Yoruba fratricidal wars. Pressured by Muslim uprisings to the north,
the Fon of Abomey to the west, and the Portuguese slavers, the Yoruba
found themselves turning on one another. Prisoners of war were most
often sold as slaves to be transported to the New World. When the
British abolished slavery, they assumed responsibility for rescuing these
slaves and repatriating them at Freetown. The task, though difficult, was
blessed with British optimism and confidence.

The private correspondence between the chief superintendent of the
Liberated African Department, Lieutenant-Colonel Dixon Denham, and
R. W. Hays of the State Department reveals this optimism and the extent
to which rationalistic thought had inspired the founding of the colony.
In January 1827 Denham wrote:

> That the liberated Africans will not only very shortly support themselves
> but become independent settlers as the Maroons are at this moment I have
> not the slightest doubt, but with the assistance of his Majesty's Government
> they will in the course of time do much more than this and I do hope that

you will take into your serious consideration the question of Experimental Farms which from the observations I have already made in two of the nearest Negro Towns that I have visited I am confident will be attended with the greatest benefit both to the Colony and the very interesting class of persons Great Britain has taken under her protection. There are two farms within three miles of Freetown where the crops of coffee, arrow root and rice have for several years not only paid the proprietors all their expenses of cultivation but also paid for the building on the land very pretty and comfortable habitations and one of these farms under the direction of the proprietor is now managed by a liberated African who receives about one pound [perhaps pence] a day. A farm of this description should be established in every liberated African village without delay and an arrangement made for all freed men to give their labour for a limited period to the Experimental Farmer his service [sic] on the recommendation of the Master his own allotment should be given him and after a year's trial of his industry and capacity either confirmed to him and his heirs for ever or otherwise according to his merit. . . . The soil is I am confident capable of producing almost anything but there is no one here at all acquainted with either European or Tropical Agriculture and men of colour natives of the West Indies are for many reasons preferable to Europeans for commencing this most important Experiment. Sea Island Cotton and Coffee should in the first instance be tried.[9]

In addition to the purely economic side of this important experiment Denham's correspondence points to the importance of the settlements surrounding the city as places for occupation of the liberated slave. (See figures 2 and 3.)

In spite of the governing role played by the Established Church and the Methodist Missionary Society in the surrounding villages, these settlements also proved to be a good home for practice of the religion the freed slave brought from his native land. The large portion of repatriated Africans of Yoruba descent meant that much of the subsequent history of Freetown and, later, of the modern state of Sierra Leone would reflect Yoruba culture.

Much of Denham's enthusiasm in September 1827 was tempered by the reality of Freetown:

I think I may venture to say that no Colony of its extent has so many unfinished government buildings falling into decay as Sierra Leone. These are of all descriptions hospitals, churches, government houses, barracks, stores and yet it is with difficulty the governor and a few clerks in the public offices are lodged even by renting houses of the maroons and other settlers, some of them at rents of £4 or [£]500 a year and the service of the established church is performed in the room over the gaol while the Wesleyan Methodists and Baptists have all neat and commodious Chapels. My own premises in Freetown were robbed four times in ten days during the dark nights and heavy rains.[10]

FIGURE 2   The gate of freedom through which the expatriated slave passed on the way to an experimental farm or an apprenticeship in Freetown. Photo credit: John Nunley

If the colony was not successful in its building program, it was because the colonists were busy adapting to the new land and establishing their own form of governance. Denham's depressing observations concerning the Established Church were essentially correct; however, he overestimated the success of the other missionary movements. An extract from a missionary journal from 1820–22 indicates some of the many frustrations faced by these men of God. The writer, G. Lane, vituperously concludes:

> This is *killing* work! our country-built chapels require great exertion of the lungs in order to make the words distinctly to be heard. They are made of a kind of lath, worked, like wicker-work, and clumsily plastered inside

FIGURE 3   Regent, one of the rural settlements near Freetown, where the agricultural component of the Great Experiment was planned. Courtesy of the Church Missionary Society, London.

with a brown mud, the roof is of grass roughly put on round sticks as they are cut from the tree, without any trimming, the pillars which support the *tie-beams,* are like the rafters, impolished; and having the bark on them. After this description of an African temple it must be seen that there is nothing in it to act as conductor, Nay, it is as unapt to *sound* as the african's mind (generally) is to comprehend.[11] (See figure 4.)

In the colonial mind the success of religion and government were represented by imposing architecture; and where these institutions were absent, the obvious conclusion was failure. (See figures 5 and 6.) What colonial officials did not comprehend was that an African social organization with its own religion and government was forming at a less obvious level. It was not characterized by large-scale architecture. It had its roots, not in the Nova Scotian or European experience, but in the African homeland of the liberated settlers. The colonial government and the church alike saw this movement as a manifestation of idolatry and as part of Satan's plan. Religious prejudice masked the real concern of political administrators that an alternative political system was developing. If the words of the gospel were quickly absorbed in mud and wattle walls, the sound of traditional Yoruba music and dance echoed across the stretches of the new colony.

One observer made note of the inadequate means for controlling the conduct of the liberated Africans after they were once located. He

FIGURE 4   An example of the mud-wattle construction technique used in building the early churches of Freetown. Picture credit: Historical Pictures Service, Chicago

concluded that it also did not seem likely that a way existed for channeling their labor.[12] It appeared that the plans for the great experimental farms were, indeed, at a standstill. It was also clear to those persons in charge that more missionaries would be needed if the colony was to succeed along the lines originally intended.

With the lack of leadership and effective governmental control, youthful "indulgence" in traditional culture posed another problem. J. Courties reported in July 1827:

> Amongst the youthful peoples of the population religion appears to have no place, they are generally abandoned to revelling, shouting or cohorting, drumming and dancing in which they frequently spend whole nights, very few attend a place of worship, nor is there to our views . . . an instance of real conversion among them.[13]

Part of the problem was noted as stemming from unemployment. However, to credit this alone as the cause of what seemed to the British as disobedience and degeneracy is to miss the point. What is significant about Courties's comment is his conclusion that very few youths attend a "place of worship." What seemed to the church missionaries to be reveling, shouting, dancing, and drumming were actually forms of tra-

FIGURE 5 Bishop Crowther Memorial Church. Churches like this, constructed of permanent materials, amplified the Word of God in fixed interior space. Photo credit: John Nunley

FIGURE 6   In buildings like this rare example of early nineteenth-century school architecture the freed slave learned the ways of Western civilization. Photo credit: John Nunley

ditional worship, at places of worship that were defined by the extent of the activity.

Here was a major misunderstanding: where the European mind contemplated religious expression within walled space, the African mind found its expression of spirituality in music and dance, which themselves defined the sacred space. This basic difference proved an insurmountable obstacle to European religion, because African cultural expression could not be suppressed in a geographical sense. African congregations, places of worship, and kinetic forms of cultural expression thwarted the attempts made by Western churches to control religious life in the colony.

In May 1843 the Reverend R. Amos recorded the European view of

the African dance ritual. In Freetown he had been writing at about 8
A.M. on a Friday, when he heard dancing. The devil of the Egungun or
Hunting society was in procession on the principal street near Amos's
residence. It was scorching hot, Amos noted, but he nevertheless pursued
the masqueraders down the streets of York, one of the many liberated
African villages surrounding Freetown. The procession was without doubt
what today is called *caroling,* a Creole term for a practice in which
hunters masquerade in the morning to announce forthcoming festivities
in the evening. Apparently a member of the masquerading society who
had been shipwrecked and drowned was to be commemorated.

The reverend confronted the entourage and spoke: "If his [the dead
sailor's] sins were forgiven, and his heart changed in this life he is gone
to heaven—but if he died unsaved he is gone to hell." When he warned
the masked procession that the devil was in the image of Satan, they
replied: "It was nothing to do with white man, it was their country-
fashion and to that they must keep." Then, the reverend recorded, "They
shouted pooh! pooh! and struck the tomtoms with redoubling fury, their
hellish appearance and internal gesticulations harrowed up my feelings."[14]
In defense of York, Amos noted that of the four thousand or more
residents, the people could not raise a masquerade procession. He continued: "The persons who celebrated this horrid custom were hired from
Freetown. The York *Aku* [a term noting the Yorubas in Sierra Leone]
devil is turned from the power of Satan to God he's burnt the devil
dress."[15] But the Hunting societies of York and Freetown had already
established bonds in a colonywide social organization that could be called
a form of governance. These colonials close to the scene were aware of
the threat such a group, rooted in Yoruba traditional culture, might pose.

One reason for the colonial government's inability to control the
settlements was the colonial policy itself. The *Missionary Register,* a
newspaper of the Church Missionary Society, printed an article entitled
"Peculiar Difficulties of the Mission" in its 1828 issue. It noted that the
government's decision to take the native schoolmasters and mistresses,
who were formerly in the mission society, and put them in the service
of the government would decrease the influence of the church at the
community level. As these instructors were relieved of civil and spiritual
authority over the inhabitants of Freetown and the surrounding villages,
a new class of officers, called managers and submanagers, took their
place. These mostly colored men were, as the article implied, of a lesser
religious persuasion and more supportive of the repatriated peoples'
traditional religion of the Hunting and Egungun societies. The article
concluded, "It was only known, that the missionaries had no more civil
power; and the people, feeling that the restraints formerly put on the
public observance of heathenish rites or noisy amusements no longer
existed, followed the natural leading of an evil heart."[16]

The purpose of the transfer of authority to the colored group was to alleviate the financial responsibility of the colonial government. Indeed, the governor of the colony, George Canning, in 1825 complained of the white man's burden. He declared that no matter how laudable were the efforts of the English, the burden of civilizing the African should be a joint venture. "England should embrace a wider sphere of action, we should not be, however laudable, alone the protectress and instructress of these collected people."[17] The governor blamed the slow progress of the colony in part on the inability of the administration, which included the missionaries. Concurring in this view, Governor N. Campbell reported in 1827 that the Reverend Wilhelm of Waterloo was, like many missionaries, a broken man unable to control his village. (See map 2.) Campbell also noted that five of the liberated Africans of that community had joined in an attack on a small "timanee" (Temne) village nearby. These five individuals, who had previously served in the Royal West African Corps, had taken their weapons with them to Waterloo. The Reverend Betts informed Campbell that such men were leaving the villages and forming their own independent settlements.[18]

Such was the state of affairs in the colony by the 1820s. It had held its own despite the colonial government, which saw failure in its inability to control the repatriated Africans and to bring to reality its experimental farms. What the British philanthropists, the Sierra Leone Company, and the government had accomplished was the settlement of Freetown and the surrounding villages, which held to traditional African religious practices. The mistrust of the Maroon and Nova Scotian toward the Sierra Leone Company and the crown was shared by the liberated Africans who established a culture based on their own traditional principles. By the time these liberated Africans had children, Yoruba culture was firmly established in the colony. The descendants of the liberated Africans, called Creoles, were to develop an attitude of superiority over the indigenous Africans of Sierra Leone. Thus the dialectic between the government and the governed continued.

A Culture Transplanted

Many elements of the ancestral religions of the repatriated Africans have survived in Sierra Leone. The Ibo, Ibibio, and Nupe traditions of Nigeria (see maps 3 and 4) are only a few tribal religions upon which the colony drew in its development. The Yoruba traditions, however, were by far the most influential. In this section the circumstances of the slave trade that led to the expansion of the Yoruba cults will be examined. The specific elements within these traditions as they relate to contemporary culture of Freetown and Sierra Leone will be discussed.

The hardships many of the liberated Africans endured are recounted

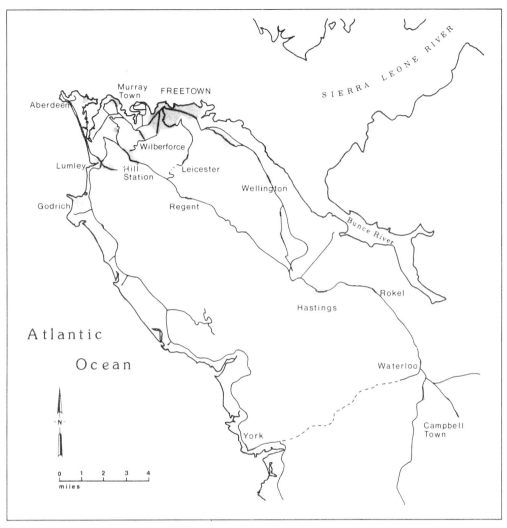

MAP 2   Freetown and Proximity   Credit: Ryntha Johnson

in an autobiographical account of a Yoruba man's memories of the slave wars.[19] Though brief and sometimes difficult to read, the sketch conveys, through the eyes of a Yoruba boy, the memories of ritual in present-day Nigeria, as well as the events leading to his capture, enslavement, and release in Freetown. Although the account is written from the point of view of an older man who has been converted to Christianity, it nevertheless fully reveals the Yoruba traditions.

Joseph Wright was born sometime in the second decade of the nineteenth century. He recalls having heard at age ten about the 1820 wars in Akkoo that pitted Yoruba against Yoruba. Seven years after he first heard of the wars, the bloodshed reached his own town. Wright's family consisted of his two brothers, his father, and his father's two wives. His

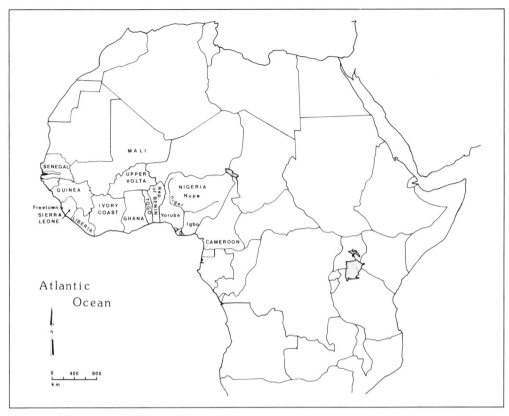

MAP 3   West Africa   Credit: Ryntha Johnson

father was an important man in the community because of his membership in the men's council, the local Ogboni society.

Years later, as a Christian, Wright expressed the view that his country was destroyed by war because of its resistance to Christianity. Its persistence in pagan traditions was punished by God. When the wars reached his town, neighboring Yoruba armies set siege to the settlement, and for seven months Wright's people prayed to the local gods, to no avail. After several months the food supply was depleted, and the men of the town were forced to leave the area to search for supplies. During their absence the enemy stormed the town, taking plunder and slaves. The invaders transported the prisoners, Wright and his brothers among them, to a place called Imodo, where they were sold to the Portuguese.[20]

Wright describes the burial practices he observed during his journey to the coast: "In this manner they dress the dead. If the dead been dressed by the council they would take all his valuable cloths, and dress him carefully, with all costly apparels, the dress will make him about seventy large pieces of costly cloths besides those that they lined the wall where the dead man lie."[21] If the deceased was not a slave but a member of

MAP 4   Yorubaland   Credit: Ryntha Johnson

the household, he was buried in his room instead of a cemetery. Another person would then occupy the room so the body of the deceased would not spoil. This latter custom, Wright stated, was commonly practiced in Freetown. When slave raiders came to these graves, they stripped the corpses of the rich cloth and the coins that lined the interior walls of their graves.[22]

Two features of Wright's description compare with present traditions in Sierra Leone: (1) the emphasis on cloth as an aesthetic and prestigious commodity in masquerades and everyday dress, and (2) the use of coins in burial rites. The aesthetic of fanciness as developed in subsequent chapters originated in the settlers' love of cloth, and one of the primary ways in which respect is shown to the ancestors as manifested in masquerades is to shower them with coins. In light of the latter tradition, ancestral spirits are said to eat wealth.

From the encampment at Imodo, Wright's new owners, the Portuguese, transported him to Ikko, where he observed the following customs:

> Their king [of Ikko] was very sick. Then the business of his attendance is to ask the diviner, whatsoever he commands to be done for the recovery of the king's health, immediately attended to during the time of the king's sickness, the slaves often met with goat or sheep sacrifice and many put on the top of the sacrificed beasts to appease the god of their land, this money the slaves always take as good luck for the money general amount of tooo [two] half penny £4–3—4. This large sum of "jukay" they used to put upon the top of the sacrificed beasts, and this one? Jukay is worth as much as English half-penny. Alas, the worthless prophet with all their edodowas and abbahtahlahss so they call their god could not able to do any good for the king in regard to his recovery.[23]

Several points are of interest in the above description. Most important is the marshaling of dancing, masquerading, and sacrificing in the maintenance of health. The king, after consulting with the diviners, was compelled to sacrifice goats and sheep. The heads of these were carried in procession on top of the attendants' heads to the accompaniment of drums. In Freetown, among societies that have sprung from Yoruba tradition, the practice of carrying an animal head on top of a dancer was, until recently, very common. At present the skull and horns of an animal or a carving are used. Sickness in the colony was a primary reason for the retention of masquerades. Faced with yellow fever, smallpox, cholera, and other diseases, the Yoruba sought comfort and healing in their traditional practices honoring the gods and the ancestors. This meant sacrifices and masquerades.

Wright's memory of ritual also points to the ancestral cult of the Egungun, which he indicated was dedicated to the worship of a god called Larrowah. This deity was attended by a priest dressed in a white gown and white cap. The priest, accompanied by other "ministers," paraded through the streets of the town warning women to give way or face the possibility of death by execution. Women were not allowed to see the men in their *ministerial dress,* a term commonly used in Freetown today to describe certain Egungun costumes. The white costume also is a common feature of many Egungun branches in Freetown. The proscription against women watching men parade was once practiced by members of a Freetown ancestral cult called Oro. This society was located on the west side of the city, where men paraded through the streets spinning bull-roars over their heads to imitate the sounds of the ancestors. As was customary in Nigeria, the women of Freetown who witnessed this event were killed, sometimes by stoning.

In Ikko, Wright wrote, the Portuguese worried that in the event of the king's death their newly purchased slaves might in turn be sacrificed. Thus, one day after the celebrations and animal sacrifices, the Portuguese loaded their human cargo and set sail for the Western Hemisphere. The second day at sea they were sighted by a British man-of-war and were escorted, over a period of one month, to Freetown, where Wright and his companions were liberated.[24] Joseph Wright's recollections vividly demonstrate the impact the traditional Yoruba rituals had upon the young. Such memories would serve in the reconstruction of Yoruba tradition in Freetown.

The success of the British liberation policy compounded the first settlers' problems. There were the added difficulties of placing the new arrivals and finding jobs for them. Moreover, the growing expatriate African community, with its own political and cultural infrastructure, challenged the hegemony of the already weakened colonial regime. Before this challenge the men of God and the king were helpless. The "General Census of the Persons Inhabiting the Colony of Sierra Leone," July 1820, indicated that from 31 December 1818 the population of the colony had increased by 2,956. This figure included 943 Africans liberated from slave vessels, 85 persons from Barbados and Honduras, and 1,030 discharged soldiers and families of the second and fourth West India Regiments and Royal African Corps. A small portion of the increase was due to births and migration of natives outside of the colony.[25]

For the same period the exports of the country included rice, elephant tusks, coffee, gum, timber, camwood, and gold dust.[26] Rice and coffee were plantation crops for which the British had great expectations. Agriculture did employ many of the liberated Africans. Yet, as they were set free, many of them traded their rations to the indigenous peoples in return for gold dust, ivory, palm oil, and other goods from which middle men might make a profit.

The problem of what to do with the large numbers of repatriated Africans plagued the British. To make matters worse, slavers captured on the high seas often had up to six hundred slaves. Thus the flow of liberated men into the colony was occasionally interrupted by large, erratically spaced numbers. Most of the records pertaining to the capture of slave ships are in the Public Record Office at Kew Gardens. A typical report, taken from the proceedings under the British and Portuguese Mixed Commission at Sierra Leone, reads:

> The brig "Avizo," under the Brazilian flag, Luis Pacheco da Silva, Master, arrived at Sierra Leone on the 8th of November by his Majesty's ship Maidstone, Commodor Bullen, in Latitude 1 33″ North and longitude 7 07″ East, and had four hundred and sixty five slaves on board. The commissioners passed a sentence of condemnation upon her and decreed the emancipation of her slaves on the 19th of November 1824.[27]

Many ships contained far fewer slaves, but the overall increases were significant, and the erratic increases compounded the problems of repatriation. Rather than depend upon British philanthropy, liberated Africans took the initiative by relying upon traditional economic and cultural practices to secure an existence.

Many of the elements of material culture of the Yoruba also appeared to have been carried aboard the slave ships and brought to Freetown. One of the more concentrated areas of Yoruba settlement was Grassfields, at the west end of the city. Of that area the Reverend T. Dove of the Methodist Missionary Society wrote:

> This appeal is made to you in behalf of a part of Freetown, by far the most populous, the most depraved and the most necessitious. The population of Grassfields and its immediate neighborhood cannot be less than five thousand; and this mass of human beings consists almost without an exception, of liberated Africans. They have brought with them from their native country their own filthy idols; they are given up to idolatry and superstition, and the most abominable practices.[28]

To redress this ill-favored imbalance between tradition and Christendom, Dove suggested that a larger, more permanent church building be constructed. Here again, in the eyes of the missionary, the solution was the erection of large and imposing architecture, as the underlying kinesthesia of the Africans was underestimated. This sense of kinesthesia no doubt was of considerable aid to the liberated Africans, who could take their rituals to spaces outside the reach of a church.

For every Yoruba and other ethnic affiliate who found a new home in the colony and converted to Christianity, many more remained faithful to the African religion. Although Joseph Wright converted to Christianity, his conversion was not without difficulty. Whenever he began to feel the peace of God, temptations would commence. His friends spoke all manner of evil against him. He wrote, "My employer begin go say that I now became one useless Psalm singer." Friends and backsliders offered him money so that he might return to the traditions of the Yoruba. He resisted their offers with the power of prayer, which he declared was the proper medicine against evil.[29] Wright's successful conversion may be accounted for in part by his upbringing at York under the tutelage of B. Pratt, the village manager. With Pratt he learned to read and write, and he regularly attended church. His faith swayed between traditional pagan and Christian beliefs for five to six years; then miraculously, on 24 December 1834, he obtained a final peace from God.

Wright's contemporaries were not so willing to convert. Banding together in ritual they opposed the efforts of the missionaries. In 1839 Reverend T. Edwards described his encounter with the masked processions. On the evening of 20 June he heard the sound of Yoruba drums, which were played in honor of Shango, the Yoruba god of thunder. A heavy thunder and lightning storm transformed the evening sky, which otherwise was thick and motionless during the rainy season. The minister, anxious to quell the fires of Shango and his devotees, marched directly to the hut where the celebrants (men, women, and children) participated before a "small Idol of mean appearance and small dimensions decorated with beads and other things." Edwards confiscated the image, while reciting Psalm 135 for his own protection. He recorded the response of the Shango worshipers: "Des big tunder come kill. Thundes come too much Debble angry Debble angry too much me no sabby white man's God. Me belong to Debble." After this confrontation the reverend lifted the image high above his head and hurled it to the ground, breaking it into a "thousand pieces."[30]

The bravery or, perhaps, ignorance that stirred the missionaries to such dangerous acts was countered by the unrelenting will of the liberated African. Several years after these early attacks on their traditional culture, the African elders of the colony maintained their resistance to Christian practices. R. Dillon of Wilburforce, a few miles to the west of Freetown (see map 2), described a routine check of the village in search of idolaters:

> We called on another idolator living in the Wilburforce Road, but we could not persuade him to abandon his idols, for he clings most tenaciously to them. When he first came to the colony 40 or 50 years ago [a few years earlier than Joseph Wright] he attended our chapter for about 9 years and was, I believe, a member. He said the reason why he left was, that one evening he was in chapel, and while on his knees he fell asleep, and dreamed that one of his feet was burning in fire. When he awoke be believed his dream was a sign that the idol he once worshipped was angry with him for following the Christian religion.
>
> I told him of the exceeding sinfulness of idolatry; also that living in the colony so many years where the gospel is faithfully preached he was left without excuse and that unless he repented he would be punished in eternity for his sins. He replied he would ask God what he had done. I argued the point with him a long time — but his invariable answer was that what I said was very good, and what he did was very good too.[31]

Traditional Medicine

Underscoring African music and masquerade was an unshakable faith in the healing power of the Yoruba gods. As early as 1837 the missionaries realized that to win the battle for Christianity the flock would have to be convinced of the superiority of Western medicine. The *Missionary Register* published, it believed, a shocking article entitled "Disease Worshipped as God." It described how the Aku peoples worshiped a smallpox spirit called Shapouna, to which they sacrificed sheep.[32] In an article about witchcraft, J. Warburton observed the widespread belief that most sickness was caused by sorcery and witchcraft. He noted the belief that witches could make themselves invisible and could move through the walls of the dwellings of their intended victims to suck their blood or perpetrate other malevolent acts.[33]

One effectual African method of fighting ill health was to treat its source in witchcraft. Toward this end, the Yoruba cult of the Gelede was introduced into the colony by the repatriated Africans. Gelede mask performers now dance to entertain and thereby appease witches; and with the aid of Gelede medicine, the fertility of female members is assured. In Freetown and Nigeria the male celebrants of the Gelede cult dress in elaborate male and female costumes and mask carvings.

In 1837 Warburton described a scene at Kissey, just east of Freetown, that could be mistaken for a contemporary performance in the Mountain Cut area. The performance was accompanied by two drums and was commenced with the sacrifice of sheep. "One of [the heathens, as Warburton called them,] who was dancing for the amusement of the company surrounding him, was partly dressed in woman's clothes, with a wooden mask of rather ingenious make, representing a human head covered with a helmet, which had for a crest, a snake in the act of killing a bird."[34] Soon afterward the missionary went to the house where the dancers had taken refuge and spoke of the evils of paganism. Inside the compound he found several other persons dressed in the manner described above endeavoring to conceal a number of masks of a more frightful form. One wonders if the ingeniously carved masks were brought by the liberated Africans from their homeland or if they were carved by Yoruba craftsmen in Freetown. Whatever their source, it appears that the Gelede society, with its impersonation, emphasis upon expensive, fancy cloth, and belief in the healing power of Yoruba ritual was seeded early in the life of the country.

Twenty years later, the adverse circumstances faced by the missionaries had changed little. R. Dillon of the Methodist mission wrote in despair:

> We have lost about the same ratio: so has the mohammedan, and the other heathen portion of the people. There are many idolators in the place, who in order to drive away the sickness as they foolishly imagined, made a sacrifice by killing a sheep, spreading over it a white cloth, — surrounding it in a circle, and repeating over it heathen incantations, after which they mingled its blood with palm-oil. It went round to the different houses and induced the people to dip their hands in it to keep away the disease from them such is the power of superstition over the African mind; they finished their proceedings by laying the sheep in a grave previously prepared.[35]

This ritual would not be unfamiliar to the people of Freetown today. White cloth is used for protection against witches and is commonly hung from the center of house ceilings. The mixture of blood and palm oil is part of the medicine currently used in the Hunting and Ode-lay societies. This medicine, called *soweh*, is an important part of contemporary masquerades. It is carried by one member of the masking party, who

FIGURE 7 This old market, from its beginnings, served as an emporium for medicines of local origin and for animal parts used in Hunting masquerades. Photo credit: John Nunley

sprinkles it on the masquerader for his protection and also offers it to other members, who rub it on their hands and bodies for the same purpose. (See figure 7.)

In one of the numerous references to the cult of Shango, the Reverend E. Marke wrote that, when he passed Foulah Town just beyond the new burial ground, he observed two basins, one filled with palm oil, the other with palm wine and some "spitted" (chewed and spewed) kola nuts. This part of Mountain Cut, near Allen Street, is still the most ritually active part of the city. The reverend saw several similar basins in houses, one of which belonged to a foreman of one of the town's leading business firms. He observed the foreman talking loudly before the spitted kola and many men who demonstrated their attention with gestures and mannerisms.

Marke was informed that these men were Shango or thunder worshipers, who were easily identified by the white strings of small beads they wore around their necks, hands, and feet. They had gathered together to consult Shango to find a cure for sickness and death that had swept the area. A sacrifice or *saddaka,* consisting of palm oil, palm wine, and kola, had been prepared for Shango.[36] The term *saddaka* is now used for sacrifices to the devil costumes prior to their appearance in processions. The offering assures the safety and well-being of the masqueraders as they proceed through the town amid the sorcerers and witches in the neighborhoods through which they pass.

The Egungun Society

Besides the cult of Shango, the ancestral Egungun cult was practiced. In missionary correspondence the word *Egungun* is spelled in a variety of ways, one of the most common being *agoogoo*. The masquerades of the Egungun society were part of life in Freetown since very early times. (See figure 8.) Like the medicines of Shango, those of Egungun were intended to protect and heal members while inflicting sickness and hardship on outsiders. A contemporary illustration depicting a missionary stripping the costume from an Egungun dancer (figure 9) bore the following legend:

> This represents a scene now almost impossible in the colony, though it was common enough forty years ago — a heathen "greegree" or "charm" man — at that time a visit of a "greegree" man was terrible to the people. The greegrees were men, covered from head to foot, to whom particular pieces of ground were held sacred. Their deeds of darkness and secrecy were as little called in question as those of the inquisition were, formerly, in Europe. In 1833, an egugu came into Freetown, Sierra Leone, with a party of drummers. This missionary, Mr. Beale, determined to expose the cheat. He ran out, seized the egugu, and dragged him into the mission yard. Mr. Beale tore his upper garment to shreds, and drew his gown over his head. When the crowd saw that the egugu was only a human being like themselves, and known to many, they raised a loud shout of derision. The man was delivered to the constable.[37]

Ironically, the Church seems to have given up on the devil societies and blanked them from their minds, for in 1887 in Freetown the Egungun were more active than ever before. Clearly the Europeans saw the Egungun as being associated with the devil; therefore, they, like the proprietors of the Inquisition, were motivated to great extremes to rid the colony of these masquerades. In *Things Fall Apart,* a novel by Chinua Achebe, the stripping of the costume from an Egungun dancer was climactic, for it symbolically resolved the inescapable situation of its protagonist, who represented the passing of Ibo tradition. The unveiling of the cultural secrets represented by the masquerade was symbolic of the disintegration of Ibo culture. Unlike Achebe's victim of colonialism, such attempts by Christians to destroy traditional beliefs and practices in Freetown met with strong resistance.

Another Egungun performance was reported by Mr. Kissling of the Church Missionary Society in March 1838. He witnessed a frightful "Agoo" dressed in a long garment, composed of a pair of sheets, with various pieces of colored cloth sewn on it. The costume terminated at the top in a conical cap that was made of baboon skin and had a place left for the eyes, which appeared to have glass or net work in them. In

FIGURE 8   An early rendering of Egungun masqueraders and musicians carrying the
Yoruba traditions of ancestor worship to Sierra Leone. Picture credit: Historical Pictures Service, Chicago

his hand, the Agoo carried an ox tail, which he flung about in the manner
of the animal to which it belonged. Several other characters of somewhat
less hideous form performed also, with similar gestures, at a distance
from the "old Agoo."[38]

This description, once again, could be mistaken for a contemporary
Egungun masquerade. The old Agoo may well have been a masker called
the *agbaru agbadu,* who is also draped in animal skins in what the
missionary might have termed "a very hideous appearance." This masquerader currently visits the ancestors in the cemeteries and from these
locations proceeds to the Egungun performance area to commence the
celebrations. This character is often seen with a machete or sword illusionistically placed through the body or head of the dancer. In procession this character may be accompanied by other masqueraders of less
hideous mien dressed in colorful cloths, without animal skins, medicines,
and metal blades. The missionary also noted several flags that marked
an area where another company of Egungun were performing.[39] Flags
are used today, also, to mark a sacred area for dancing.

At a location on the outskirts of Freetown, Kissling saw another
conspicuous flag and suspected it was intended to distinguish the house
of an idolater. He entered the house and found its wall painted white
and black and smeared with blood. On a raised section of ground close
to the wall was a country mortar painted black and covered with blood.
On top of the mortar was a plate covered by a cloth. In front of the
altar was a three-foot stick, two inches in diameter, which the owner of
the shrine said was a spirit of thunder. With a spoon he fed this stick

FIGURE 9   A missionary attacks a masked Egungun dancer to expose the human being masquerading as a spirit or devil. Courtesy of the Church Missionary Society, London.

the contents under the covering on the plate. Kissling added, with his own empirical sense of dismay, "I was in search of Thunder's mouth and could find none, they all bust into a bold laugh."[40]

From this description we may establish a historical connection between the Shango cults of Nigeria and Freetown. The Shango of Nigeria was often represented by carved sticks, with double-crescent tops, and the elaborately carved mortars. (See figures 10 and 11.) However, by the time the liberated Africans introduced the cult to Freetown, the deity was represented by the stick and the mortar and was no longer elaborately carved. (See figure 12.) The mortar also became an integral part of the Egungun masquerades. A dancer in special costume, representing the spirit of the deceased at the traditional forty-day funerary ceremony, stands on the carving and in a shrill voice, muffled by the costume, sings in Shegita, the language of the underworld people.

In the Ode-lay societies, which are in one respect a composite of the Egungun and Hunting societies, the mortar plays yet another role. It is the object on which the costume and headpiece are assembled and first offered a sacrifice. (See figure 11.) After this sacrifice the costume is lifted from the mortar and placed on the masquerader. Thus, by extension, Shango survives in contemporary masquerades of the Ode-lay.

Ogun and the Hunting Societies

The worship of Ogun, the god of iron, in the Hunting societies represents another principal Yoruba tradition. Most of the Yoruba descendants I met traced the origin of Ogun to the Egba Yoruba of Nigeria (see map 4).[41] These people were decimated during the slave wars. Whether or not the Hunting costume as a representative of Ogun belonged to a distinct society apart from the Egungun in Yorubaland is open to question. Whatever the case, by the time it reached Freetown, the Hunting and Egungun masquerades belonged to different societies.

One of the earliest references to a Hunting masquerader is found in the journal of a Mr. Schön, which was published in part in 1838. Schön forcibly entered the house of a suspected idolater and detailed what he saw there. "The mere view was enough to fill the mind with horror. The large idol actually represented the devil, with blood-stained face and two horns; before him stood a water-pot, half filled with blood of animals."[42] The idol that "actually represented the devil" in this account no doubt referred to the common Christian representation of Lucifer with horns. This scene might well describe Ode-lay practices today.

In the past, Ogun guaranteed hunters safety and a rich bounty. The society paraded with its devil before and after the hunt, and on occasion to honor deceased members. The fierce aesthetic and militant style of these processions have been incorporated into Ode-lay performances. J. G. Macaulay of Murrytown, a western suburb of Freetown (see map 2), provided a detailed description of Hunting traditions that is similar to current explanations of the society.

> Ogun, the god supposed to preside over iron, implements of war, and hunting, is worshipped by hunters. It consists of an iron stone buried in the earth, representing the anvil on which the smith beats the iron of which their hunting implements are made. Whenever they are going out to hunt, every one is required to be present at a meeting to be previously held at the residence of the man in whose yard the Ogun is buried. Each is to take with him his gun; kola-nuts and a bottle of palm wine are brought on entering the yard. All the guns are laid on the sacred spot, the kola-nuts split, and libations of wine poured; these are performed to secure good luck. Hunters, through fear of this god, are scarcely found trespassing on the rights of another; for they generally swear by him, and should any swear falsely, on being accused of having done anything such a one will ultimately be killed by a wound received from any iron. When any of them die, it is customary for the rest, on the seventh day, to collect themselves together in pursuit of the remaining game, supposed to be left untaken by the deceased when alive, for it is a prevalent opinion among hunters that they have each a share of animals in the field. Before leaving for the field, Ogun is resorted to, as above mentioned; but, besides, the deceased's gun is delivered them and that portion of it on which the trigger acts is taken

FIGURE 10   A Shango mortar pedestal (Odo Shango) from the expatriated slaves'
homeland in present-day Nigeria. Courtesy of Dr. and Mrs. Phillips and the Birming-
ham Museum of Art.

and hid; it is then turned upside down and a young branch of palm tree
tied to the stock—a sort of charm to frighten away the spirit of the
deceased lest he should take it up and with them into the field, and thus
prevent them from taking any game; for disembodied spirits are believed
to possess keener sights, and to handle with greater dexterity their hunting
implements. The gun having been rendered useless to the deceased, by the
removal of the lock for striking fire, and the barrel and stock preserved
by charms, they go in search of the deceased's portion. Should it happen
that no game is taken, it is believed that he has killed his share while alive.
The funeral obsequies being over, an effigy of the deceased is made, and
put in the road wherein he had been in the habit of passing to his farm.
On this occasion, a dog is killed, and suspended by means of a cord to
his neck. His gun, if old, is broken and thrown on the spot; but, if new,

FIGURE 11   Shango dance wand (Oshe Shango) with double-celt motif at the top. In the collection of Robert and Nancy Nooter. *African Arts* 16, no. 2 (1984): 33.

FIGURE 12 A Freetown witchgun in the shape of a Shango dance wand with dou-ble-celt motif at top. The cruciform pattern at the bottom indicates the touch-down point for the spirit of Shango. Photo credit: Robert Kolbrener

is sold and a bow and arrow substituted in its stead. Should they fail to perform this duty, it is believed that he would bring such bad luck on them, that from henceforth they should never take any game when they go out to hunt.[43]

In the Hunting shrines of Sierra Leone, the symbols of Ogun are buried at the center of the *igbale* (shrine house) in a small circular pit. These include stones, bits of metal, and sometimes the skull of a sheep. Ogun is synonymous with medicine. When an applicant joins a society, he must eat the medicine of the Ogun. It is believed that if he should reveal the secret, his belly will swell, and on the seventh day after divulging the secret he will die.

The ritual use of the gun noted by Macauley on the seventh day after the death of a member may still be practiced today. The gun does play an important part in Hunting and Ode-lay masquerades. I observed several Hunting celebrations held in honor of a deceased member where costume dancers took a carved gun from the *bila* man, the person who escorts the masquerader, and imitated the actions of the hunter, killing him in the enactment of a role reversal. In this instance the reversed behavior is most likely symbolic of death. In African funerary rituals, daily activities are often acted out in reverse form to represent death.[44] In the Ode-lay societies the carved gun has taken on added significance, as the members see it as an emblem of the military. To emphasize this theme, they dress in military fashion, with boots, berets, pants, and bandoliers with empty cartridges. They act out the ancient rites of the god of iron and war while relating their experiences to the armed forces under the control of the All Peoples Congress party.

The Emergence of a New Society

The Yoruba-rooted secret societies, medicine men, and traditional Yoruba deities provided the liberated Africans, especially the Aku, with a sense of identity. The Aku were the most troublesome Yoruba group from the point of view of church and government. They seemed to parody the church by picking times and places for celebration that were awkward for Christian worshipers. This, no doubt, intimidated new converts to Christianity. Reverend T. Edwards tells how on one occasion a divine service was interrupted by loud screams and discordant voices, as several hundred "Akoos" gathered to propitiate a Shango devil outside the chapel to celebrate the death of two of their number who had been struck by lightning. The minister, unable to continue the service, challenged the competing group of eight women, who were seated on mats "destitute" of clothes, their skin glistening with palm oil.[45] This manner of disrupting services was common. It served notice to missionaries and the colonial administration that another form of government, rooted in African concepts, might well exercise sovereignty over the liberated Africans.

That the colonial government was aware of the potential organizing force of the Aku was acknowledged much earlier, in 1827, in an episode involving "King" Potts and his "African" government. In this case the interrelationship of economics, religion, and politics was clear. The integration of these elements in an African government strengthened the hand of those liberated peoples who plotted a course of self-determination. John Peterson's portrayal of the Potts case emphasized the strength of the traditional culture of the liberated Africans. He considered the persistence of Potts and his "companies" a sign of that culture's vitality in its struggle with colonial rule.[46]

In July 1827 Governor Campbell returned from Gambia to review reports about a "king" who had organized a group that could exact fines and inflict punishment on its members. This was the first group to systematically oppose the British government. Though the so-called king claimed he could not read or write, letters allegedly in his handwriting revealed the extent of his organization. In one of these, the king requested that individuals suspected of opposing the society make an appearance at the next quarterly meeting to give testimony in their defense. He referred to his organization as the *company,* cited the members who had paid their dues, and added that individuals who left the company forfeited their contributions.[47] In a subsequent letter Potts excused some members for not attending a meeting and requested new members to pay ten shillings. He warned that if they refused to join, they would be taken off the company's list. This letter was signed by the headmen of company branches at Freetown, York, Regent Town, Wellington, and Waterloo (see map 2). Potts boldly signed the document "the king of the society."[48]

To the Aku this movement represented a means of gaining economic independence. The company was based on a Yoruba commercial organization called the *asusu,* which functioned like a commercial bank. The members of each asusu made a contribution at each meeting. Any member could draw upon this financial pool, provided he showed just cause. Reasons for borrowing from the reserve included personal hardships, such as the death of a relative, fire, or sickness. In a letter Potts mentioned that his company paid nine pounds to another company in York to help defray funeral expenses of a deceased member.[49] Here again we see the African's penchant for combining economic, social, and religious functions in a single organization. Though not mentioned in the letter, funerals given by the Aku community would have included celebrations of Ogun and the Hunting devils.

Members also used the organization's accounts to buy goods for retail and wholesale operations. In this respect the asusu functioned as a bank, through which the liberated Africans gained a firm commercial foothold in the colony by trading fancy cloth, beads, and kitchenware for ivory, gold, and other provincial goods highly valued in European markets. This economic capability and the fact that the company formed a network justified British fears concerning the Aku.

The government deemed the situation so critical that an inquest was called, at which Potts was compelled to appear. In a transcription of the proceedings, Potts carefully described the societies of which he was considered the head. He revealed that the society was established on 7 October 1824 to create funds by subscription and fines for misconduct and drunkenness of its members.[50] These funds were to provide relief for the sick and survivors of deceased members. Potts wisely denied the title of king, but he did acknowledge that the company was divided into four branches, each with a headman or president. These branches were presided over by the head of the Freetown branch, who was Potts. Rather than being called king and thus challenging the authority of the English throne, Potts was legally on safer ground with the title of headman of the leading branch of the company.[51] To the additional charge that the society at York had flogged members for refusing to pay fines for misconduct, Potts did not respond.

The constitution of the company was described in the private correspondence between Campbell and Goderich. The preamble read:

> George the fourth by the grace of God Sierra Leone October 7th 1824. This society is to be made with law and the law shall be read to the whole of the brethren of the said society understanding this society is made for the purpose of helping each other in trouble, and in death, to bury each other, to have and keep ourselves from the trouble of this world by the help of God.[52]

The laws governing the conduct of the membership during celebrations stipulated that no man should get drunk in the street, argue with his brethren, or steal from them. It provided that the *box* (treasury) bury the deceased and that those individuals leaving the society forfeit their previous contributions. The box also provided for the widows and children of deceased members. Care was taken in wording the passage that specified crimes committed *within* the society be prosecuted by the society and offences committed *outside* the jurisdiction of the society be reviewed by the justice of the peace of the colony. This distinction between inside and outside offenses was established to avoid a head-on collision with the British government's jurisdiction over its subjects.

At the inquest Sergeant Potts confessed that he was unaware of anything illegal about the formation of such a society and that his constitution had been submitted for approval to colonial officials prior to its activation. This submission was significant in two respects. It revealed the liberated African's ability to adapt the Western concept of the social contract by creating a document that stipulated the rights and obligations of its members. It also established for secret societies the practice of formulating constitutions that were sent to presiding authorities for approval.

That the government was caught unprepared for this development was clearly seen in Governor Campbell's response. His own investigations confirmed his worst fears that this ostensibly harmless benefit society was capable of forming the basis of an extralegal government. In reaction to this threat, Campbell ordered that Potts be removed from his government position, that the headmen involved in the companies be tried in the civil courts, and that members who were discharged soldiers lose their pensions. Campbell specifically outlawed the asusu and all networks of intervillage benefit societies. He ruled that a society could deploy its funds only to members in distress. This made loans to branch groups illegal and therefore weakened intervillage alliances. Alternative associations were to be limited to one hundred members and a treasury of no more than twenty-five pounds. Thus, by limiting the amount of funds a group might collect, the colonial authorities hoped to curtail the influence of such traditional forms of social organization.[53]

In the belief that the lack of a savings institution was the primary cause of the asusu expansion, Denham suggested that a savings bank be established to fill the void left by the legally impaired asusu. As Peterson noted, Denham's observation was partly correct, but it did not consider that the root of the problem was a void in matters of colonial governance. The administration could not provide a social contract broad enough to meet the needs of its people; at this the secret societies of the liberated Africans were more adept. By serving notice on the government, the secret societies provided the government with "a fearsome and potent example of the extent to which the colony citizens would go to assume control of their own affairs."

Potts's ideas were acted upon by other Yoruba groups. The missionary records contain numerous references to Hunting and Egungun societies performing for each other in a network of secret societies. These exchanges betrayed the existence of an ad hoc government that met the expressive needs and economic and political demands of the colonists. That the benefit societies were somewhat coercive in their membership drives, there is little doubt. Missionaries noted that new converts who had once worshiped idols in "country fashion," as pagan practices were labeled, were quick to thank them for their efforts. They had wished to give up their idols but had feared reprisal from the secret societies.[54]

Reports concerning secret societies and traditions introduced by the liberated Africans decreased during the 1870s. By this time the Established Church and numerous reform branches were ensconced in the colony. The missionaries were more concerned with the political infrastructure than with African customs. Members of the Methodist Missionary Society, for example, expressed the most concern about personnel problems and matters of administration. Attempts were made to consolidate the regulations of the churches and the mission schools. Confident with the growing number of converts, the missionaries turned their efforts to the protectorate and to the source of the religion of the liberated African in Nigeria.

If the majority of the Sierra Leone reports gave the impression that the civilizing mission had been a success, individual observations contradicted this impression. Writing on the day after Christmas in 1870, E. Dannatt of Wilberforce (see map 2) reviewed the progress of the Methodist Church. "In the case of the old people—those during the greater part of their lives have been brought up in the midst of heathen practices—much superstition is mixed up with their religious ideas; as might be expected, still I believe the root of the matter is in them." As for younger people, he continued:

> One would have thought that after receiving the advantages of a fair primary education a religious training by all the inestimable blessings resulting from a stated Christian ministry, the young people would have thrown off the superstitions after their fathers but alas, it is far otherwise. It is utterly astonishing to hear them talk of the almost miraculous powers of their doctors, enchantments, apparitions, etc. and do what you will, you cannot get these abominable ideas uprooted.[55]

As a testimony to the strength of traditional African culture and a foreshadowing of events in politics and art in the twentieth century, Dannatt concluded that the church and, indeed, the colonial government were quite helpless with respect to "tribal" influences in the country.

> Mr. Boyce in his letter asks what of the tribal influences yet existing in the colony, a sort of secret government within a government? Is that true? Is it dying out? I may say in reply that the tribal influences are as strong as ever. In this village there are three distinct tribes; they inhabit separate parts, seldom intermarry, and have but little communication with each other except in the way of business. Mr. Boyce defines the system well: it "is a secret government within a government." . . . I believe it will be a long long time before they dye [sic].[56]

It is apparent that African forms of social-political organization had taken up the slack left by the colonial administration. These African organizations were firmly imbedded in the religion of the liberated slaves, who expressed their beliefs with masquerades. That Dannatt called it a secret government within a government is a remarkably farsighted observation, one that is relevant to the current situation in Sierra Leone. Dannatt also observed very little mixing among the various tribes except in matters of business. This may well describe the relations between the Creoles and persons who migrated to Freetown from the countryside. Relationships between the settlers and the natives have seldom been cordial; their settling in proximity, however, was the first step in the formation of a protonational culture that would one day integrate a number of cultural elements of the Creoles and the peoples of the provinces.

By the end of the nineteenth century, the Creoles were the dominant class in Sierra Leone. They professed Christianity and were the most educated. They occupied the best jobs and commanded considerable political authority. Economically solvent both in the mountain villages and Freetown, they built large wooden houses with stone foundations and hired the natives for domestic work. They had effected their own Krio language and African cuisine. They sent their offspring to private and public schools in London. Many of these privileged children returned as doctors, lawyers, and members of other professions. On the religious side, Creole culture was mixed. Despite their professed allegiance to the church, the Creoles nevertheless retained their roots in Yoruba culture. If at one level the Creole was uneasy in discussions about paganism, he saw no contradiction in celebrating the funerals of deceased at the local Hunting lodge. This might be done with or without the knowledge that at the base of the Hunting society was the cult of Ogun.

A New Identity

The Creoles had developed a strong sense of Yoruba identity, and this necessarily reinforced the practices of the mother culture. Creole nostalgia for Yoruba custom probably sprang from the threat posed by the influx of peoples from the protectorate and from the fear that they themselves had become too apingly Western in their beliefs and lifestyles. Many of the native missionaries of Yoruba descent expressed a longing to return to the homeland. One, Mr. Thorpe of Hastings, the original site of the Hunting and Egungun societies of the colony (see map 2), expressed his feeling:

> Grave responsibilities might possibly attach themselves to my strange and perhaps isolated situation amongst a people like the egba who are as notable for their sagacity and wisdom as for their jealousy and suspicion, and the tenacity and profound sacredness with which they hold their ancestral rites and mysterious superstitions.[57]

The attitude of this new generation of missionaries toward the traditional religion of the liberated African had shifted dramatically toward the positive. It is difficult to imagine the first missionaries using words like *sagacity, profound,* or *sacredness* in connection with "pagan" peoples. These terms characterized the Creole's new and positive African outlook.

On the surface it seemed that Creole culture was imitative, but the truth was that the African elements had been transformed, with the original creative impetus remaining the same. An article described a womens' auxiliary that was faintly European and strongly affected by Yoruba aesthetic sense. In a review of the "Soirée of the Red Riding Hood Club," the reporter wrote that except for the president, the members were uniformly clothed in cream-colored dresses richly trimmed, with badges and headgear of red, which "though producing an admirable effect cannot be exactly described, as it is neither a hat nor cap, neither a diadem nor a crown, but it is a distinguishing something, which marks out at once a member."[58] The president was dressed in a black silk dress with the indescribable headgear.

By the end of the century the Creoles were securely at the top of the social ladder, using their education and Christian outlook to maintain that position. In their fondness for lavish display of costume for the purposes of group identity and aesthetic rivalry, the underlying African sensibility was close at hand. The Great Experiment had yielded surprising results.

2

Freetown

The first settlement of Freetown, as surveyed by the Sierra Leone Company in 1797, was composed of three main streets running east and west, and nine smaller streets that intersect them at right angles.[1] (See map 5.) The coastal plain and steeply rising hills have prevented expansion to the north and south, thus the city has primarily spread to the east and west. With only a few streets connecting the east and west, the city has developed serious traffic problems, which at times make it impossible to travel by vehicle from one end of town to the other. Moreover, since most government offices are on the west side of Tower Hill and New Englandville, east-side residents must take lorries, which frequently stop on the narrow streets, thus aggravating the traffic problem. People who live in the core area of the city depend on the lorry service for transport to the industrial part to the east, an area that promises to be a major outlet for continued growth. Freetown's harbors are also located here, at Cline Point, and along Fourah Bay. Each morning and evening Freetown is faced with a traffic snarl as residents crisscross the city going to and returning from work. As settlement spreads along the east-west axis, commuter problems persist, causing one to wonder if future planning will correct the situation.[2]

The main geographical features of the city include hills, mountains, coastal bay, and a flat coastal plain. The east and west wings of the town are joined together at Tower Hill, the site of the parliament and Fort Thornton, the oldest fortress of the city. The main east roads—Fourah Bay and Kissi—feed into the central business district, which is on the north side of Tower Hill. Circular Road circumvents the hill, as it connects the east and west sides of the city. Pademba and Kroo Town roads are the primary west thoroughfares. In the business district, banks, embassies,

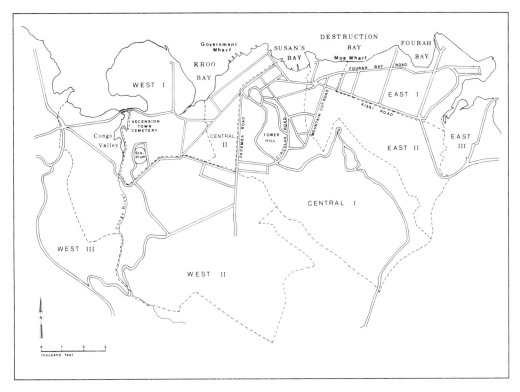

MAP 5   Freetown   Credit: Ryntha Johnson

department stores, and large clothiers compete for space in the original
site of the town. A little farther east, along Kissi and the adjoining smaller
streets, are Lebanese shops and local markets. Within this area both
Lebanese and Africans rent apartments above commercial space. As might
be expected, the population density is quite high in the central area.

In the eastern section of Freetown—the Fourah Bay area—most businesses are located along Kissi and Fourah Bay roads. To the south of
the latter street are shantytowns of Mende and other migratory groups,
whose housing is the poorest in the city. These dwellings have cement
or dirt foundations and are clustered tightly together at varying elevations
on the side of the hill. As a result, waste from the upper elevations
surfaces in the yards and rooms of the houses farther down the hill, and
health conditions are poor. The more affluent descendants of the Yoruba
at Fourah Bay occupy an area between Kissi and Fourah Bay roads. There
the evenly spaced apartments and houses suggest early town planning;
and many of the old Creole houses, some in excellent condition, are still
occupied. (See figure 13.) Concrete and stone-block houses are the most
common types of residences in this area.

Population density at Fourah Bay is extremely high, and one suspects

FIGURE 13   A rare old Creole wallboard house between two later structures.
Photo credit: John Nunley

that the population will continue to increase.[3] Many homeowners have
built additional levels onto their residences. Some have built pan-bodi
houses on the back of their lots to rent to rural migrants. This settlement
pattern has accelerated the population-growth rate and, of more critical
importance to the environment, has put a strain on the city's infrastructure. Traffic, sewage, adequate and safe water, and power supplies
have all become major problems in this area. Fourah Bay remains a
stronghold for Yoruba Muslims — the Aku — who have maintained some
of the oldest secret societies in Freetown.

On the west side of the city, the streets are broader and traffic is
reduced. This area, which was originally intended for farming, is uniformly
divided into plots, and roads that were planned to border upon each
plot give the neighborhood a spacious and orderly appearance. The
housing in this section is of a higher quality than that in the eastern

section. Drainage is less of a health hazard, since most of the residences are on level ground. Private homes of expatriots, government officials, and wealthy members of the Sierra Leone business community are located on the western hills. The army barracks are also located there, at Hill Station and Wilberforce (see map 2). Hill Station was once the quarters of the British colonial staff. The British ambassador's residence is currently located nearby. Government offices have been built in the west section, at New Englandville and along Pademba Road, the location of the city's prison. Other offices have been built at Tower Hill.

Residential expansion in Freetown is of three types: (1) the intensified pattern, in which new housing and additional levels have been squeezed onto existing occupied lots; (2) entirely new settlements that might loosely be referred to as squatter settlements; and (3) the homes of the affluent built on the hills to the east and west.

The most difficult persons to place are the recently arrived immigrants. The new arrivals are usually underskilled and at the bottom of the economic hierarchy. If an unskilled male is fortunate, he will secure a menial job that will support him and his family in a small rented space. Many migrants reside on government property, where rents are informally arranged at low prices. Some of these squatter settlements are located at the east and west fringes of the city, along Destruction Bay, Susan's Bay, and Kroo Bay. (See map 5.) Others are along the river valleys that drain the Sierra Leone Mountains to the south. One river-valley settlement is located on the hillside facing Ascension Town Cemetery, the residence of the Ode-lay group called Bloody Mary. Another settlement has risen along the Congo Valley on the west end.

The Congo Valley settlement exemplifies the problems that have been caused by migration. Until a short time ago this valley was essentially uninhabited. A few people bathed or washed clothes where the river spills over large rocks at the valley bottom. Today the area is settled mainly by Limba migrants. They may be evicted by the government at any time, but their large numbers make this action unlikely. Several years ago a man who worked for the Lands and Survey Office conceived the idea of moving into the valley and building pan-bodi houses for rent.

As a way of concentrating capital for the building of the pan-bodi houses, a distillery was built at the valley bottom. The Limba, who have enjoyed a reputation for palm-wine tapping, have now extended their industry to the related art of distilling homemade gin or *omoli*. The product, which consists of yeast, sugar, and water, is boiled for several hours on the first day and then allowed to simmer for eight days. Afterward it is siphoned through a coiled copper pipe submerged in cold water. The cooled gin is then poured into five-gallon plastic containers. In 1978 the drink cost forty cents a quart, which was well within reach of the migrant population and the members of the Ode-lay societies.

FIGURE 14   Pan-bodi construction with balanced-stick frame used in the Bloody Mary settlement. Photo credit: John Nunley

With the capital from this cottage industry, the Limba developer purchases fifty-gallon drums from Rural Transport and other government agencies for about four dollars each. These containers are cut into strips for siding. Poles from monkey-apple and cottonwood trees are used to construct the house frames. (See figure 14.) Over these balanced wooden frames the flattened drum sheets arc nailed. (See figure 15.)

Pan-bodi technology has made some progress in the use of materials. For example, it has been recognized that the monkey-apple tree is well suited for frame construction because of its resistance to termites and ants. Despite this knowledge, however, poor design makes for uncomfortable conditions in the houses, especially during the hot season, and fire is an ever-present danger. At $10 a month, however, the three-room units are very desirable.

Because the valley is steep, most of the housing is pitched on hand-built rock terraces. Large portions of the hills are terraced; and where sizable rocks intrude into the landscape, they are heated with old rubber tires and cracked with hammers. The rubble that results is used to construct battered walls, which support the front of each terrace. Since

FIGURE 15   A finished pan-bodi house constructed by members of Bloody Mary.
Photo credit: John Nunley

terrace building is not practiced in Limba country, the technology has
been developed by trial and error. Some of these terraces have collapsed
because of the rains and consequently pose a threat to the occupants
farther downhill. But in spite of these setbacks, new terraces continue
to be built, giving the impression that the entire valley will soon be
occupied.

Pan-bodi settlements like the Congo Valley community are on the
increase in Freetown. In the short run they reduce the population pressure
of the inner city, but their growth will create new problems. If the
government does not respond to this settlement pattern, a crisis may
occur. The cutting down of trees to accommodate the new settlement
and small-scale cultivation have created prime conditions for soil erosion
and have lowered the water table to a dangerous level. The harsh urban
environment and tough lifestyle it engenders affect community organization, politics, and, unavoidably, the urban masquerades. The way in
which Ode-lay members respond to this bleak urban setting with and
without their masquerades will be an important determinate of government stability.

Before World War II

Large-scale migrations from the protectorate have been a principal cause of social and cultural changes in modern Freetown. These population movements reached their peak during the two world wars. The impact of rural migration was not restricted to Freetown, for a cluster of secondary cities, namely, Bo, Kenema, Port Loko, and the diamond towns of the Kono District were similarly affected. (See map 1.) Urban growth was to effect a new class, whose behavior was less in accordance with the traditional economy and more within the guidelines of free enterprise. This meant wage earners were more inclined to follow political movements that addressed the problems of the working man. Trade unionism and national-platform politics were to prove more attractive than the traditional chieftaincy. The chiefs were ill equipped to deal with the problems of this newly emerging class. This class was nurtured on the aesthetic of masquerade and ritual, but it had moved one step away from the traditional political sphere.

If the signs of this shift in social makeup were evident early in this century, the syndrome had not yet become clear. Robert Wellesley Cole's memories of his early boyhood in Freetown's east end prior to World War I reveal a startling picture of Creole life. Cole's grandfather was born in Kingston, Jamaica, in 1857. His father, who was born in Freetown, eventually settled in the Caribbean under the British apprenticeship scheme.[4]

Cole's ancestors were Egba Yoruba.[5] His Egba name was Ageh, which he claims is the Yoruba term for *man of iron*. His writings in *Kossoh Town Boy* describe a city filled with Yoruba tradition. He tells of a powerful *agugu* (Egungun) society, which was headed by a Christian named Abamba.[6] The society was located near his father's residence at 13 Pownall Street. That a Christian should be caught in the Yoruba tradition was not a contradiction. Even Cole's family, who were considered proper Creoles and therefore devoutly Christian, retained some of their ancestral traditions. The boy from Kossoh Town saw many celebrations and processions of the lanterns (floats) that appeared at the end of the Ramadan celebration. These objects, he explained, were constructed of paper in the form of ships, locomotives, railway cars, and giant dolls. At Easton Street a Temne pagan named Santigi (*tigi* is the Mende word for *head*) was instrumental in the creation of *wende, poro,* Bundu, and Alikali devils that paraded down Malta and Pownall streets.[7] That a Temne should be active in these masquerades is worthy of note, for it has been pointed out that this ethnic group was the instigator of the Alikali masked societies that preceded the Ode-lay groups.[8]

Kossoh Town was inhabited by Muslim and Christian Creoles and by natives of the protectorate. Everyone coexisted in this peaceful community with a mutual respect for a variety of traditions. Cole's father worked side by side with Muslims and pagans for the improvement of the community. In certain pockets of Kossoh Town, the Yoruba traditions were well insulated from external pressures, including those of the co-lonial government. Cole described one such area east of Pownall Street, beginning at Easton Street and terminating to the east at Savage Square. This neighborhood was known as Krojimi or what Cole called the Deep South of Freetown. It marked the sacred place of the Egungun mas-querades of the Aku, who had settled Fourah Bay in the nineteenth century.[9] One of the oldest and the most prestigious of the Egungun societies of this neighborhood currently stages lavish masquerade pre-sentations. The people of this neighborhood lived relatively untouched by Islam or Christianity, even though their settlement developed within the rectilinear grid of the city. This area was characterized by compounds connected by a labyrinth of dirt paths rather than uniform streets. In unplanned defiance, it carried forth the Yoruba traditions and, of sig-nificance to the future, offered living space for peoples of the protectorate and descendants of the first settlers. (See figure 16.)

The mixing of the sons of the liberated Africans and those of the native peoples did not escape the attention of the more conservative Creoles. Their reaction, quite understandably, was defensive; for they recognized the potential danger of a large electorate composed of natives. They believed that their adopted religion was far superior to the tradi-tional practices and that this superiority extended also to Creole culture. In 1919 the *Sierra Leone Weekly News* cited with disgust some Mende policemen singing pagan songs that their accompanying British officers enjoyed.[10] In this regard the Creoles believed that British recruitment of police from the protectorate was part of a policy directed against them. They perceived it as a British effort to divide and conquer. They pointed out that with the increase in number of the native police came an increase in the number of crimes. Thus the relationship between Creole and protectorate peoples became strained.

The argument that protectorate policemen were less capable of main-taining law and order in the city is one that has surfaced from time to time. Whether it is valid depends on the source of the criticism. It is a fact that the number and kinds of crimes greatly increased early in this century, especially during World War I.

In a 1917 newspaper we find reports of the first "organized" gangs of youths. We might imagine these groups as counterparts of the corruptible youths of the early nineteenth century who, the missionaries asserted, were hopelessly lost to paganism. One difference, however, was that the gangs were composed of Creoles and peoples of the protectorate and not exclusively the former. A newspaper wrote that a group called Foot-A-Backers, composed of urchins and backsliders from their homes, prac-ticed picking pockets and other forms of theft to the extent that it was

FIGURE 16   Descendants of the Oku Yoruba in the Fourah Bay area surrounded by twentieth-century architecture. Photo credit: John Nunley

not safe to walk the streets in certain parts of the city. "Pointers" of the group served as pimps, introducing strangers to women of the evening.[11]

Foot-A-Backers, the correspondent concluded, was a branch of a group called A-Burn-Am, sometimes known as Land Pilot. This parent society was headed by Generalissimo Yonkon, whom the article described as "mostly dilapidated." The A-Burn-Am always smoked cigarettes and carried spares behind the right ear. It is therefore easy to interpret *A-Burn-Am* from Krio as meaning *I burn them*. These groups lived at the Government Wharf beside another group called *Arms Akimbo*.[12] One has the impression that youths who migrated from the countryside early in the century joined other youths of the city to form social groups that were not unlike the older Yoruba societies. The novelty of the names of these groups and their officers as well as their style of presentation are characteristics that were to reappear in subsequent young men's associations.

This outbreak of organized crime continued after World War I. The leader of one youth group, "Money" Morlai Ankulla, and his "chief of staff" were sentenced to five years in prison for stealing nine bags of palm kernels. They were caught with the stolen property as they landed in canoes at Susan's Bay. The reporter added that crime had increased since the police were recruited from among the "aboriginies," as he called the natives.[13] The same kinds of criminal activities are still practiced at Susan's Bay, an area from which stolen goods are easily disposed of on the black market.

With the large-scale migration came the native religions that the media with its Creole bias denounced in articles such as "Native Customs."[14] Here the reporter took a position against the blending of African customs and Christianity. Despite the writer's admonishment to the contrary, many people turned to native African traditions. The media bias surfaced again in another article published later that year, in which the reporter concluded that Christianity offered the only salvation for Sierra Leone.[15] Religious controversy was stirred up by a shift in the composition of the Freetown population. This shift threatened the hold of Creoledom.

A 1919 newspaper article, in advocacy of a search for cultural roots, urged that the Oku (Yoruba) language be taught accurately. It noted that intermarriage between Creoles and protectorate persons was widely practiced, stating that, therefore, the Oku language and Yoruba customs must be correctly learned.[16] With the young Creoles' nostalgia for the old traditions, the writer predicted Freetown would be the center of a Yoruba renaissance. In Kossoh Town and other parts of the city, one could find people of diverse origins imitating Oku singing, dancing, and drumming.

In a subsequent article the reporter recorded Yoruba proverbs in what he considered to be the correct style.[17] One proverb cautioned the Yoruba and those who would imitate their traditions against excessive attention to dress and cloth, which might be called the Yoruba Achilles heel. The proverb *Ko si igbati a caso ti a ki iri ile fi wo* in translation means there is not an occasion when any new dress was made that the wearer did not have to earn the right to display it. This expression warned young people that their excessive love of fancy dress might turn them into degenerate debtors. Here we find the Yoruba rule of moderation.

If there was such a rule in Freetown, it seemed forgotten entirely by the inhabitants in their passion for ritual. Newspaper advertisements in Arabic and English, such as those placed by the Société Commerciale de L'Ouest African at Kissey Street, listed real Indian madras, Swiss madras, handkerchiefs, blue and shiny bafs, tissue blue prints, printed flannelette, fancy prints, checks, scarves, and shawls. We might imagine that these stores, which were located on the east side of Freetown, supplied the various Egungun, Gelede, and Hunting societies with fabric for their celebrations.[18] In the nearby mountain village of Regent, the Hunters celebrated the centenary with the firing of guns, dancing, music, and the appearance of the Hunting devils.[19] In Freetown the Native Comedy Company announced a fancy-dress ball for young people to keep them out of mischief. (See figure 17.) Tickets were sold to the general public and prizes were offered for the best-dressed and most accomplished dancers.[20] At Sackville Street young Muslims gathered for Egungun celebrations that ended in disappointment. One writer for the *Colony and Provincial Reporter* in 1917 challenged an Egungun group called Miratuz Zaman of Foulah Town to rise on the next occasion and not "allow the diabolical and disgusting Three Sisters Egun" to get ahead of them as was the case in their last presentation.[21]

Influenced by world news, the African Comedy Company advertised the following program in 1915:

> Exciting, amusing, and most comical. The man in . . . red coat, and hats with Uncle Sam, will be on stage. Do not miss the old fashion song—Father and Bina—the new song—Mr. Kaiser—will be rendered and all the latest rag-time songs. Come and see the goose step and the quick step back to Germany. Refreshment, sold cheap.[22]

Such new forms of entertainment were not the only features of the time, for the cinema was about to make its debut. In the same year Nicol's Electric Cinema advertised the feature *The Great German War Pictures*. This was screened at a makeshift theater at Wilberforce Memorial Hall.[23] The penchant for the aesthetic of cloth, dancing, music, and masquerade would later combine with the inspiration in the cinema to have a far-reaching effect on the Ode-lay societies.

The Yoruba-rooted celebrations of the Egungun, Hunting, and Gelede societies continued during the years between the wars. The Amalgamated Hunters Society announced its eleventh anniversary in 1939. Its service was held at Centenary Tabernacle Church along historic Circular Road, and the church announcement of the event signaled the end of the long perceived contradiction between the Yoruba and Christian traditions.[24]

During this period gangsterism was again a widespread problem. To remedy this, the acting governor, H. R. R. Blood, at the 1937–38 opening session of the Sierra Leone Legislative Council declared his intention to increase the police force. The addition of four constables was to provide more effective control of Government Wharf. The governor noted a slight increase in the number of crimes against property, but said he considered the increase in number of juvenile offenders a more serious matter.[25]

Many juvenile offenders were members of the Alikali and Compin youth societies. During World War II a Temne teacher with little political experience but a great deal of public support mobilized this network of societies to win an important government position.[26] Future leaders of the All Peoples Congress party (APC) saw in this teacher's campaign the value of organizing the youth. Creole and protectorate youths continued to join in Freetown celebrations. This integration was condemned by some and a warning was sounded:

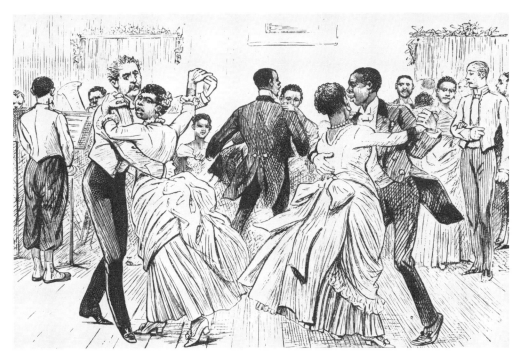

FIGURE 17   A Creole fancy-dress ball of the sort that influenced dress style and materials used in fancy masquerades. Picture credit: Historical Pictures Service, Chicago

> The pagans who took part in Christmas as a holiday beat their tom toms and drank their liquor. . . . Pagan orgies and pagan carousals to which the Creoles of Sierra Leone have gotten attached are destroying them both in body and soul and they must be aware. . . . The holiday must not be one of drunken carousals such as have brought ill-starred youths to their graves recently among us.[27]

Joint celebrations reached new heights by the time of World War II, and the warning that such combined cultural practices would destroy the Creole in both body and soul went unobserved. The forces that would end Creole domination were set in motion.

The reference to the "ill-starred" youth sent to their graves foreshadowed increasing violence and the use of strong-arm political tactics during the postwar years. This incident brought to the attention of the government the seriousness of the problems associated with the youthful secret associations. These groups contributed to lawlessness; and by creating their own constitutions they formed alternative governments. They constituted governments within the government, states within the state.

To counteract the impact of these societies, the Freetown Legislative Council introduced a bill entitled "An Ordinance to Declare Certain Societies to Be Unlawful Societies and to Provide for Matters Connected

Therewith." The *Sierra Leone Weekly News* attacked the bill as unconstitutional, claiming that it violated the rights of free assembly. In addition, it argued that adequate legislation already existed for the arrest of individuals who acted illegally. It continued: "We find it hard to believe that the executive seriously feels that any one in this Territory would wish to subvert or promote the subversion of the government. Nay, one who attempted to do so, will have his reward."[28] Threatened at the heart of their sociocultural institutions, the citizens of Freetown mounted an intensive campaign to defeat the bill. When the Freetown council discussed the measure ten days later, the attorney-general motioned to withdraw the ordinance. The motion was seconded by the colonial secretary, and it was quietly withdrawn from the agenda.[29]

The War Years

The increased pace of social change in Freetown was primarily caused by rural immigration, which was sparked by the availability of wartime jobs. Newspaper reports during World War II are reminiscent of those during World War I. It was observed that war-related industries attracted strangers, who filled the streets and wharfs.[30] Many of these so-called wastrels joined the military. Because of this the *Weekly News* cautioned Creole enlisters to be wary of protectorate persons, whose lawlessness, disrespect for chiefs, and defiance of police might be a damaging influence. The wharf-rat phenomenon posed a problem for the police throughout the war.[31] (See figure 18.)

By 1945 the number of young men who came to the city had reached an unprecedented level, and once more they had organized into effective groups capable of large-scale illegal operations. A newspaper article summarizing the decade up to the end of the war pointed to the large increase in general crime, pocket picking, petty thievery, and what it termed "big business" crimes.[32] As the war effort diminished in the colony and fewer jobs were available, the unemployed youths organized associations with scouts and intelligence branches. The *Weekly News* reported that gangs were located in the southern parts of the city at Macauley Street and Upper Mountain Cut, the home of the Firestone Ode-lay Society and a traditional reserve of the Yoruba societies. It reported two murders in the area, one involving the dismemberment of a young girl. A few months later the same paper reported "Gangs Come to Town," identified Mountain Cut as the location of the Hold-Up Gang, and—of even more significance—addressed its concern to a second generation of hooligans, who today compose the Ode-lay societies.[33] With the development of gang lifestyle came the first notices of marijuana-related arrests. This drug, called *djiamba* in Krio, would come to form an essential part of the Ode-lay lifestyle.

FIGURE 18   The followers of the Alikali masqueraders in this rare photograph were known as wharf rats. Courtesy of Michael Banton, International Africa Institute, London.

Shortly after World War II the *Sierra Leone Daily Mail* published one of the first written references to what have been called the Alikali societies, the Ode-lay prototype. It reported that Jonathan Harding was fined for wounding Moses Macauley at Ascension Town. Mr. Harding had stolen the head (mask) of an Ascension Town Alikali and sold it to a branch group in Aberdeen. In retaliation, members of the Ascension group wounded Harding, who in turn had cut Macauley with a broken glass bottle. This story emphasizes the intensity of aesthetic competition that existed in the masquerades.[34] The theft and sale of this headpiece shows that Alikali costumes were highly valued and indicates the high prestige that was attached to Freetown creations. Branch societies throughout Sierra Leone still purchase costumes from this art-producing center.

Not all aesthetic competition was violent. It also took the form of dancing events, which were staged in the more respectable quarters of society. In 1942 the *Weekly News* reported a dancing craze in Freetown. It stated; "We have invariably put in a word of caution to our young people who have banded themselves into clubs or associations and made the staging of ball dancing an essential purpose of their existence."[35] That word of caution fell on deaf ears, for it was not easy to convince the young to save money for the war effort or to take measures to protect the virginity of the young women who participated in the dances. The article pointed out that no fewer than four groups had made plans to cosponsor a dance festival in March 1942.

Secret society and public dance competitions were not the only forms of entertainment in the war years. Cinema and night clubs had also made tremendous gains. Popular films were being shown as early as 1934 in the old Town Hall. Edgar Wallace thrillers, the Three Stooges, and films with Arthur Askey played to the fantasies of Freetown audiences. Even in this early period, the theater attracted large crowds. The confusion at theater entrances, caused by anxious ticket buyers, was a matter of great concern to those persons who represented the law.[36] The Empire Cinema featured such films as *That Night in Rio* with Carmen Miranda, Don Ameche, and Alice Faye.[37] These films, scored with the heavy Afro-Brazilian beat, had a resounding impact at the Sackville Saloon Bar in Mountain Cut. This bar featured the Mayfair Jazz Band, which played at rumba competitions.[38] The Happy Eight Youth Songo Club, where the Cuban Swingers played to couples layered in fancy dress, must likewise have been affected.[39] The popular film *Weekend in Havana* also inspired these clubs.[40] Other films that were brought to Freetown included *The Princess and the Pirate* with Bob Hope, *Riders of the Black Hills*, *War of the Wildcats*, *Western Jamboree* with Gene Autry, *Under Western Stars* with Roy Rogers, and *The Three Musketeers*.[41]

One article discussed the impact of film on African dancing and music. It claimed that the medium was responsible for introducing new types of musical instruments into African ensembles and new dance steps into African dancing.[42] With later Ode-lay groups, such as Chicago, Red Indians, Gladiators, and Bloody Mary, the effects of cinema would be strong.

Through the years American cinema has consistently focused on gangster and Western-cowboy subject matter. These themes have left a remarkable impression on Ode-lay members, who have identified with the film industry's presentation of America by naming their societies, for example, Chicago, after the center of mobster activity, and Red Indian, after the primary enemy of the cowboy. The wide appeal of cinema led to the construction of the first theater in 1945. It was built on Westmoreland Street opposite the Sacred Heart Cathedral.[43] It was inevitable that the Word of God in the cathedral should find as its competition the hopes and fantasies offered by the moguls of Hollywood.

Since World War II

The 1950s were characterized by continuous masquerades and, likewise, newspaper complaints about them. One report claimed that the Egungun celebrations were in violation of the Summary Conviction Offences Ordinance, because the plays—as they were called—lasted into the "unnatural" hours of the night. The reporter criticized the city police for doing absolutely nothing to enforce the ordinance.[44] Bundu masking associations (women's initiation societies whose origins were probably in protectorate traditions) were also prevalent. (See figure 19.) Many adults claimed that the urban Bundu had actually abducted their offspring. One 1955 article entitled "What Is This Bundo?" described in detail the fattening of girls in the three-month ritual of the initiation and concluded that the ancient custom was backward and should be banished.[45]

The masked performances of the 1950s were no different than those of the war years; yet they were more numerous. Any occasion could be used to hold a masked performance. Even the Sierra Leone women's movement got into the act. On Christmas Day in 1955 members donned rubber and paper masks of European manufacture, covered their bodies in large scarves, and danced in the city streets to Wilburforce Hall. They were accompanied by the popular Calendar Band, an ensemble consisting of brass horns and native drums.[46] It is likely that Calendar (pronounced *Kalenda* in Krio) was the immediate prototype of the mailo jazz ensembles, as both groups combined traditional and Western instruments.

The 1950s were not all celebration. The increase in wage labor, rising cost of living, and growth of the incipient working class created pressures that frequently erupted on a large scale. The riots of 1955, for example, represented an extreme response to the problems of the developing nation. Many young men of the Bombali, Kono, and Port Loko districts of Sierra Leone (see map 1) declared open warfare on the state. Those active in the riots for the Kambia district were identified in a report that stated, "From these sources it is apparent that two 'hard core' gangs, remnants of demonstrators who had been dispersed by police in Magbema Chiefdom . . . remained active in February."[47] In the Bombali district, men smelling of drink attacked police with sticks, slings, and stones. Kenneth Little, an anthropologist, who more than any Western scholar has dedicated his research to Sierra Leone, reported that the Poro society was probably involved in the organization of the riots.[48] In addition to Poro,

FIGURE 19   The women's Sande (Bundu or Bondo) Society of Freetown. Photo credit: John Nunley

the so-called youth gangs that had taken their ritual pattern from the older Yoruba societies were also involved in the disturbances. Similar outbreaks occurred in 1959 in the Kono district.

The increase in diamond production attracted more persons to the eastern provinces than the industry could absorb. Young men who did not find employment organized themselves into gangs to illegally tap the diamond reserves. One local report claimed that the gangs were structured like the police riot units, with between 50 and 400 members in each branch. On Christmas Day, during a period when over 20,000 young men were unemployed, these groups fought openly with Kono police. Thus, the gang societies prospered in areas where the interests of an emerging class were best served by grassroots organization.[49] This represented a slight shift from the traditional tribal authority, in which the chiefs stood at the apex.

The Kono secret societies not only supplied their members with food and shelter, but also served expressive functions. They combined the tradition of the ancestors, African medicine, and a blend of Western and African music in an aesthetic-ritual event that mitigated the hardships of

radical and harsh social change. At the present time the Ode-lay societies
of Freetown and Kono enjoy strong intergroup relationships. By offering
sacrifices of kola nut, rum, rice, and medicines to the spirit-possessed
costumes, followers maintain a continuity in tradition. At the same time,
they learn the rules and boundaries accorded them in the urban environment, where rights and obligations are decided by the marketplace
rather than by the customs of societies in which age, sex, and lineage
status largely determine behavior.

In 1958 a news article called for a ban on all "Useless and Aimless
Clubs," claiming that their only purpose was destruction and the cor-
ruption of youth.[50] During this active period, the Sierra Leone Peoples
party under Milton Margai obtained the seat of power left after the
British granted the nation its independence. By the early 1960s, the ruling
party felt somewhat secure and scheduled the prison release of Sorie I.
Koroma, Siaka Stevens, and several other members of a new political
party called the All Peoples Congress (APC).[51] The APC, which had learned
the lesson of the 1955 riots, aligned its base of support with the youth
who had organized the "useless and aimless clubs." At the expense of
the tribal rulers, the APC would one day declare a one-party state. At
this time the Odeon Cinema was featuring films like *The Golden Idol*
with Bomba the Jungle Boy, and the Roxy showed *Frontier Rangers,
Party Girls, High School Confidential,* and *Island in the Sun* with Harry
Belafonte, James Mason, and Joan Fontaine.[52] During the 1960s a new
kind of film from India, China, and Hong Kong would attract Ode-lay
members.

The interest of the *Sierra Leone Daily Mail* in masking celebrations
heightened with its photographic coverage of the many different types
of costumes. In 1961 the paper illustrated the *gorbois* (*gobai*) and *gongoley*
(*gongoli*) maskers (see figure 20) who with the Bundu women, played for
the reception of the Duke of York.[53] In 1962, on Boxing Day (the first
weekday following Christmas, when British employers present gifts to
their employees, a day that is celebrated with sporting events) an Arishola
fancy devil was illustrated in the news.[54] A 1961 issue of the *Daily Mail*
featured the West End Holidaymakers, with banjoist Mr. Thomas of
Post and Communications and other persons dressed in female costumes,
celebrating Christmas. The instrumental ensemble consisted of a horn,
triangle, and banjo. Thus the Creoles in a secular entertainment company
recalled the Yoruba fancy aesthetic and the transvestism of the Gelede
society.[55]

The early 1960s were a time of rapid growth for the Ode-lay societies.
On each 27 April, Independence Day, the youth staged a large presentation
with many street masquerades. The *Daily Mail* described the lawlessness
and violence that accompanied these celebrations. In one instance a police
officer reported an encounter between a group called *Henganday* (a Krio
expression meaning *hang on there,* referring to the place where the edge

FIGURE 20   Country gongoli masks surrounded by red flags of the All Peoples Congress party. Photo credit: John Nunley

FIGURE 21   Detail of an Alikali masquerader in fancy dress. Courtesy of Michael
Banton, International Africa Institute, London.

of the pant leg should fall by the ankle) and another masking group at
Waterloo Street in the western area of the city. The groups fought with
stones, strips of iron, and broken bottles. The officer testified that he
asked the two groups to disperse, but that the participants turned on
the policemen. Despite the danger, the police arrested one of the group's
"most cherished devils dressed in velvet from top to bottom."[56] (See
figure 21.) Two days later a group referred to in the article as Remie
(named after the late Remie Bell, who had headed the Lord Have Mercy
Ode-lay Society) fought with a society known as Torpedo. Members of
each group were arrested.

Devil arrests have never been accepted by the populace of Sierra Leone.
Even the more conservative elements of society have questioned the right
of the police to arrest what is quintessentially a spirit, a manifestation
of the ancestors. How such an entity could be charged with a crime was
a common question. Ode-lay members were quick to point out this
problem; and sensing the contradiction, they vigorously protested gov-

ernment intervention. After the arrest of the Henganday devil and twelve society members, the Alikali maskers appeared before a magistrate's court and were charged with disorderly behavior and unlawful procession. The members stood before the court, half naked and covered with wounds, and pleaded not guilty to both charges. Over one hundred young men crowded the courtroom to voice their protests and disrupt the proceedings.[57]

The police were as concerned about law and order for lantern celebrations as for Ode-lay celebrations, and they attempted to regulate both events in the same way. A 1967 article set forth the following guidelines for lanterns:

> No political emblems or symbols will be displayed in the form of lighted lanterns
>
> The singing of any songs that are likely to cause a breach of the peace will not be permitted
>
> Lanterns shall not be destroyed
>
> 35 groups in the parade must pass the East police station in order to be judged
>
> Lanterns wearing Red or Green must ensure no breach of peace on this celebration of Eid ul-Fitri[58]

These rules bear a strong resemblance to masking ordinances, in their attempt to regulate the direction of the procession to minimize group encounters and destruction of property.[59] What was significantly different in the lantern rules of 1967 was the outlawing of political songs and emblems, a ruling backed by supporters of the Sierra Leone Peoples party (SLPP). This party felt that such an allowance would favor the All Peoples Congress party, which at that time had a well-organized system of youth clubs. Moreover, the APC was more supportive of the Muslim faction of the city than was its political counterpart, the SLPP; this, of course, was appreciated by Muslim youths, who celebrated with lanterns on a Muslim holiday. Newspaper illustrations featured Black Arrow, the predecessor of Firestone, with a lantern depicting the story of Sahida Allie and the Satan; the Foulah Town Lantern Club with a huge freight vessel; the Rainbow Lantern Club's mission of Camel Sahidal; and a substructure of the Vimto Lantern (Vimto was a soft-drink brand).[60]

A year later the All Peoples Congress party came to power and Siaka Stevens became prime minister. The following Lantern Day procession included thirty-four entries in three categories: ships, animals, and miscellaneous. The first-place winners in these respective categories were Congo Market with fifty-one points, Mighty Endeavor with seventy-two points, and Russian State and Ansaru Deen-Islam with fifty points each. The prizes were presented by the wife of the new prime minister. That same day two hundred masqueraders were arrested in Kono for disorderly conduct.[61] The mood in the provinces was reflected in Freetown. Two days after the celebration, the *Daily Mail* reported that the Bantous Nationale Lantern Club had stolen the silver cup (worth ninety-five *leones*) from Mighty Endeavor. The two clubs fought at the traditional grounds of the Egungun.[62]

At the root of this social unrest was Sierra Leone's lagging economy. This was poignantly brought home to the minister of trade and industry, S. I. Koroma, when a group of unemployed youths forced their way into his office and threatened to beat up the staff unless something was done about their employment status.[63] From this incident, party leaders concluded that the key to political success was in the effective control and support of youth and of Sierra Leone's urban secret societies. Shortly afterward Koroma organized his home constituency of Port Loko, "encouraging" the men of the area to join the Egungun society. He would use this network in Freetown and Port Loko to facilitate self-help projects.

The APC had yet to demonstrate its control over the youth, who during the previous century had proved too great an obstacle for Christian missionaries. Independence Day 1969 again exposed the vulnerability of the state political machines when two Ode-lay groups engaged in a massive brawl at Wilburforce Street. The police arrested several members, but only after some people were stabbed.[64] On the same day two other groups met at Kroo Town Road.[65] On Independence Day, a year later, a fight erupted between two groups that met at Pademba and Circular roads. When female followers of the masquerades were refused entry to a nearby house, an Ode-lay member struck the owner with an ax in a fit of anger and killed him.[66] At Christmas in 1970 the police were beaten by a "devil" group at Allen Street, the sacred home of the Hunting and Gelede societies.[67]

With Siaka Stevens's elevation to the presidency in 1971 and his appointment of S. I. Koroma as first vice-president and prime minister, the All Peoples Congress party began to consolidate its power.[68] In an effort to gain the support of youth, another APC member, Alfred Akibo-Betts, who sponsored the Firestone and Rainbow Ode-lay societies, became the president of the Western Area APC Youth League.[69] In December 1973 the minister of finance, C. A. Kamara-Taylor (later the second vice-president of the one-party state under the APC) made an appeal to the mask devils at the APC women's organization. He stated, "It is not the intention of government to restrict masqueraders and the colorful mask devils during the joyous celebrations of Christmas.[70] He also made an appeal for a new scheme of national development under the rubric of self-help. The development schemes, phrased in pararevolutionary rhetoric, emphasized grassroot efforts at the secret-society level.

At this time Freetown cinema patrons were viewing *The Big House* with Bruce Lee at the Roxy Theater and *Chauchow Boy* at the Odeon. A new oriental-film trend reflected the All Peoples Congress party's accommodating political relations with communist countries of the Far East, as well as the Ode-lay groups' interest in incorporating oriental visual motifs in their masquerades.

Despite the extreme hardships faced by the early settlers, Freetown was firmly established by mid-nineteenth century. With the rational experiment, which included a planned city, gridiron patterned streets, and satellite settlements, the British believed the colony could sustain itself while also contributing raw materials for manufacture in the British Isles. Government offices, schools, churches, and markets were built to accommodate the experiment.

But British intentions were compromised by the importation of nearly sixty thousand repatriated Yoruba slaves. The new arrivals introduced native masquerade traditions, medicine, religion, and an oral tradition that opposed the great experiment. Missionary attempts to eradicate Yoruba culture by building churches and actually confiscating masquerade accoutrements and other religious objects did not succeed. These Africans and their descendants established a Creole class, which combined native and Western traditions. As businessmen, traders, professionals, and government officials, they shaped the colony to meet their own needs rather than those of their colonial benefactors.

Freetown grew rapidly in the twentieth century. As a crown colony it attracted a new wave of immigrants from the countryside. Their culture and customs collided with those of the Creole class. Many of the young immigrants formed associations that newspapers labeled gangs and hooligans. These groups evolved in a truly urban landscape of overpopulation, unemployment, poor health conditions, lawlessness, and a news media consisting of radio, telephones, film, and printed materials. The admiration of the new arrivals for the accomplishments of the Creoles brought them to seek entry into the Yoruba-based secret societies, but they were rejected because of their low status, lack of education, and religion. They then formed their own associations, borrowing largely from the Yoruba Hunting, Egungun, and Gelede traditions. The so-called Ode-lay societies evolved after World War II and a second wave of immigration. These groups provided identity and security to the young immigrant, who otherwise found survival in the city difficult.

3

Ode-lay Organization

The origins of Ode-lay organization are found in the Yoruba-based Hunt-ing, Gelede, and Egungun traditions, as well as in general concepts of Yoruba religion. The concept of medicine and the position of medicine men also derive from these sources. Although the Ode-lay flyers an-nouncing forthcoming masquerades and countless lists of officers appear very contemporary, written in a Krio language affected by popular records, films, and books, the offices have traditional functions and are linked to the past. From church flyers to Hunting announcements to Ode-lay flyers one can see a clearly evolved notion of society organization.

The concept of society medicine is deeply imbedded in Ode-lay as-sociations. It, too, has roots in Yoruba and native religions. Medicine composes a world view. It can be used for destruction, protection, good and bad luck, and healing — in brief, for every aspect of living. By ingesting the secret-society medicine upon initiation, Ode-lay members become an organic part of the group. Moreover, the masquerader and masquerade materials also contain the medicine and thus are far more than mere symbols of the group; they are the metaphysical extension of each in-dividual member and of the group as a whole. This view of medicine, in Freetown called *juju* or *oogun,* has recently been introduced to New York, Miami, and Chicago, where Caribbean immigrants have settled. They share a common background with the repatriated Yoruba of Sierra Leone.

All of the secret societies, including the Ode-lay, have medicine men. Since the nineteenth century these persons have maintained a traditional sense of justice, protected members from opposing medicine practitioners and secret societies, and performed miracles. By maintaining the purity of their society membership and of the masquerade accoutrements, these respected individuals allow the participants in their ceremonies to reach ecstatic states.[1]

Offices

In the *Awodie* (the Freetown word for *hawk*), the oldest and most prestigious Egungun branch, the head officer or *agba* leads the masquerade processions and opens and closes the mask presentations. His assistant, *kaykayray agba*, is the chief organizer of the society and the one most expert in the society's medicines. The treasurer, *olukortu*, collects the gifts and monthly dues and summarizes the club's financial status at monthly meetings. In electing such officers, Ode-lay societies often use the Egungun names to describe them. Like the Egungun the Ode-lay also designate a masquerade dancer *onifakun* and medicine man *babalowu* or *juweni* man.

It is clear from Egungun plays that the agba acts as ceremonial head. He stands before the audience, moves between masqueraders, and at times leans over, one ear to the ground, listening to the masked ancestral spirits who speak in a deep, gutteral trill called *shegita,* the language of the underworld people. The agba greets important patrons of the society and frequently plies his guests with hard and soft drinks. The kaykayray agba, the masquerade director, keeps the rituals moving at the correct pace. He works with the chorus and drummers to coordinate their parts in a well-timed presentation. He also keeps an eye out for trouble, as audience and members alike may fight in the intense atmosphere created by the music and masquerades. Liquor is a major cause of such altercations. Assistant agbas are most anxious about the appearance of their groups during the holidays and often complain about the bad effect of alcohol. The assistant heads also attend other Egungun celebrations, to compare ritual presentations with their own. Ode-lay officers with these titles have similar responsibilities.

The Egungun medicine men are discreet in masquerade performances. It is their task to contact the ancestors before the play, to provide the medicines that protect the masqueraders and membership during the course of the performance, and to detect witches who may be intent on harming the actors or participants in the celebrations. The difference in meaning between the terms *babalowu* and *juweni man* to describe these officers is not clear-cut. Although Ode-lay groups prefer the latter title, these expressions are used almost interchangeably. They differ, however, in that a juweni man is less likely to consult clients about personal health problems and is more concerned with using power to obstruct or destroy certain individuals on behalf of his clients. The babalowu not only safeguards the society to which he belongs, but also serves as a diviner who consults patients with physical and social illnesses. One babalowu explained that a juweni man is one who calls the dead with medicinal leaves and herbs—mixtures that were first made in Nigeria.

Often it is the confrontation of juweni men at the celebrations that decides the fate of a masquerade. A society's medicine man is able to detect the presence of other such men who visit performances, often taking an invisible form. A defending juweni, it is claimed, can "smell out" the evil, which sometimes has the odor of gunpower, perfume, or even goat fat. If an outside juweni has come to do harm, the defending medicine man might shake in convulsions, thus alerting his companions to the potential danger. When asked why or how a juweni man can become invisible, the answer was, "*Oku aberi ashoh*" (A dead man does not ask for clothes). The implication is that the juweni man is close to the ancestors and like them can appear invisible, the only manifestation being one of smell.

Another officer of the Egungun that also is found in the Ode-lay societies is the leader of the house or *e lay fiki*. He conducts the initiation of members and the sacrifices inside the lodge or *igbale*. Other officers include the secondary personnel who support the primary appointments. These include the first vice-president, the first secretary, and the first treasurer. If particularly large ceremonies are held, a special coordinator is elected. All the officers, except the medicine men, are elected by the membership once a year.

Female officers of the Freetown secret societies are called, according to the group's preference, *e ya a ga*, mammy queen, or *digba*. The origins of this office for the Ode-lay are both indigenous to Sierra Leone and external, coming from the Yoruba Gelede society.[2] Michael Banton has noted that the female counterpart to the leaders of the young men's societies of the 1930s and 1940s were the mammy queens, who were named after the popular Queen Victoria.[3] It is probable that the title represented a nominal transformation of the *e ya a ga* of the Gelede. It is the belief of Hunting and Gelede members that women have the most powerful medicines. Their powers are rooted in the female's ability to reproduce. As the Ode-lay groups of Freetown became more aware of Western culture and conscious of new trends in dancing and dress, they changed the title of this Yoruba officer to the more fashionable mammy queen.

Ode-lay mammy queens are prominent female members who participate with the executive male officers in the sacred sacrifices presented to the spirits prior to each masked performance. This officer, so far as is known, does not make society medicines as does her counterpart in the Gelede societies. The mammy queen often lives in the Ode-lay settlement. She collects membership dues from both men and women, and she has the authority to raise special taxes for annual celebrations—a considerable expense—for she must provide the drinks, rice, salads, beans, and other food for the occasion. She is often assisted by several other women in making these preparations. It is noted that the late mammy queen of

Bloody Mary, Mammy Yoko, was the *soweh* or leader of the Western Area Bundu Society. As of 1978 a female officer was also the leader of a Bundu group. Her shrine is located in proximity to Bloody Mary, across the Congo River. It appears that some knowledge acquired by Bundu leaders has been adapted by Ode-lay groups in the office of mammy queen.

Ambas Geda (translated *we have togetherness*), the dance society of the 1930s and 1940s described by Banton, formed a brotherhood among migrants, mostly Temne, who were attracted by the city's industries. Their selection of officers reflected the older Yoruba institutions, as well as the latest trends. They constituted a bridge between the older traditions and the Ode-lay. The list of officers in descending order of importance included the sultan, mammy queen, second sultan, second mammy queen, judge, doctor, manager, second manager, commissioner or inspector, provost, cashier, clerk or secretary, leader of dances, conductor of the band, sisters, nurses, woman doctor, collector reporter, and bailiff.[4] These offices had many parallels in Yoruba positions. The most significant difference between the two groups of organizations was that the Temne-based Ambas Geda did not have masqueraders. Yet their uniform dress, called *ashoebi,* and stacks of Tyrolean hats could be considered a kind of mask costume.

The present structure of the Ode-lay has parallels in the Yoruba cults. Although some office titles have changed, the office functions have remained constant. The officers of the Bloody Mary Ode-lay Society, for example, include the agba, assistant agba, mammy queen, olukortu, onifakun, bila man, and the juweni man. For some occasions the Ode-lay groups elect a large number of program officers to organize special events. The programs for these events are intended to impress the public with a fashionable display of knowledge about social organization. (See figure 22.) A devil celebration of Civilian Rule demonstrated the extent to which the Ode-lay strive to make such an impression. The list of its officers follows:

Orbanks, director general
J. K. Conteh, deputy director general
Augustine-O-Neto, director for defence and communication
Willi-ro Jesus, high priest and special envoy from Jah
Foday Santama, permanent representative to the security council
Offi Toeh, special assistant to director general
Kobbo, permanent representative to the United Nations
Nabieu, chief imama
Henry Lewis, permanent representative to the Under World
Thompson Dad, adviser to the director general
Emmanuel Akpan, special envoy from the O.A.U. [Organization of African Unity]
Togar, press attaché

Mission Bloody Mary will be out again

on Tuesday, 22nd November, 1977 in full Festac swing

Musically you will hear the deep Throbs of The

Ancestral African Matoma and Soko Cultural Beat.

Also all the Brothers and Sisters of the Bloody Cult will be there like:

Agba Wonti	The Philosopher
Small Twin	The Wild West
John Shaft	The Free Thinker
Mr. Bond	The 'Business Man'
Mr. 'T'	The Simple Man
Joe Tex	The Rasta Preacher
Wortor	The Sister of Virgin Mary

Bloody Mary Festac 77 gonna be like it never used to be before

We are advocating for Peace, Equal Rights and Justice.   Take off is at 1.30 p.m.

Mary's just too Dreadful so Dreader than Dread
Join us at the Carnival so that peace can prevail
We don't want no Babylon to stop the Carnival

All the Dreadlocks from the Ghetto Shake off your natty dreadlocks and join the Carnival

Dreadwagon to cloud 9 nine. Security BATHUNORO 'nor scarede' Admission see:—

Wanti Junior,	Lily Nabbie,	Marshall,
Agba.	*Soc. Sec.*	*President.*
Mr. Bond,	Mr. 'T'	'Momoh C'
Org. Sec.	*Pub. Sec.*	*Sec. Gen.*

FIGURE 22   An Ode-lay society notice with expanded list of officers. Courtesy of Bloody Mary Ode-lay Society, Freetown.

Foday Headboy, special assistant to the permanent representative to the Under World

Gay to Gay, foreign exchange controller

Abondamay, chief military officer

Joboh Sherrington, chief executive secretary

Bavon Marie-Marie, chief of protocol

Ringo Blues, entertainment adviser

Alpha Bololo, commerical attaché

Daniel Carew, envoy from Las Vegas

Sebleh, envoy from the World of Athletics Council

Solo, representative from the Peoples Republic of Thailand[5]

Recruitment to the Ode-lay societies is also based on the older Yoruba institutions. This involves several steps, including application, evaluation of applicants' credentials, and assessment of sponsor support. A candidate's acceptance is the responsibility of the executive officers. The initiation ceremony is intended to protect the applicant from other societies and to safeguard the secrets of the particular lodge in which membership is sought. It should be noted that all Freetown societies recruit without regard to ethnicity, with the exception of Gelede, which maintains its selection of new members on a tribal basis. Gelede membership is restricted to offspring of Yoruba mothers who belong to the society.

The description of initiation obtained from members of a Hunting society is identical with the Ode-lay ritual, but this particular Hunting group was at one time an Ode-lay group. According to the group's informants, the *ashigba*, the Hunting term for *head of the society*, first received the initiate and then passed him to the *ajade* (second officer), who in turn passed him on to the care of the *olukortu* for the *sa* or swearing in. (See figure 23.) With one person standing in front of the candidate and another behind him, the ashigba and the ajade lead the initiate to the shrine of Ogun. There all three men face the olukortu. The applicant offers wine, red rum, and a small entry fee to the olukortu. who gives the offerings to the ashigba. Then four persons drink some of the wine and pass the bottle to other members. They then sing:

> *Enia ashigba de de low, de de.*
> *Ouwu shuku ouwu.*
> *Eberi te mo ka.*
> *Te been tie.*

> Let the ashigba stand up.
> The medicine is more than a medicine.
> A stranger has joined the society.
> We are satisfied that you are a member.

After the song, the initiate drinks the medicine, which he believes will cause his belly to swell and will cause his death on the seventh day thereafter if he should ever reveal the secrets of the society. In this way

THE AKU HUNTER'S SOCIETY
WATERLOO
Motto;- U N I T Y

Under the very Grand Chief Patronage of:-
Hon. Alfred A. Akibo Betts
(Special Parliamentary Assistant Ministry of Social Welfare)

AND

Grand Chief Patronages of:-
Dr. G. Devenaux *ph.D*

AND

Mr H. N. Fergusson
(*TOWN CLERK, Freetown City Council*)

A Thanks-giving Service Will be held on Sunday
5th, March 1978, at 3.30 p.m. at the ST. Mark's
Church Waterloo

Preacher:-Mr. N. H. PABS GARNON

At 1.30 p.m. A Procession of Hunters will leave the
Hunting yard for the Cemetry, before Proceeding to
the Church for Service

The band of the Methodist Boys High School
will lead both processions.; from the Church
to the Hunting Yard. Light Refreshments will be
served

Collections will be lifted up by Distinguished
Collectors & Recievers. A Cordial invitation
is Extended to all. Please bring a friend with you.

J. B. Pontis	J. V. Thomas	G. E. Wolfe
Chairman	*Olukortu*	*Ashikpa*
Balogun Sawyerr	J. B. Davies	C. A. Priddy
Ajadeh	*Ekpamor-Owo*	*Akowae*

FIGURE 23   A Hunting Society notice with list of officers. Courtesy of Aku Hunter's
Society, Waterloo, Sierra Leone.

the Ode-lay societies demand complete loyalty from their members. This potion is just one example of the power attributed to medicine in the Ode-lay society.

Medicine

Medicine men, called in Freetown babalowu or juweni men, are often held accountable for the personal health, vitality, death, and disease of others. These practitioners are also held responsible for the safety of masqueraders and society members as they parade the streets subject to hostile actions of medicine men of competing societies. From this it may be seen that the function of medicine and the role of medicine men within the secret societies are of pivotal importance.

The term *medicine* as we use it is perhaps too narrow to be applied to the African concept of *juju* (the Krio term for *medicine*) or *ogun* (oogun) as the Freetown Yoruba call it. The wielding of power or the ability to effect change in both the natural and supernatural realms might better describe what "medicine" *does* in the African sense. Apart from the definitional problems surrounding any discussion of the subject, we must consider the sensitiveness of the topic from the African point of view. Medicine is often a secret and private thing, and this discussion of it must therefore remain at a very general level.

Medicine is at the very foundation of each of the Freetown secret societies, including the Ode-lay. To know the medicine of each group is to share its secret. By eating the juju, initiates become one with the society. The juju most frequently mentioned in Freetown are *soweh* and *alé*. Ajagunsi, a famous juweni man from Hastings, explained that his Yoruba ancestors stored these medicines in their stomachs on board the slave ships. *Soweh*, a greenish mixture of crushed vegetable fibers and water or palm oil and blood, is carried in a calabash or tin cup by an attendant of the masquerading devil. With a medicine-soaked hand-broom, this person sprinkles the solution on the devil costume. Members of the society also rub this juju on their hands and foreheads. (See figure 24.)

Alé is a general classification for a number of medicines that cause severe skin problems. It is used by juweni men to protect Hunting and Egungun masqueraders. In one instance this solution was used in a clash between two Egungun societies from Hastings. The leader of one of the groups used a type of alé called *weregbe* to harm members of the other group. Enraged, Ajagunsi countered with a medicine called *fangay,* which belonged to the Limba people of Sierra Leone (see map 1). This mixture caused severe pain in the head of the opposing leader, who later died from its effects.

FIGURE 24 Masquerade attendants, with broom and basket container of soweh medicine (*right*), with ronko medicine hat (*second from left*), and with bila gun (*left*). Photo credit: Hans Schaal

Freetown medicines are derived from Nigerian as well as indigenous sources. Since the migrations from the rural areas to the city, other types of medicine have also appeared. The Limba-cloth shirts or *ronko,* of which there are many kinds, are worn as medicine by masked dancers. The shirt is generally made of dark-brown country cloth printed with several small designs. Amulets and other talismans are sometimes attached to it for protection of the dancer, who otherwise is vulnerable to actions of witches and juweni men of opposing societies. Still other medicines appear in the form of powders and ointments. These mixtures are hidden in the horns of the costumes and on the grounds of the play area. One such juju I saw consisted of three sheep horns stuck in the ground at one point so the horns formed an inverted tripod, at the center of which was placed an egg. Next to this medicine were two kola nuts, one white and one red, each split in half. Egungun members touched this object with their fingers and rubbed its juju across their foreheads.

Some juju is used specifically to contact the ancestors. Although the nature of these mixtures remains obscure, it is understood that these medicines are used in ancestral sacrifices performed before the devil costumes preceding a public appearance. This ritual is generally performed at a grave by the executive officers and a juweni man. The juweni man tosses four or six kola-nut halves on the ground. If the halves land face up and down in even numbers, this is taken as an indication of the ancestors' blessing upon the performance. The officers can then return to the shrine house to complete the sacrifice.

Other medicines are classified as "miracle inducers."[6] They are related to the *onidan,* miracles of the Egungun masqueraders. As the rains approach, the Egungun societies become anxious about the effects bad weather will have on the performances. Since masqueraders appear at the forty-day bereavement of deceased members, the collision between weather and performance is sometimes unavoidable. Ajagunsi recalled Jaybus Henry, the famous Egungun leader of Hastings (see map 2), who was the *ogboni* agba (*ogboni* in Freetown refers to an important elder, not to the Nigerian society of that name to which the sons of chiefs belong). Jaybus practiced his miracles before the "Kaiser's war" (World War I). Using three ogboni drums and some secret medicine, he moved the rain to a place outside the play area; and when the devils finished performing, he brought it back. Jaybus placed this juju in a plate in the dance area and set it on fire. As the concoction smoked, he walked around the performance ground inscribing a square in the dirt with his foot, thus identifying the spot where the rain would be prevented.[7]

The most powerful nineteenth-century Egungun medicine man at Hastings was Aku Charles (*Aku* in Krio means *dead man*). Although the dates of his life are not known, it is believed that he practiced juju during the mid-nineteenth century. Aku Charles had a magic wooden box, which he carried to Egungun performances. To "pull" the devil, Charles placed the box in the center of the play area and tapped it. Soon afterward smoke appeared above the box and in it were the devils. Aku Charles could also tap the ground with a fly whisk to make the masqueraders appear. It is believed that his medicine is buried at Hastings in a sacred place that is now surrounded by an iron fence and that each year the juju causes smoke to rise from the ground.

Other miracles involving the sudden appearance and disappearance of masqueraders in confrontations with missionaries are described. One popular account that occurred in Hastings tells of a certain clergyman who tried to interfere with the processions. He entered the performance area and whipped the dancers in an attempt to show the people that the devils were not ancestors. To his surprise, the story is told, he saw nothing underneath the garments but a fly whisk (a broom as the missionary purportedly reported), which followed him mockingly on his retreat.

> One day Graf went out with a whip in his hand to end an *Agugu* dance. He began to castigate [the dancers]; but he only flogged a mass of empty Egugu clothes. The bodies inside the clothes had mysteriously and inexplicably vanished. The missionary marched back to the Parsonage; his whip had dropped, but a broom belonging to one of the . . . Egugu escorts, followed him to the Parsonage, gyrating in fact executing a little dance of its own behind the worthy Cleric's back. However, when [he] turned round flourishing a Bible, it disappeared.[8]

The miracle of appearance is also associated with the Egungun mask of *oku walelo*. This is a tall devil that has a cane substructure and a cloth cover. Inside this boxlike costume, the dancer changes the height of the figure by adding or subtracting cane sections. In this way the costume seems magically to ascend and descend to various levels during the performance. *Oku walelo*, which means *Di man grap back* (The dead man gets up again), was performed for a forty-day ceremony at Hastings in 1978. The performance, given at dusk, was difficult to see. Prior to this masquerader's appearance, the crowd became silent in expectation of the miracle. An ordinary cloth Egungun masquerader bent over in the center of the dance area and assumed a chameleonlike position. Another performer moved toward this masquerader (who represented the dead man) and covered him as he changed into the costume of the oku walelo. The discarded costume was hidden by the assistant under his own cloth. Then, standing on a mortar, oku walelo ascended to a height of about fifteen feet. Its movement was spellbinding. At dusk the spirit of the deceased seemingly arose and slipped past the twilight into the world of the dead. After the ceremony the crowd dispersed and the relatives of the deceased followed its reincarnation back to the sacred shrines singing the song of Oku:

Lead singer (*Awoko*): Oku, dead man
                          Oku
                          Oku
                          Oku Walelo.

Chorus: [Name of the deceased], Walelo
                         Moshigbie, we are parting, we are finished with each
                              other.

The curative medicines of the first settlers of Freetown and the cults of Shango and Ogun were at the base of most healing substances and rituals. Several nineteenth-century shrines built for Shango have been described. One of the most interesting was a mortar-shaped idol.[9] One needs only recall the widespread use of the mortar in the ceremony of oku walelo. In this ritual the assistant masquerader sportingly tosses a mortar in the air and occasionally slips it underneath his garment in playful gestures. In this manner Shango may have been incorporated in the Egungun ceremonies.

Likewise, one description of Shango worshipers may point to a connection with the fancy attire of the Ambas Geda dancers, whose costumes might be considered a transformation of Shango dress. A clergyman who worked in the colony noted that Shango devotees dressed in female attire and carried axes on their shoulders. He also observed that the men wore two or three feathers of white, red, and black.[10] This description suggests a connection with the Ambas Geda, where the women wore feathered caps, and also identifies the Egungun devil *agbadu agbaru* with Shango, for the latter masquerader also carried an axe.

Respect for traditional medicine is a characteristic of Ode-lay practices. Young juweni men are believed to be spiritual seers who are capable of communicating with the dead through powers and strengths derived from juju. According to a member of Bloody Mary, the juweni man possesses a gift only God may confer. He has the power to waken the dead and to make ordinary men stop still. Given the appropriate medicines, the juweni man has control over anyone in his society. For the 1976 Eid ul-Adha festival, two members of Bloody Mary and their juweni man "wakened" the dead in graves at the Ascension Town Cemetery. After forty-five minutes of preparation, the juweni man brought forth two spirits. The first one to appear was evil, its shape and force made manifest by the wind. One observer described the other spirit as wrapped in white cloth and, like a deceased Muslim, his thumbs and big toes were tied in submission to Allah. On behalf of those officers present at this ritual the juweni man asked this spirit for a peaceful masquerade, prosperity, and progress for the group.

The dangers of Ode-lay masking processions make it imperative that medicines be placed in the right parts of the costumes. (See figure 25.) These medicines, made by the juweni man, must protect the devil from witches or other medicine men. With his "four" eyes, two focused on this world and two on the supernatural world, he is able to see dangers that are not visible to ordinary persons.

Hunting societies have little respect for these Ode-lay practices. They consider them mere imitations of their own traditions. The Ode-lay juweni, however, do claim knowledge of Hunting and indigenous medicines. The juweni man of Bloody Mary, for example, processed local herbs and leaves to make an ointment that was placed on the graves of the dead to make them appear. An informant commented, "We were four together in the cemetery. We had guts to stand. You can only see the miracle of the walking dead if you are strong-minded and can stand it. Before we got the juweni man we were hot tempered. But now we

FIGURE 25   Back to Power society members wearing pendant amulets as protection against witches. Photo credit: John Nunley

are reformed because we got two guys who perform miracles."[11] Whatever the cultural ties are between traditional and Ode-lay medicine man, it is clear that in the new societies, as in the old, this officer is very important.

A comparison between the traditional medicine man and his Ode-lay counterpart underscores the difficult tasks faced by the latter. Since Ode-lay masquerades are held in public-street processions, which may change direction at any moment, the juweni man cannot with any success plant medicines along the course. Because the Egungun and Hunting play areas are restricted and selected in advance, it is relatively easy for their medicine men to discreetly place their juju to protect their devils. The Ode-lay juweni are assisted in the difficult task of defending their masqueraders by several persons armed with clubs, broken bottles, and occasionally even small firearms.

Ode-lay social organization has its roots in Yoruba and Ambas Geda models. The elaborate list of officers in the Ode-lay societies was not a mere imitation of the preceeding Freetown organizations. The lengthy list of officers for the Civilian Rule Ode-lay society, for example, indicates a willingness on the part of the young men to shape their own identity.

Ambas Geda officers, such as lawyer, doctor, and nurse, do reflect Western traditions. As Banton observed, these societies kept strict account of the dues and taxes of the members, along with foodstuff, clothes, and other items that were required for the wakes of deceased members. Such accountability put emphasis on the contractual arrangement of the society. This, Banton claims, was the essential lesson for migrants, if they were to learn the principles of behavior within the urban context.

Durkheim noted that the primary distinction between human relationships of the urban and rural environments was in what he termed *organic* and *mechanical bonds*. Organic bonds, he explained, described relationships in which human beings exchanged a variety of goods and services. This was done to create an improved lifestyle. By Durkheim's use of the term *organic,* we understand that his metaphor is meant to be biological. Each unit within the social network is engaged in organic relationships to ensure that the larger body will survive.[12] The mechanical bond may be exemplified by classical Maya. In the Peten of Guatemala the land mass was uniform and settlements everywhere produced the same products. There was no need for small groups to unite into larger bodies, yet that happened. It has been suggested that the human impulse to form large structures is centered on the spiritual needs of humans to identify with larger social bodies.[13] Without economic ties, these bonds were fragile, for they do not contribute to an improved lifestyle for the participating subgroups. Thus these bonds had to be enforced by coercive means, in this case by the Maya elite.

Banton has suggested that the contractual arrangements written into the Temne association's constitutions represent an attempt made by the youth to reshape relationships based on the urban model.[14] The shape of these new relationships was determined by the rules and regulations of membership. The societies provided the youths with examples of organic bonds, which could also be applied outside Freetown. The Temne traditionally engaged in mechanically bonded relationships in which rights and obligations were enforced by traditional authority and not by rules of market exchange, which, Durkheim maintains, regulated organic relationships. In this respect youth organizations, functioning instrumentally, taught members how to live in the urban context.

Ode-lay societies have also emphasized the contractual nature of social relationships. Members must abide by a written constitution in return for society benefits. That problems exist in the adoption of the contractual notion is seen in the intragroup fighting that often occurs between the leadership and the general membership.[15]

4

The Ode-lay Societies

Freetown is divided politically into wards, from which members of the parliament and city council draw their constituencies. The primary division of the city into the eastern, central, and western wards once again reflects the city's east-west axis. The western wards have the greatest number of Hunting societies, whereas the eastern wards have the greatest number of Egungun groups. The Ode-lay groups have a slightly higher concentration in the Central One Constituency. The Hunting units are composed predominantly of Christian Yoruba who are descended from settlers who occupied the central and western wards. The Egungun societies drew upon the Aku, who settled in the eastern wards. The most important district for the Ode-lay societies is the East Two Ward, where the prestigious Firestone and Eastern Paddle societies are located. See map 5 for the political-ward boundaries of Freetown and appendix 1 for a list by ward of the mask societies in Freetown.

Between 1977 and 1978 approximately ninety-six masquerade societies were active in Freetown: twenty-four Ode-lay; twenty-nine Egungun; twenty-five Hunting; and eighteen other, including Gelede, Jolly, and fancy-devil societies. The Egungun groups have enjoyed the largest following, in a trend that continues as the city swells with migrants who are, for the most part, Muslim. As the migration of youth increases we may also see an increase in the number of Ode-lay societies, yet some of the older branches currently seek recognition as Hunting groups. The hunting units (the term *unit* here is a Krio equivalent for *branch*) have maintained their number and no decline is expected. It is interesting to note that of the three types of urban societies, the Ode-lay and Egungun groups have extended their reach to rural areas, whereas the Hunting societies have been restricted primarily to the Freetown area. The inability of the Hunting organization to become part of the countryside is a result, in part, of its primarily Christian membership.

The most noted Ode-lay societies of the East One Ward are Mau Mau and National, the latter sometimes called Back to Power. Less prestigious groups are Gladiators, Education, and Tagbota. In East Two, Firestone and Paddle occupy the center of attention, and Kalabush recruits the members rejected by the other two. East Three includes the Liner, Mexico, and Apollo societies, which are all equal in prestige. In the central wards are Rainbow, the most famous; followed by Sanghai Joe and Kai Bara City with equal memberships; and, finally, the smaller groups including Japan, Tetina Boys, and Sukuma Boys. In West One the most powerful Ode-lay society is Civilian Rule, followed by Red Indians, Bantus, and Nongowha. West Two is controlled by Bloody Mary, with Black Stone playing a supportive role. In West Three only Dortington represents the Ode-lay, the poor representation accounted for by the fact that this area is occupied mainly by upper-class Sierra Leonians and wealthy expatriots.

The primary Ode-lay settlements from west to east are Bloody Mary, Civilian Rule, Paddle, Rainbow, Firestone, and National. These groups have settled at the periphery of the city. Unlike the Hunting and Egungun groups, many of them occupy public land. Bloody Mary is settled at Ascension Town Cemetery and at Pike and Phillip streets. The population density of the original settlement at Pike and Phillip was quite high in 1978, so some members moved to "Heaven City" (the cemetery), where they found greater privacy and freedom from police harassment.

With the exception of Back to Power, the Ode-lay settlements are located on the coastal banks or southern hills, making them exceedingly difficult to reach. Firestone is located below Mount Aureol, separated from the nearest community by a fast-moving stream, and its only means of access is a narrow log. Rainbow and Civilian Rule are established along coastal banks, where it is dangerous to walk after dark, thus affording protection against outsiders and police. In these neighborhoods Ode-lay members are free to sing, dance, and hold activities without fear of police raids. Graham Greene observed that even the African police were reluctant to patrol these areas.[1] The police today show the same caution; but when they do raid one of these places, the incident is reported with a great deal of hyperbole.

The number of Ode-lay societies is constantly changing: some disappear because of lack of interest, a few become Hunting units, and others are created through a process of fission or amalgamation of existing groups. We will here consider the societies that are most influential and best exemplify the Ode-lay lifestyle.

Firestone

Firestone evolved from a lantern-building society called Black Arrow, a Mountain Cut group that celebrated occasionally with Jolly fancy devils. Its members made lanterns for Eid-ul-Fitry and became famous for their creations. One member, who is now a well-known artist, won several prizes for his work. During the 1950s Black Arrow attracted local youth and those who migrated to the city. With a shift in ethnicity and age of membership came the issue of marijuana smoking. Older Black Arrow members had only contempt for the drug, but younger members—who were referred to as *youngbloods*—quickly took to its use. One of these men, Brama Denke, organized a faction of the youth into a new society called Firestone. Denke derived the name for this group from his experiences in Monrovia, Liberia, where the Firestone Rubber Company played a significant role in the economy. There he had been impressed by the dominance of the company. As the older members of Black Arrow gained higher economic status, their interest in lantern building declined. The society was eventually dissolved, and its remaining members joined other fancy-devil, Egungun, and Hunting societies.

Firestone was named officially in 1967, one year before the APC consolidated its power under President Siaka Stevens. It claims as its sacred shrine and settlement address 101 Red Pump, off Owen Street, a property allegedly owned by a member of parliament. Shouts of "Firestone! Firestone!" greet a visitor on the way to and from the settlement and define the society's territory. These calls may be heard along Mountain Cut Road and its cross streets, increasing as the area is approached and decreasing as it is left behind.

In 1978 Firestone claimed about ninety members and over three thousand masquerade supporters who annually gathered for the Eid-ul-Adha celebrations.[2] The head of the group, the *ashigba,* maintains the group's Ogun shrine with sacrifices of kola and rum. Other officers include secretary, treasurer, mammy queen, and masquerade dancers. Like most Ode-lay societies, Firestone has its own song leader or awoko; but it hires one of the popular mailo jazz bands to accompany its masqueraders. The employment of a separate professional music ensemble distinguishes the Ode-lay from other more traditional societies, whose reputations were made by their own musicians. The general membership or *bobo* of Firestone identifies itself, like that of the older Yoruba societies, by the untranslatable password *ansay* and its response *asrbaoona.* Firestone members also belong to other masquerade associations. Though initiates are primarily recruited from Mountain Cut, this is not a criterion for induction. Individuals of all ethnic groups are invited to join.

The Firestone settlement recalls that of the Ambas Geda:

Most companies build a shelter in the yard they rent. It has bamboo uprights around the sides and bamboo benches; leaves and fronds are plaited into the walls and sometimes into part of the roof to provide a cover. Sometimes there is a flagpole to which a flag is hoisted when the company is meeting. At the headquarters occasional practice dances are held to teach the members new dances and songs; on these occasions members of the public may be admitted free, but for a dance to celebrate some particular event a charge may be made.[3]

This description makes an important point with respect to property use. The Temne societies leased land from private individuals, whereas the major Ode-lay groups in most instances settled on crown land. This privilege is bestowed by individuals in the government, who have allowed the societies the use of public-domain lands in return for political backing. The groups described by Banton apparently had the finances and co-operation of the membership to insure the collection of monthly dues for rent. Ode-lay leaders have less control over financial matters, their members on the whole being mistrustful of their officers. This land-use pattern is indicative of the close relationship between Ode-lay groups and the current political regime. Although the earlier Temne societies did not obtain the same degree of intimacy in matters of government, elected officials did not ignore their political potential.

Owen Street, which leads to Firestone, is narrow and especially difficult to traverse during the rainy season, when parts of the road are washed out. Adjacent to the road are several pan-bodi houses, which line a path to the settlement. Upon crossing a single-log bridge, one has entered 101 Red Pump. There members of Firestone are usually seated in the various shelters in the morning, some engaged in a game called shoot shoot (a form of craps), while others still have not recovered from the events of the previous evening. At about 10:00 A.M. the neighborhood girls bring hot foods, including meat and fish sauces prepared in palm oil. In 1978 portions were sold with a small loaf of French bread or rice for about thirty cents. Usually the leaders are served first; others who could not afford a meal depend on the generosity of members who leave small quantities of food on their plates to be passed on. Mornings at Firestone are restful. Some people tend flower gardens, which they compare to the city's Victoria Park, while others sit under bamboo shelters for protection from the hot morning sun. The sound of traffic and the din of shoppers at the markets rise from below. The location has a full view of the ocean, and breezes move refreshingly through the settlement.

In 1978 Firestone had three bamboo shelters, two of them round and one square, and a large cane-mat-walled enclosure in which costumes were prepared for holiday processions. These structures were built around a large tree decorated with mask carvings and a telephone that was used to contact the ancestors of Heaven City. Slogans and names of society members were painted in white on large rocks located throughout the settlement. The slogans were often framed in a street-sign format. In one example "Giveway 100 M.P.H." was painted inside an inverted triangular border similar to a yield right-of-way sign. The message expresses the freethinker's self-image concerning quick thinking and fast reactions. It implies that if one could not move a hundred miles an hour or faster, one had no business on the road. Another sign stated "101 Red Pump, go on with Firestone!" Phrases such as *Equal Rights* reflect the influence of reggae music and a song with that title by a popular Jamaican artist named Peter Tosh. (See figure 26.) Alias names of society members painted on the rocks reveal the impact of adventure films shown at the local cinemas. Two code names associated with films are Lt. Colonel Colt and FX08 RSFI. The slogan *De foe ko!* (They should fuck off!) is signed "The Major."

This Firestone settlement was destroyed by fire in February 1978 as a result of a dispute between the youngbloods and the *taingaise* members (older officers).[4] For some time after this incident, the younger members planned to build a new "Revolutionary Firestone" settlement farther up the mountain. But the intended area was very steep and did not afford much land for construction; consequently the young dissenters returned to the original site and rebuilt the shelters. The circular building used for gambling was reconstructed first. The profits from this activity financed many society activities, including the construction of other buildings.

The gambling shelter was made of monkey-apple and bamboo vertical supports, with plaited grass and palm fronds composing the conical roof. These materials were supported by a crisscross network of smaller bamboo sticks. Several stones, each about the size of a concrete building block, were placed in a circle for the players to sit on. In its combination of African concepts of medicine, concretization of expression, and use of objects to express ideas, the shelter was well designed to control the behavior of the game's overexuberant participants.

At the center of the conical roof hung a large old key and a pair of crab pincers; an electric iron was set at the roof's edge. The key was "used" ceremonially to open and close games and the settlement during the sacrifice to the ancestors and for other important occasions. On a stone opposite the electric iron was the word *Go*. A game of shoot shoot was played like craps, and the same rules were applied to determine winners and losers. The players, who were seated on the stones, each took a turn in a clockwise direction. If one player threw craps, he as the loser might curse the pincers and the "house." The person who represented the house would tease or chide the loser through the mediary pincers. Symbolically, the victim of the house was helplessly caught in the grasp of the scavenger's claws. When a player lost a large sum, he

FIGURE 26   This slogan in a Ghanaian bar compares with those painted on rocks in
the Firestone settlement. Courtesy of Charles D. Miller III, Long Island, N.Y.

cursed the electric iron, which symbolized the wealth that once was
mined at the Marampa Iron Works and the old iron rods that once
served as a West African currency. The association of abstract ideas with
concrete objects was to show itself again in the smashing of 45 RPM
records at a sacrifice in honor of a "record-breaking" masquerade. When
tempers flared, some players were asked to leave the game. This was
indicated by directing attention to the stone with the word *Go* on it.
When one could no longer play the game, it was a matter of *Kopo no
de,* i.e., "There is no money."

Shoot shoot is a popular game in all the Ode-lay societies, but the
elaborate procedures followed by Firestone are remarkable. The use of
objects to mediate relationships of a potentially hostile nature is an
ingenious way to maintain order in what seems to be a very unstructured
environment. The *crab* (a pun for *craps*) pincers metaphorically recall
that losers are caught in a pinch or are trapped by the laws of chance.
Winners form pincers with their fingers and imitate crabs as they subdue
their opponents. The use of the electric iron demonstrates the ease with
which Ode-lay members incorporated Western objects into their lifestyle.
Firestone members were at one and the same time amused at the pun
between iron and money and admiring of the modernity of an electric

appliance. Many migrants, before coming to live in Freetown, had seen only the coal-heated iron.

In addition to the nightly games of dice, Firestone members and their girlfriends dance to radio music and ply their appetites with drink and marijuana. A few drummers and a *mbira* (the so-called thumb piano) player occasionally accompany the dancers. Young children of the neighborhood follow older youths to the settlement and join them in songs that recall past performances of the society.[5] Log fires and kerosene lanterns light the night sky. By 3:00 A.M. most people are asleep. Others have returned to their rented rooms nearby.

Paddle

The Eastern Paddle Society was formed at Magazine Wharf on the east side of Freetown. The members first met at a place called Devil Hole, a cave on the side of a cliff located at the north end of Hagan Street. The Clock Tower by the police station on the southern end of Hagan Street and the cave on the north marked the territorial limits of Paddle.

Older members of Paddle claim the group was founded by James Kortulu, who resided in the Devil Hole in the early 1950s. He furnished this natural shelter with table, chairs, bed, and stool. Records show that during this time he served several prison sentences for theft.[6] It was alleged that he worshiped a two-headed snake called Sama-Roof that also resided in the cave. This monster, which currently is the spirit of the society's bush-devil costume, was described as "a terrible snake with cowries on the head. The cowries appear to give this creature a double head, which makes it all the more fearful. It has not been seen for the past five years. Apparently it is dead or has found its way out."[7]

Kortulu is remembered as a dangerous man who killed adversaries in street fights. It is likely that he pirated goods from the docks and hid them in the cave until they could be sold on the black market. Thus he carried on a tradition that had become established at least by World War I. The proximity of the cave to the loading docks must have contributed to his decision to live there. Moreover, the site was on government land, and as a squatter he avoided the payment of taxes and rent.

The fearsome character of this founder and the legend of Sama-Roof caught the attention of nearby residents. An aura of mystery surrounded the cave and was furthered by the belief that this shelter led from the wharf to Mount Aureal and opened somewhere on the college grounds. Such an underground passage, it was explained, was used during World War II to smuggle diamonds out of the country for wartime industries. Devil Hole also served as a hiding place for political refugees during frequent turnovers in government.

The sacred character of the spirit of Sama-Roof, Kortulu, and numerous stories about the cave have established the reputation of Paddle. Prior to Paddle's registration with the government and the establishment of its written constitution, the society was mainly a one-man affair. An officer of the society explained its origins:

> During James Kortulu's time the Paddle Society was just a one-man affair. Subscriptions were not collected as such. One man would sponsor the building of the devil and on the day of the procession, others would join to swell the ranks of the crowd. In effect, at the end of the procession, the money collected would go in the pockets of the person who sponsored the building. Sometime in 1960, the headquarters of the society was removed to Foulah Town but was transferred back to the Devil Hole again. James Kortulu was residing in the Devil Hole. He initiated most of the older members presently in the society.[8]

The origin of Paddle exemplifies the formation of other Ode-lay groups in that in each case an individual with a fearful personality was identified as the builder of the first devil costume. For most Ode-lay groups, including Paddle, the early years are characterized by a lack of organization. In the beginning Paddle did not hold regular meetings, and it did not elect officials. It was, in fact, a "one-man affair." Persons who discussed the history of the group recalled that the wharf was used by some neighborhood boys to study comfortably by the cool water and moonlight. Other youngsters played soccer there. When Kortulu pulled his devil, the youth joined the procession in a spontaneous celebration. Later Kortulu initiated some of the older boys into the mysteries of the cave and thus established the founding membership.

After the initiations the celebrations became larger, the costumes more fearful and elaborate, and the music more effective. The first extravagant presentation was held on Boxing Day, 26 December 1958, which is traditionally celebrated with sporting events. Before the mid-nineteenth century, horse races were held on this day in the eastern part of the city along what is now called Race Course Road.[9] After disease killed the entire racing stock in 1850, the sport never recovered. Soccer games and Hunting society celebrations are currently held on this occasion, and on this day in 1958 Paddle and some sixty members also paraded with its masquerader. The group proceeded from the cave to the Eastern Police Station, to Fourah Bay Road, and to Bombay Street. There it encountered a Hunting society known as Pa Yorick, and a fight ensued, for which Paddle claimed victory. This incident enhanced its fierce reputation.

To avoid future altercations with Hunting societies, which were mostly Christian in membership, Kortulu in 1959 decided that the masquerade should be presented on the Muslim feast of Eid ul-Adha. By associating Paddle with a Muslim holiday, the group attracted larger crowds than it had previously. The Ode-lay appeal to young migrants of the Islamic faith provided a base for people of the city and the rural areas to develop ties. This joining of urban and rural peoples in a single association would have important implications in future politics.

In 1968 Paddle was organized formally, with elected officers and official recognition by the government. A notice of its registration under the Friendly Societies Act was published in a local gazette. Its name was given as the Eastern Paddle Society; and the names of the assistant financial secretary, treasurer, and financial secretary were listed. Its aims were stated as (1) to render pecuniary assistance to members in times of difficulty and (2) to foster relationships among members.[10] The emphasis on pecuniary support for members recalls the goals of the first Temne benefit and dancing societies and also the early nineteenth-century associations controlled by King Potts.[11] It is noteworthy that the president and vice-president of Paddle were not listed in the gazette. Exposure of these individuals would have revealed the intentions of certain political parties.

The secretary of Paddle single-handedly reorganized the association, conducted elections, and initiated the tradition of taking minutes at meetings.[12] Drawing upon the support of better educated youths, the organization now prides itself as the Ode-lay of the intelligentsia. Its members look down on their less controlled brothers.

The first Paddle minutes, dated 11 February 1968, reveal a strong interest in the society's performances. Members met at the Devil Hole to discuss the kind of masquerade and uniform dress they would use at the next procession. Some members suggested the Deer Flat-Top head (carved antelope head) as a suitable costume; others wanted the more traditional horned costume, the *alankoba*. Supporters of the more fashionable headpiece suggested a carver from Mountain Cut for the commission.[13] The members agreed to wear an *ashoebi* or uniform dress consisting of a white T-shirt, blue pants, and grass hat of the kind worn by hunters. This modern dress style is most popular with the Ode-lays.

At this meeting it was also debated whether to "pull" the devil from the bush or from the Devil Hole. Some persons wanted to imitate the Hunters by starting the masquerade in the bush, but the majority decided that the location at the wharf was more appropriate. Ten pounds were allocated for costume materials, five pounds for alcoholic beverages, and five pounds for soft drinks for temperate Muslims in the group. A Muslim member objected to the use of spirits, pointing out the disorder they caused in past performances. Another five pounds were allocated for the cost of obtaining a government permit for the masquerade procession; it was agreed that the society would contact a captain of the Royal Sierra Leone Military Forces to help obtain this document.

At the second meeting of 1968, members discussed devil construction: whether to use bag, country cloth, or fancy material for the pants and shirt of the masquerader. Traditionalists urged the use of bag, while young persons, who also pressed for the Deer Flat-Top headpiece, wanted to use fancy material. At this meeting, which was attended by a well-known government official, the names of VIPs were selected to receive the written requests for financial support. A political guest expressed concern about the route the procession would take, and it was decided that it would pass by his house. Anxious about the security of the devil, the members selected a subcommittee to clear grass and rocks from the front of Devil Hole so a gate could be built at its entrance.

During a meeting in March 1968, one faction urged that the society hire professional dancers to improve the masquerade dancing. The majority objected on the ground that it was a privilege to be considered for mask dancing.

Much of the information in the Paddle minutes indicates the seriousness that characterized the discussions about the masquerades. The minutes of 2 November 1970, for example, record several questions regarding the performance for the Eid-ul-Adha celebration. It was declared that the mailo jazz group Sabado of King Tom would represent the society. As a matter of courtesy and as a warning, Paddle also agreed to send a letter to its crosstown rival, Lord Have Mercy, declaring its intentions for that holiday. The devil dancers were also selected at this meeting, and the points along the route where masqueraders would exchange the costume were chosen. These stations included Cline Town, Mountain Cut, and the house of a member of the mailo jazz group. The soweh men and money collectors were also designated.

The meetings of 1971 addressed the issue of proper devil dress. One controversy centered over the use of traditional bag or Limba cotton dress (ronko) having magical powers. The hotly contested issue caused one member to faint during the debate. Afterward it was decided that the uniform dress for that year would include a black vest, jeans, and a black tie or ribbon tied around the arm in mourning for deceased members. The question was raised about the society's legal right to the property around Devil Hole, and it was decided that a certain amount of money would be deposited in a bank to lease the area.

By 1972 Paddle had gained prestige and a substantial membership, which generously increased its treasury. At the first meeting of the year, in preparation for the masquerades, the society allocated sixty leones (about sixty dollars) for the engagement of a mailo jazz band, and compensation was allotted for the dancers. Some female followers of the group had informally circulated examples of uniform dress materials for male approval. Strong opposition was expressed to the idea of women participating in what was considered a men's affair. The men decided that they and not the women would select the appropriate materials for the masquerade. The acquisition of the masking permit was left to one of the society's strong political supporters.

The minutes of 1973 reveal growing political support for Paddle and an increase in organizational efficiency. That year the society printed posters to advertise the masquerade and obtained money from government supporters to pay for the musical entertainment. An internal dispute regarding the leadership was brought before the executive committee. In this matter a leading member was charged with damaging the carved gun carried by the bila man in a performance and with attacking the devil with a knife at the cave before the morning carol, but the committee excused the individual because of drunkenness. During the year Paddle enlisted the support of six prominent politicians to obtain a permit for the Eid-ul-Adha holidays.

From the north end of Hagan Street, above Devil Hole, the closely spaced pan-bodi houses are visible, and the serious drainage problems once again become evident. A descent via a precipitous and irregularly stepped stairway and paths that connect at right angles finally reaches Devil Hole. On the left side of the stairs is an unfinished apartment building, which had it been rented would have threatened the society's occupancy of the area. On the right is a cane-mat enclosure fifteen feet square in which members hold dance celebrations. This structure is attached to a concrete-block building that is connected to the entrance of the cave.

A plan of the cave reveals its division into two compartments. The space adjoining the concrete building is about eight feet wide and not quite high enough to stand straight. The interior chamber has a higher ceiling. In this section, before the sacred shrine of Sama-Roof, new members are initiated. In this interior, sacrifices are performed and costume pieces are assembled.

The quality of construction of the settlement is poor. Cracks in the concrete are a source of considerable leakage and floor damage. Bamboo benches, like those described by Banton for the Ambas Geda, are placed in the members' room, but these also are in poor condition. Except for meetings, processions, and initiations, the cave is seldom occupied.

Devil Hole was primarily used for initiation, which the group leaders proudly claim is very systematic. Before the procedure was established the society was ruled by what members called "the law of the jungle." The first step in the initiation process requires applicants to write the secretary requesting permission to join. The second step, if the candidate is considered, is his appearance with a sponsor before the society. Upon approval he is invited to the cave and instructed to bring red rum, kola nut, biscuits, ground nuts, sweets, mints, and an egg. The egg is thrown at the entrance to the cave. Within the interior chamber, a place called *yara*, the initiate and attending members perform the initiation rites. The manager of the society performs the induction ceremonies and informs the initiate that if he betrays the secret of the society he will be punished by the manager before the shrine of Sama-Roof.

Bloody Mary

The western wards of Freetown are the home of Bloody Mary, an Ode-lay society that has long held a reputation for being the most feared young men's society. Bloody Mary was originally intended to be a short-lived organization, its sole purpose to take revenge on an opposing group.[14] Its devil proved so popular, however, that the society survived. Adding to its fierce reputation, the group has received more press coverage than any other Ode-lay group, especially in its confrontations with police. Bloody Mary headquarters are along the banks of the Congo River, Ascension Town Cemetery, and Pike Street. The last location was the first meeting place of the group and the residence of its founder, Wanty George.

The first young men's masquerade group in the area, called Big Time Jolly, was established in the mid-1950s. Another group, Yoncolma, was derived from this Jolly society, which at times displayed thirty or more costumes of the pumpkin-head or Alikali type.[15] Through the years the growing unemployment and inflated prices of costume materials have made it increasingly difficult for Big Time Jolly to compete in masquerades. As a result the group abandoned these fancy displays.

This Jolly was replaced by a society called Texas, which was named for the many cowboy movies shown in Freetown.[16] Texas took the format of the Ode-lay in its adaptation of the Hunting costume and organization. The devil head, according to a member named Johnny Shaft, was constructed of a freshly cut sheep's head; the remaining parts of the costume included a front and back hampa with traditional Hunting materials, a bag-cloth shirt, and pants. The devil made its annual appearance on New Year's Day.

The Texas society was formed at the suggestion of an APC official who wanted to commemorate the rise of Siaka Stevens. Unlike the friendly Jolly parent society from which it evolved, Texas was known for its fierceness. The society, it was said, "sent many people to the next world." Shaft explained, "We sent them to Heaven City." Public outcry against the society resulted in the exchange of the Texas bush devil for one of the fancy type. With the support of government officials, many fancy-devil costumes were constructed, and the society changed its name to Yoncolma.

Yoncolma met at a place called *Bapayor,* which Bloody Mary claims is a Limba word meaning *do not be afraid.* The location was Ascension Town Cemetery, where—it was pointed out—the living and the dead reside together in peace. Yoncolma paraded with its devil on Easter Monday and Republican Day. Its most popular masquerade character, Fat Mama, was described in this manner: "The Yoncolma devil is a mother devil—a fat woman. All side beef. When you hold it like this, you get so many steaks." The reputation of Fat Mama and its builder, Mr. Edmund, who was also a member of Bloody Mary, spread rapidly throughout the country, particularly to Kono, where the center of the diamond industry is located. (See map 1.) Yoncolma members were often recruited from this area.

The relationship between the youths of Freetown and Kono have been strengthened by the sister societies that have also been founded in the diamond districts. The Freetown Ode-lay realize considerable profit from successful masquerades; and as word spreads of an exceptionally well built costume, its value increases greatly. Yoncolma sold its first Fat Mama for about $200 to a Kono society. Many of its costumes and those of other groups have been purchased by political sponsors, who donate them to the Ode-lay groups in Kono.

Although Fat Mama was acclaimed for its fancy aesthetic, its sacrifice was the kind usually reserved for the fierce bush-devil costume of the hunters. Before the appearance of Fat Mama, a select part of the membership made a sacrifice that consisted of bread, uncooked rice, and pepper whiskey, which were placed on a winnowing tray. Such trays are used to fan the devils in procession. A red cock was sacrificed above the tray. The rice was offered in an uncooked form, because—it was explained—the invisible one does not eat cooked food. Such a reversal of a life practice to symbolize death is reflected in other West African customs, especially those involving the use of the left hand in funerary ceremonies. Sisala sculptors of northern Ghana, for example, use their left hands to carve a figure in honor of a deceased carver at his funeral. The use of the left hand instead of the normal right symbolizes the deceased carver's entrance to a spiritual world that is considered in many respects to be the opposite of the natural world.[17] After the sacrifice, two kola nuts were split in half and tossed before the costume to determine if the spirits had given approval of the procession. If the kola appeared face up and down in uneven numbers, the ceremony was repeated until an even combination was attained. This was interpreted as a positive sign from the spiritual world.

Yoncolma practiced Hunting rituals with the fancy devil until the group was attacked by Rainbow and Firestone, both of the central wards. After its final performance, the Yoncolma members met at Ascension Town Cemetery and declared a task force, SS117 Mission Bloody Mary, to take revenge on the attackers. To represent the power and fierceness of the new organization, it was decided that the society would be represented by a bush devil. It was explained that Bloody Mary, unlike Fat Mama, would be a bush devil—a devil that doesn't take shit![18] The new society's adoption of its name from a film entitled *OSS117 Mission B.M. Operation Lotus Flower* again reflects the impact of cinema on the youth of Free-town. Also reflecting this impact are aliases used by the group's founders, including James Bond, Fernando, and Sam Cook (a famous deceased black American vocalist).

Bloody Mary was organized like the Hunting societies, except for the addition of the office of mammy queen. This officer was to organize women followers and collect taxes for sacrifices and food for the celebrations. The creation of this new role for women in the group represents a sharp departure from the traditional Yoruba societies, with the exception of the Gelede. In Heaven City, it was stated, things are different; men need women in society affairs.

The members of Bloody Mary spent much time in their settlements. At about 10:00 A.M. they could be found preparing for the day after a long night of drinking, smoking, and dancing. If funds were available, they bought palm wine or marijuana to commence the day. Records, played on a portable hi-fi powered by an automobile battery, accompanied morning rituals with rock, soul, African, and reggae music.

The Ode-lay lifestyle has been influenced by the Jamaican inspired rastafarian philosophy as espoused through reggae music and lyrics.[19] Bloody Mary members, however, in expressing their views of the reggae-rasta movement, explain that a Freetown rasta is better described as a freethinker, one who is more intelligent than his Jamaican brother. The freethinker dressed in the carefree manner of the rasta but did not wear the *dada* or dreadlock hairstyle, because it was not neat in appearance. Unlike the rasta, the freethinker worked within the established order. "I understand a *freaker* [freethinker] by his appearance," Johnny Shaft said. "He is always a winner, because he works his ideas fast, making his living, hustling jobs in hotels, offices, and government departments." Freakers, he added, take a stand against the legalization of marijuana and, thus, are in opposition to Peter Tosh and the Jamaican rastas who rally behind his popular song *Legalize It!* "If everyone smoked dope," Shaft said, "it would be a disaster; it would add confusion. Fools can't handle it. They would let topics like money and inflation bug them, and they would turn to crime."[20]

Despite the differences between freaker and rasta lifestyles, Ode-lay identification with the reggae music of the rastafarians points to a gap between the older and younger generations in Freetown.[21] The reggae-rasta movement set the tone of the Ode-lay lifestyle, much to the irritation of the older generation of the city. If the rasta life was not emulated in detail, its cry Equal Rights! was on the minds of all members.

The government's refusal to grant permits to Bloody Mary, Firestone, and Paddle for the 1977 Eid-ul-Adha holiday and the police raid on the Bloody Mary settlement at Pike Street reshaped many members' thinking about settling at the cemetery. Even though the Pike Street location, with its intricate network of paths and houses packed together, provided a good defensive position, in 1977 the police overcame the Bloody Mary society there and confiscated its devil. With this is mind, the majority of the membership relocated at the cemetery, the original site of Yon-colma. There the Congo River, the steep embankment, and the cemetery offered better protection against the police, and the small residential population of the area left the society free to carry on late into the night.

Two economic factors also contributed to the resettlement. The first was a new soccer stadium built by the Chinese next to Ascension Town Cemetery. Shaft and other society members built new residences and a bar near a point of access to the stadium. They believed the bar would attract a great amount of business on soccer days. The second economic factor was fishing. Bloody Mary had built several pan-bodi houses below the cemetery along the mouth and east bank of the Congo River. This was an ideal location for a fleet of small plank-sided boats. One of the members, a fisherman, possessed the skill and knowledge to build these vessels.[22] The bar and the fishing fleet, it was hoped, would provide the society with a means of livelihood and thereby reduce its reliance on illegal activities for economic gain.

In return for the support of an APC candidate in a special election for West Two Constituency, Bloody Mary received enough funding from the government to build four additional residences at the cemetery. Two were under construction at the base of the embankment and two others were completed at the top in 1978. The structures, in pan-bodi style, were built on pumice rubble. Shaft's thirty-five by twenty-foot house was divided into four rooms: one room for himself, two rooms for rent, and a parlor that also served as the bar. Cassava crops and garden vegetables were planted around the house to supplement the fish and rice diet. Locally distilled gin and palm wine were the only drinks sold in the bar. Beer and Guinness stout were the preferred beverages, but the group could not afford to bring in electricity to refrigerate them.

Johnny Shaft was the member responsible for the society's small-scale entrepreneurial enterprises. He had considerable leadership skills and a broad background. He had once been a representative for the labor and cooperative studies program at the Ministry of Labor and National Resources. In that role he had been sent by Public Services International of London to Washington, D.C., and Israel to learn about international labor relations. Individuals like Shaft, who are well acquainted with the network of Ode-lay societies and possess leadership qualities, might in the future coordinate the energies of the various Ode-lay groups and express their demands to the government. (See figure 27.)

Civilian Rule

Civilian Rule is the dominate force in the Kroo Bay area and in the markets above the bay. The road approaching the society's quarters is often cluttered with garbage, sewage, and dead animals. During the rainy

FIGURE 27   Bloody Mary society members pose in their meeting house before solidarity posters brought back by Johnny Shaft from a young people's conference in Cuba. Photo credit: John Nunley

season, the passage is extremely slippery; and the frequent run-off presents health problems to the residents below. In the bay the tin-tapping sounds of tinkers can be heard from the cluster of bamboo enclosures. Here smiths and their assistants fashion buckets, pans, charcoal burners, and pitchers for home use. Housing is mostly of the pan-bodi type, with an occasional concrete structure. A few mosques offer places of prayer. At the foot of the main entry to Kroo Bay, a sewage drain, which carries debris from the market, attracts young children. Some people use the drain to wash clothes. This is one of the most impoverished parts of Freetown. A few yards east of the drain is the Orbanks City Bar, the home of Civilian Rule. In the veranda of the bar are several rotted, overstuffed chairs and the metal frames of car seats. These furnishings are usually occupied by Civilian Rule members, who watch young boys play soccer with a small, punctured rubber bladder. The players move vigorously across the field, splashing in and out of the drain.

I paid several visits to this settlement, at first without success. The head of Civilian Rule seemed always to be out on business. Later it was disclosed that the spectators of the soccer games guarded the entry to the Orbanks pub and warned its owner of the arrival of any outsider. Once invited into the high-fenced yard of the establishment, however, in the leader's absence, I was introduced to an assistant to the head of the society. A questionnaire I presented to this representative was challenged by several members, who questioned whether the interview was worthwhile and wondered how they might profit from it. Although this was not an unusual occurrence in my work, the objections raised in this case, especially those raised by the secretary of the society, were very articulate. This member, it turned out, was also the personal secretary to the minister of trade and industry.

The small facade of the pub masked a surprisingly large interior space with a slightly raised stage at one end. This was used by dance bands and by members who assembled mask costumes. At the front entry to the pub was a small wire-caged room containing several cartons of beer and a refrigerator. Adjacent to this space were two other rooms, one a parlor for the head of the society, the other his sleeping room. The doors to these rooms were kept locked. A large collection of mural paintings covered the dance-hall walls before the stage.

These brightly colored enamel paintings of life-size subjects on sheet rock revealed much about the lifestyle of the Ode-lay. In one corner of the room was a depiction of an Ode-lay youth, with head down and a bottle of beer on the floor in front of him. This icon was said to represent a "stoned" youth. (See figure 28.) To the left was a painting of two Third-World characters dressed in Chinese garb. Beneath them on the same panel was a seascape with a cluster of traditional African circular, mud-wall, thatched-roof dwellings. This painting was influenced by the

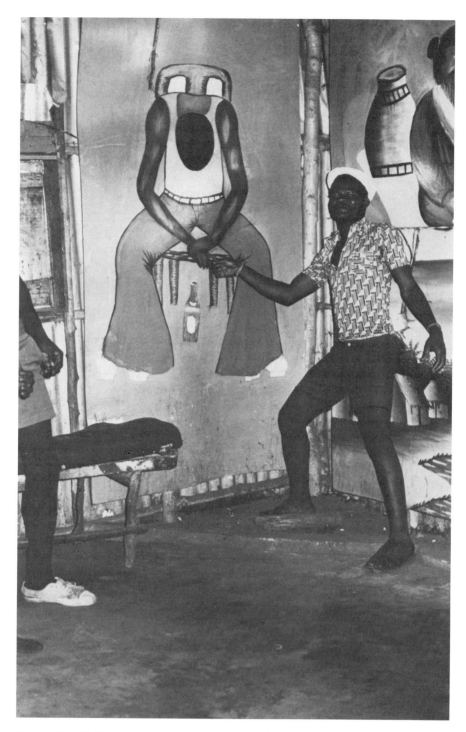

FIGURE 28 Civilian Rule member with pub painting of young man overcome by alcohol and marijuana. At ritual times these murals are removed and the pub is transformed into sacred space. Photo credit: John Nunley

posters in the windows of local travel agencies. A half-length military figure juxtaposed to a bikini-clad female in a centerfold pose was located on another side of the room. The standard female nude pin-up was also represented. A large seascape with villages and fishing boats covered the major part of another wall. In westernlike perspective, the painting depicted a road, lorries, and cityscape. A life-size portrait of a Sierra Leone traditional musician was painted on the door facing the private yard. The ceiling of the dance hall was decorated with 45 RPM records.

The paintings represented an extension, in the two-dimensional realm, of the Ode-lay environment. Each time I photographed the youths in their surroundings, they made gestures uniting themselves physically, if not spiritually, with the illustrated figures. The identification of one member of Civilian Rule with the freaker in figure 28 makes the point. All photographs of the members show effects of the cinema. The martial arts poses are in imitation of kung fu films. By posing in these martial positions, Ode-lay members bridge the reality of their world with the fantasy world of film.

After two months of working at Kroo Bay, I was introduced to the agba or leader of Civilian Rule; he had been present on many of my previous visits. During this introduction he gave me permission to work with his secretary only on the history of the society. The society's masquerades and costume construction were not to be discussed.

The Civilian Rule Society, originally called Civili in reference to the "civilized" youth who typically joined the society, was founded by Bankole Koroma in 1961. After the All Peoples Congress party came to power, the society changed its name to Civilian Rule. Some members claim the society was founded to offer an alternative to the Hunting societies to which many of the youthful members' fathers belonged.

The officers of Civilian Rule include the agba, the general secretary or *ashegba,* a financial secretary, and two mammy queens. The group has no vice-president. In 1978 the financial secretary was absent; he was in a Japanese prison for killing a sailor. Because the group recruits mainly from among the Kroo, an ethnic group with a long history of seafaring, many of its members are sailors.

In Civilian Rule, more than any other Ode-lay society, power is centralized in the person of the agba. He drew his strength in part from lucrative businesses. He owned two bars and a lorry transportation service. He was also an important member of the Old Rising Egungun Society. When this group celebrated, he allowed the Egungun members to prepare their costumes in the bar at Kroo Bay. He also contributed drinks on these occasions. Thus, as a middle-aged, successful business man, an Egungun member, and provider to youth, he enjoyed undisputed control of his group.

The secretary of Civilian Rule was confident that he would obtain a masking permit for the Republican Day celebration in 1978. The agba believed, also, that since he had staged a large and peaceful Egungun celebration the previous month, the government would comply with the request. In preparation for the celebration, the murals were removed from the bar, to protect them from damage by high-spirited youth. A commission for the costume headpiece was given to John Goba, a prominent carver at Mountain Cut. It was to consist of three large skulls painted white, with the red letters *APC* on top of each carving. Projecting from the top was a smaller skull with a bird's head on either side. All skulls were studded with cowrie shells, and three large gourds impaled with quills filled the spaces between the skulls. (See figure 29.)

The headpiece was attached to the hampa, which was draped over a wooden barrel. It was made of animal skins, medicines, cowries, mirrors, land snail shells, and quills—the same materials used in making Hunting costumes. The difference between the Hunting and Ode-lay costumes was in the greater complexity of the Ode-lay hampa, which unlike traditional Hunting costumes contained mask carvings.

During the week prior to Republican Day, the Orbanks City Bar was transformed into a shrine house in which the parts of the costume were assembled. The double-stepped dias forming the stage was screened off from the rest of the bar with cane mats. Behind this screen the leader assembled the costume. On the opposite side of the stage, a plastic statue of an angel decorated with Christmas tree ornaments was erected. Thus, Creolized religion, drawing upon Yoruba and Christian heritage, found itself within a saloon setting.

After word reached the agba that the desired permits would be issued, his secretary prepared a flyer announcing the celebration of Civili. The flyer stated:

> *LAVAY' LAVAY' LAVAY' LAVERSE*
> *BRAVO' BRAVO' BRAVO' A.P.C. WEST I*
> *REVO' REVO' REVO' REVOLUTION*

> Revolution is brought about by men who think as men of action and act as men of thought.
> Indeed the A.P.C. will be exactly 10 years in power on Wednesday 26th April, this year. What a great, great change in society during the [*sic*] the last 10 years. On that day A.P.C. West Ward I Youth League will once more parade along the streets of Freetown in grand style, with "Civili One Party Rule" the accredited spiritual representative from the land of ancestral mask devils.

> Music by: 1. Bantus Jazz
> 2. Mathomah
> 3. Bondo Drums
> 4. Kabba Kaylay

> Members should spend the night at the sacred shrine where consultation will be held with ancestral spirits.

FIGURE 29   A Civilian Rule bush-devil headpiece with carved skulls painted with the logo of the All Peoples Congress party. Photo credit: John Nunley

The group hired four mailo jazz bands for the procession, including the popular Bantus and Matomah. Civilian Rule was well known for its songs. The lyrics, such as *Nor lie pan me nor to me gee you beleh* (Don't tell lies on me I did not make you pregnant), reflect the shantytown lives of the group's followers. The Civili also popularized songs about Ode-lay street life. Examples of urban-tempered songs are *Around the Turntable,* to which the masked devil danced around circular junctions, and *Pole to Pole,* to which, propelled by the mailo beat, he moved with reckless abandon from light pole to light pole.

This celebration, which attracted a crowd of one thousand spectators, was very successful.[23] The Civili masked dancers outperformed those of their rival, Rainbow. This led to a fight between the political sponsors of the two groups. Rainbow members felt they received too little support from their political backers. Civilian Rule members, unlike the members of Rainbow, worked in the diamond areas, which enabled them to form strong ties with the Ministry of Trade and Industry, through which they received funds from the ministry. Civili members also raised revenue (as Rainbow did also) by selling their old costumes to branch societies, such as Santo, Kono Spark, and Lahay, in the Kono District. These branch societies used the costumes in demonstrations to frighten non-APC voters at the polls.

Rainbow

The informal gathering of youths at Susan's Bay (see map 4) observed by Graham Greene during World War II[24] coalesced into the Rainbow Ode-lay Society in the early 1960s. The "wharf rats" who composed Rainbow were known for illegal business activities, which included pirating, gambling, and robbery. Little detailed information was obtained regarding the early history of this group, but the group's agba (see figure 30) said it was founded by a Temne man and a Limba man. This group brought people of the wharf together. Soon after its formation, its dancers and musicians were invited to perform for the country's first prime minister, Milton Margai, at Hill Station. In the late 1970s the society played for the first vice-president, again at Hill Station; and in 1976 it was invited by the vice-president to play for a visit of President Tolbert of Liberia. Rainbow currently parades with its devil on Republican Day and after the death of its important members.

The Temne founder of the society, Pa Savage, a former member of an Egungun society in the Kambia district, organized Rainbow on the Egungun model and used Egungun titles for the officers. He chose the name Rainbow because it symbolized the group's recruitment pattern, which reflected the many colors of the rainbow in the multiplicity of its ethnic

FIGURE 30   Okin, the agba of Rainbow Ode-lay Society, in his Creole sideboard house, with his wife and a society member. Photo credit: John Nunley

groups and like the rainbow combined them into one form. The agba explained that, like the ancestors of Heaven City, the rainbow loomed in the sky, appearing and disappearing in the air. In like manner the society was linked to the ancestors.

The society became popular for the devil-dance step called *Mass tree lef foo, three lef four* (March three, stop twice, march three, pause four). This step was partly affected by the youths' observations of British and West African corps regimental marching. However, the cadence was shifted from 4/4 time to a syncopated beat, a jazzlike march well suited to street processions. This beat was made popular in 1961, at the first Independence Day celebration, by a retired soldier named Mahan. Mahan, who was known as a *kresman* (crazy man), frequented a bar on Mammy Oko Street near the Bombay Market. When intoxicated he often marched through the streets to this syncopated rhythm. He also mixed his marching style with popular songs. The Rainbow Society parodies this marching style in its masquerades, its devil staggering uncontrolledly backward for every few steps forward. One observer stated that Mahan marched in his best style when he got drunk. A flyer advertising Rainbow's last masquerade celebration in 1978 read: "Ride on to the underworld with peace and love. Mass tree lef foo three lef four." (See figure 31).

A long history of fighting characterized Rainbow. The agba recalled one incident that occurred at Mountain Cut Road between his society

Rainbow Hunting Society

HO – LA – LA If you want to enjoy the Republican Anniversary on the 19th of April, 1978.. look around for the "MIGHTY RAINBOW"– watin! Na rainbow dae go so if you tinnap e go lef pan you tangains ho! Young blood ho! Ride on to the underworld with peace and love. Mass tree lef too three lef four.

We are strictly against violence pilfrage, robbery and larceny. Any one who make any will be in serious trouble. Who get yase for yere leh e yere.

By Order Of
Agba Okin.

FIGURE 31 A flyer advertising the Rainbow masquerade for 1978. Courtesy of Rainbow Hunting Society.

and the Lord Have Mercy Society. Some "traitors" of both groups provoked the fight by sending letters that were alleged to have been written by the society heads. One letter stated that Mercy was prepared to attack Rainbow if the two groups should meet on Republican Day. Rainbow met this challenge by parading into the western part of the city, where the fight took place. The guards of the Rainbow devil were bigger and stronger than Mercy's, so the society was able to escape from the battlefield by taxi and thus save its devil. Another fight occurred in 1972 between Rainbow and Civili, when the two groups paraded even though no masquerade permits were granted. The first passing was peaceful, but a fight ensued near Christ's Church on Circular Road on the second encounter. An innocent bystander was killed. The head of Civili was arrested but was released soon afterward.

During this time Rainbow earned a fierce reputation, which even intimidated the police. Before staging the 1972 performance, members bought a coffin from a mortuary store at Lumely Street, the group's old headquarters, and carried it on the top of their shoulders to the Eastern Police headquarters. This served as a warning to any officer who might prevent the group from masquerading; such an attempt would send the over-enthusiastic officer to an early grave.[25] To strengthen their fierce reputation, Rainbow initiates received knife slashes across their chests.

The officers of Rainbow lived with the agba in an old Creole house on Fisher Street. Access to the residence was obtained by making one's way along narrow paths between closely spaced houses or by a rocky, almost impassable road. The residence was well protected. Like the Civili shrine of Ogun, Rainbow's shrine was located next to a bar that was decorated with murals, but the Rainbow murals were less sophisticated than those of Civili. A dog's head was buried in the center of the Rainbow shrine. The keeper of this Creole house, whose name was Okin, collected the rent for the owner in return for free lodging for himself, his two wives, and his children. The house was in poor condition: paint was badly chipped, and many floor and wall boards were missing. The downstairs tenants, who occupied what was once a storefront, complained about leakage from the floor above.

A 23-year-old Rainbow interviewee came to Freetown in 1962 with his Susu parents and joined the group in 1971. He was first employed by one of the largest department stores in Freetown as a security guard, but he was terminated after three years. At the time of our interviews he worked as a city-market tax collector and also earned income from gambling, con games, and theft. He disclosed two of the illegal means by which members of Rainbow survived. One was called *Three Card*.

"Three Card is a very popular technique. If there are five or six of us from the same society and in the same position moneywise, but one of us has twenty cents we play the game. One person takes three cards and chooses a winning card. These cards are shown to the person who has the twenty cents. He must try and keep track of the winning card after all three cards have been shuffled and turned face down. Sometimes the cards are shuffled in downside position. This man knows the winning card because the cards are marked, but it appears to everyone passing by that the man is making a lot of money, he is a winner. Other people from outside the society begin to play, but they lose more than they win."[26]

The other was called *Finger Pocket*.

"If six of us are moving together on a Saturday, we go to the market and look for a woman with a bag. Three of us will walk in front of her and three behind. We eventually close in and make it appear that there is much congestion. Then we take the purse after bumping her."[27]

Rainbow members were also active in harbor thefts and in commerce with visiting sailors. One way of profiting from the harbor traffic was called *Bonga Canoe*. (Bonga is a favorite local fish that is dried and prepared in a sauce.) The society used its five canoes to carry leopard, snake, civit, and monkey skins; parrots; pineapples; and other exotica. These items were exchanged with sailors for money, clothes, shoes, and other personal items. Another profitable enterprise, referred to as *pirates,* was stated to be a very dangerous business, for in its pursuit some people had been shot. The details of this operation were not disclosed, except that it occurred after midnight. Items such as refrigerators, electric irons, hi-fi systems, radios, televisions, cotton goods, paint, rope, and drums used to store palm oil and wine were taken from ships and were easily disposed of on the black market.[28] In another form of theft, "Money" Morlai Ankulla and his chief of staff of a certain society were arrested with stolen property as they beached their canoes at Susan's Bay and were given five years each for stealing nine bags of palm kernels.[29] Today Rainbow controls such activities at the bay.

The Freetown black market is extremely lucrative. In 1978 hi-fi sets with cassette recorders sold for $300, half-size refrigerators for $80, and storage drums for $8. Because of the excessive import tax on such goods, their legal prices often exceeded the buying power of the public. Compared with a half-size refrigerator sold on the black market, one at the retail level might sell for up to $500. Rainbow sold over $2,000 in stolen goods each month. The complex mechanism by which these products were distributed was a carefully guarded secret. The items were widely dispersed among low-, moderate-, and middle-income groups. Although these activities were unanimously condemned by the public and the press alike, the service thus provided by Rainbow was greatly appreciated in the face of high inflation and unemployment.

Because the sponsors of Rainbow included two of the most powerful men in the city, there was little doubt that the group would be granted a permit for the 1978 Republican Day celebration. In preparation for the event T-shirts with the society name and crossbones were imprinted in front and back. Jeans and tennis shoes completed the costume. The devil costume was prepared at the residence of the agba and was later taken to the shrine. The evening prior to the holiday, the officers and several members gathered at the bar on Fisher Street to eat, drink, and smoke marijuana. They sold T-shirts to neighbors and to others attracted by the activities. Dancing and merriment continued through the night at the Ogun shrine.

On the morning of the procession I observed the Rainbow masquerade from the second floor of a two-story apartment building on East Brook

Street, one block from the society's shrine. The agba and his assistant urged me to be discreet in taking photographs, so as not to disturb the general membership. By 9:30 A.M. a few persons dressed in society uniform were seen moving about the area near the old railway bridge. The Navy Egungun society, with its members dressed in full-length white Muslim attire, processed nearby.

At 11:30 A.M. one of the Rainbow members pulled a *kaka* or shit devil called Old Papa.[30] This character clowned in the streets and collected money from spectators. The costume, which was said to have come from the Congo (Zaire) was formerly used by an old man of the area, who paraded in it when drunk. Privately owned kaka devils often performed before the appearance of the Ode-lay masquerades. Like the Mende mask clowns known as gongoli (see figure 20), these characters added a spirit of frivolity to the celebrations. After performing for about an hour, Old Papa disappeared into a pan-bodi house off Brook Street.

Then a government car appeared with several of the society's important sponsors. These persons, along with some members of the Internal Security Unit troops, went to the Ogun shrine to sacrifice to the devil and make a financial contribution. Later more troops arrived. By 12:15 P.M. the state car and military escorts departed, immediately followed by Dr. Olu and his mailo jazz band. Viewed from above, the impact of the celebration, heightened by the earth-shaking, wall-thumping bass-box drum, could be fully appreciated.[31] The sound of the mailo jazz instrument reverberated off the walls between the buildings, accelerating the aesthetic intensity.

The Rainbow devil appeared from below the path leading to the shrine, as followers yelled and cheered. Their sounds echoed through the streets. Although the devil was far less elaborate than others, its effect was more compelling. The aesthetic of this masquerade was predominantly fierce. Its simple lines and projecting horns, uncomplicated by fancy ornaments, emphasized the linear movements of the dancer. The construction of the costume was similar to that of Hunting Society costumes.[32] The masquerade continued through Fourah Bay to Mountain Cut, across Tower Hill, to the west side of the city, and back to Fisher Street. The procession met without incident until the finish at 8:00 P.M.

After the festivities ended, the devil costume was returned to the house of the agba to be stored until it could be sold, as was the case with most Rainbow costumes, to another group in Kono, Kenema, or Makeni. Groups in the last named town included Endeavor, Sparrow, Paddle, Rainbow, and Republicans.

The foregoing descriptions of the Firestone, Rainbow, Paddle, Civilian Rule, and Bloody Mary Ode-lay societies provide insight into how and under what conditions the societies are established, as well as into their functions, leadership, masquerade activities, and settlements. Enterprises such as pirating, picking pockets, gambling, selling goods on the black market, and trafficking in marijuana testify to the illegal side of these groups; wheres activities such as the establishment of a bar and fishing fleet by Johnny Shaft of Bloody Mary and the successfully run bar of Civilian Rule reveal their desire for a respectful position in society. Members' contributions made to benefit individuals in time of stress are drawn from the Yoruba asusu and the box that helped the early Creoles through difficult times. Minutes of the Paddle Society emphasize the importance of the selection of costumes and membership dress for masquerades as well as the importance of political patronage in obtaining masking permits.

Most of all, the descriptions of these groups give insight into the Ode-lay lifestyle. The Ode-lay members, with their embrace of the equal-rights messages of reggae and their freethinker philosophy, meet in secluded locations. Their subculture is spreading to outlying districts of major cities and to secondary cities. Although the groups show the influence of Western media and lifestyle, they depend upon the masquerade, which has become an indispensable part of their function, for their own identity and for communication with each other.

5

Ode-lay Aesthetics

The Ode-lay societies use the characteristics of fanciness and fierceness to heighten the effect of their masquerades for participants and spectators alike. These aesthetics have their origin in specific Yoruba costumes of traditional secret societies. The richness of cloth, the strong sense of contrasting colors, and the attraction of sparkling and bright materials constitute what in Freetown is called fancy dress. In contrast, fierce costumes are made primarily of animal and vegetable materials that were first used in Hunting costumes and in certain kinds of Egungun costumes. Together these opposing aesthetics stimulate a full range of emotional feelings on the part of masquerade participants.

The first scholar to report on the concept of the fancy aesthetic was Michael Banton, who observed it in the Ambas Geda Friendly Society.[1] Though Banton did not use the term *fancy,* the concept is nevertheless implied in his descriptions of the fine dress, stylish music, and dancing of the youth groups. In addition, his comments on the Alikali societies and masqueraders note that these were of a maleficent or fierce nature. Thus the fancy and fierce aesthetics were already part of Freetown's youth organizations.

The Fancy Aesthetic

Banton's classification of a society called Boys London as an Ambas Geda type of society establishes a historical link between the traditional and Ode-lay versions of fancy masked costumes. According to one source, there were two entertainment groups: Big Boys London, established in 1943, and Small Boys London. These groups did not parade with masks, but they did dress in uniform costumes for public presentations. Both men and women of these groups participated in dance competitions for which the leader or sultan played records and at times blew a whistle to indicate a change in the music and dance style. He often created a new step, which the dancers then followed. This routine strongly resembles the 1970s Western disco dances. A comparison of my informant's description of Ode-lay dancing with Banton's description of Ambas Geda dancing elucidates the origin of Ode-lay fancy masquerades.

> The Ambas Geda dance starts with a line of four men and four women circling the floor to a slow tempo. Then the Leader blows his whistle and the men and women separate so that they dance opposite to one another, several yards apart. In the next phase they dance up to one another: right hand to right, left to left, backing and advancing; then they change places and repeat this much in the way of English square dancing—indeed the dance of one company markedly resembles 'The Lancers.' After more whistle blasts any persons present may come on to the floor where they dance together in mixed couples in what is said to be ballroom fashion and to a much faster tempo. A woman may dance with two or three trilby hats on her head and a man with a woman's *lappa* or shawl, round his shoulders; these are presented to them for the dance by their admirers.[2]

During the Christmas season of 1945, the Boys London societies were in such a dance competition, which ended in a fight. The dispute was taken before Beebee Kamara, an elder of Big Boys London and its founder. The fight involved a father and son and appeared to be a conflict brought about by differences of opinion between the two generations. Kamara advised the younger members involved in the conflict to establish another society so as not to compete with Big Boys London.

The younger members complied with Kamara's suggestion and established a new society called Small Boys London, which was represented by a masked devil. This group had been impressed by a new mask costume called *ajo* that was introduced by a Nigerian during World War II and now wished to adopt the new costume type. However, they did not have sufficient funds with which to build this fancy devil, so instead they built a Jolly costume that required fewer costly materials. The members of the new society never lost sight of their original intent to build a complete fancy devil, and in 1953 they accomplished their goal. This fancy costume was made with a popular and expensive material called *golden box*, which was then the rage in Freetown, so called because the cloth came wrapped in a shiny gold paper. As the young boys matured and took steady jobs, they could afford to prepare more expensive costumes. Their new stature demanded such display. One artist remarked, "Because we had an intention, we wanted more respect, and Jolly was only for 'teddy' or 'rowdy' boys." The new fancy devil was named *arishola*, which means *beautiful head*. This became the name of the society. (See plate 1.)

PLATE 2   Fancy Egungun costumes of Yorubaland with headboard construction. *African Arts* 11, no. 3 (1978): 24. Photo credit: Marilyn Houlberg

PLATE 3   A Freetown Egungun costume with headboard and Yoruba-inspired veil.
The headboard suggests this costume is of the alabukun type. The red image at the
center is symbolic of the rising sun, the symbol of the All Peoples Congress party.
Photo credit: John Nunley

PLATE 4 The complex design, bright colors, porcupine quills, and rams' heads in this Ode-lay headpiece exhibit both fancy and fierce characteristics. *African Arts* 14, no. 2 (1981): 56. Photo credit: Hans Schaal

PLATE 5 (facing page) A Jolly devil masquerade costume and face carving created by Ajani. *African Arts* 14, no. 2 (1981): 57. Photo credit: Hans Schaal

PLATE 6   Robot masquerade costume inspired by the Shawl/Alexovich film *Who Can Replace a Man?* created by John Goba. *African Arts* 15, no. 4 (1982): 43. Photo credit: Hans Schaal

PLATE 7 An individual (right) carries a 45 RPM sacrificial record for the Juju Wata fancy-devil masquerade in Hastings. Photo credit: John Nunley

PLATE 8   A bush-devil costume used in the unsuccessful Firestone celebration at
Mountain Cut. Photo credit: John Nunley

The first ajo devils were also called *pumpkin heads*. These gourd-shaped headpieces were crowned with stocking caps, from which several silk scarves or headties were hung. The body of the costumes consisted of a cotton gown decorated with loops of fancy colored materials. These loops have given way to more fashionable machine-made lace, which is popular with the fancy-devil builders of today. Like the ajo or Jolly, the Arishola masqueraders rarely parade in the streets. Arishola celebrations are held in a vacant lot at 54 Sackville Street and the home of Big Boys London.

What is striking about the Ode-lay fancy masked costumes, of which there are many today, is their original derivation from Yoruba culture (see, for example, figures 32 and 33) and from the Ambas Geda, Arishola, and Alikali groups. Although the Ambas Geda associations did not masquerade as such, they did use what might be considered mask substitutes in their uniform costumes. The passage from Banton cited above interestingly notes that Ambas Geda males wore female's shawls and that the women wore two or three men's trilby hats. The emphasis on costume in this context is clear, yet the description invites interpretation. Why, for instance, would women wear a stack of trilby hats, which are usually a part of the dress worn by men? Why, too, would men wear women's shawls during plays? Beyond the mere presentation of gifts from admirers, such behavior constitutes male and female impersonation, both prevalent themes in Yoruba masquerades.

In the Gelede societies of Freetown, male dancers imitate females, as well as the double impersonation of females imitating males. These transvestites dance in "male and female" pairs around a private residence or in an area especially marked for them. The dancers stand opposite and move to three drums, at times drawing close together, but stopping just short of touching. At this point an attendant places a fan between the dancers so they do not touch, for this would be a serious breach of spiritual etiquette. Instead the dancers rotate around the fan-holding attendant in a square-dance style that is close to Banton's description of Ambas Geda dancing.

The use of trilby hats by women represents less an imitation of European civilization than the African penchant for fine materials and masquerade. Banton did not describe the configurations struck by the hats, but it may be assumed that combinations of three colorful specimens of plumage and velvet, of which the hats were made, must have struck a complex arrangement. The fancy devils currently display complex headpieces that look more like hats than face masks.

Another feature of the trilby hat that must have attracted the Ambas Geda players is the arrangement of Tyrolean feathers on them. The lustrous quality of the plumage viewed against the velvet lackluster is an aesthetic motif found by Robert Thompson in the Yoruba art of Nigeria.[3] Perhaps of more significance than this aesthetic parallel is the symbolic

FIGURE 32   The costumes of these Egungun masqueraders from Nigeria are remarkably similar to fancy-dress costumes of the Jolly and Egungun societies of Freetown.
Courtesy of John Pemberton III.

FIGURE 33   Freetown gbegi costumes found in Egungun and Jolly masquerades, with
the masquerader on the right carrying the initials of the All Peoples Congress party.
Photo credit: John Nunley

reference of the Tyrolean feathers, which at another level represent birds. In West African tradition the bird is associated with witchcraft. One can see this in Yoruba art, where the ibis is perched on Gelede masks (see figure 34). In Senufo traditions antiwitchcraft masks often have birds carved on their tops. Among the Temne the witchbird is a common carrier of bad fortune. The Temne consider old and unkempt women to be perpetrators of witchcraft. Such persons, they believe, send witchbirds to make children ill.[4] Since the majority of Ambas Geda members were Temne, they must have recognized the significance of the witchbird in the feather projections of the trilby hats. In this respect the Temne also adopted the feather-covered Yoruba witch-hunting mask called *ayogbo.* Many such masks formed part of the Temne-based Egungun associations in 1978.

Fancy clothes, transvestism, feathers, and dance of the Ambas Geda are all prefigured in the Yoruba Gelede tradition. (See figure 35.) Although the Ambas Geda denounced masked performances, it is argued that their own presentations were merely transformations of the mask at a less conspicuous level. Thus the traditions of Ambas Geda served as an immediate source from which the Ode-lay societies drew their own cultural expressions and organization. The fancy aesthetic appeared long before the Ambas Geda, however, early in the life of the colony. It arrived with the Yoruba implantation of the Egungun and Gelede.

An early reference to Gelede costumes demonstrated that the fancy aesthetic tradition was already in existence by 1837.[5] Costumes used to entertain and appease witches were a source upon which the Ode-lay societies drew for the construction of their own costumes. Despite the seemingly all-male cast of Gelede players, the principal object of worship is the *mammy juju,* a feminine medicine called *ife.* The mammy juju is built of beaten bark mixed with rum, blood, and other materials formed into the shape of a woman. Gelede members believe this medicine is more powerful than that of the Ogun of the Hunting societies. During Gelede presentations only members may take donations from the medicine or soweh cup and then only if given permission beforehand; otherwise, it is believed, they will go mad or "off head." Members of Hunting societies, however, take from the cup freely, without fear of the medicine. An expression used by the Ode-lay societies to indicate the power of women is *woman tote man.* This phrase was used to describe a Civilian Rule Society headpiece depicting a woman with a man on her shoulders.

Forty days after the death of a Gelede member the masqueraders appear in a play for the bereaved, which may last as long as a week. The Gelede also perform one week each year for the benefit of the society. In all performances three large single-headed drums of varying pitches form the ensemble. These instruments are called *ako, etu,* and *agbo.* Rattles or *aja* are shaken by attendants who escort the masqueraders to and

FIGURE 34 This carved Egungun mask from Nigeria has the same mask-cap design as Gelede masks from Freetown. Courtesy of the Art Institute of Chicago.

from their chairs. These attendants also separate the masqueraders with fans when contact seems imminent. The female impersonators and female impersonators impersonating males remain separate in erotic dancing. The female impersonators dress in real and imitation satins and silks to effect the beauty of the play. The Gelede dancers wear several shawls (recall the Ambas Geda males' costumes) and layers of fine cloth. The female impersonators, like the Gelede of Nigeria, wear masks and artificial breasts that project prominently from the chest. The masks, which years ago were imported, are now carved by a local Freetown artist (see figure 36).

The Freetown mask carvings are not properly considered casque masks, since they do not extend over the back of the head as the Gelede masks from Yorubaland do. The masks of Freetown display the Yoruba pattern of scarification on the sides of the cheeks and forehead, as well as large, almond-shaped eyes, with white-enamel retinas and black pupils (see figures 37 and 38). The heads and foreheads are usually decorated with birds but sometimes with bands of bottles or horns. To complete the costume, "female" dancers wear white gloves and carry flywhisks or *asha*. The rattling sound of ankle irons or *elu* as they stomp the ground complements the sound of the drum ensemble. The feet are wrapped with several layers of cloth and covered with white stockings to prevent the large rattles from slipping off. The dancers wear bustles to accent the shape of their derrieres, which they swing as they move their arms in a delicate feminine manner, often affecting female finger and hand gestures.[6] (See figure 39.)

The Gelede males impersonating females who impersonate males dress in nearly the same fashion, except that the bottles and horns of the masks are replaced by stylish coiffures. Perhaps this distinction, which was not explained, symbolizes the right of women to wear medicinal objects. This would be in keeping with the tradition of the Freetown Gelede, who celebrate the medicinal power of women over men. Male costumes do not include carved breasts, and the cloth panels that hang from their waists, unlike those in the female costume, are tied in knots at the bottom.

The impulse behind Gelede celebrations is the entertainment of witches. The lavish display of cloth in the fancy aesthetic is meant to placate individuals who are believed to cause sickness among children by witch-craft. Since witches are said to have the power to control menstrual flow, it is also a common fear that they regulate fertility in women.

The Gelede celebrations begin an hour or so before sunset in a vacant lot that adjoins a member's house. First the drummers strike a beat, as the head of the society sprinkles medicine on the ground to protect the spirits of the masquerade, and some attendants play the *aja*, which in Yoruba means *dog*. The sound of the aja calls the devils. The masqueraders

FIGURE 36   Gelede carving from Freetown with mask-cap design similar to that in figure 34. Photo credit: John Nunley

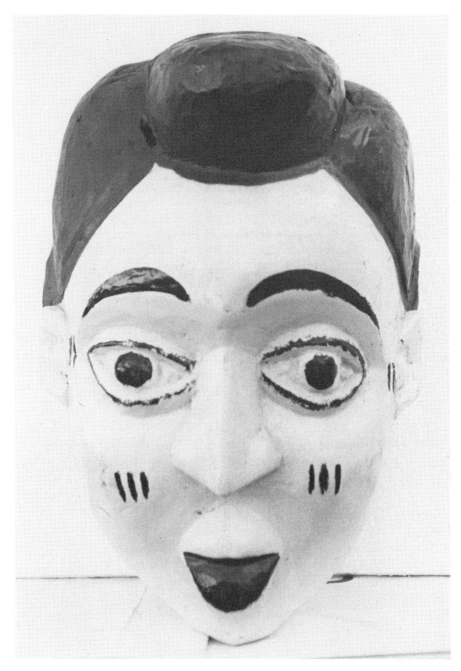

FIGURE 37   A Gelede mask carved by Ajani for an offshoot of the Autta (Ota, Nigeria) Gelede Society of Freetown. Photo credit: John Nunley

FIGURE 38   A Gelede mask from Nigeria carved by Olabimtan Odunlami in the early twent
century. Photo credit: Henry John Drewal and Margaret Thompson Drewal

FIGURE 39   A Gelede masquerade costume featuring a bird on top of the headpiece.
Drawing by Linda Horsley-Nunley.

usually depart from the house adjacent to the play area, enter the arena single-file, and take chairs near the musicians. When the music is played well and the first pair of dancers, male and female, performs before society members and guests, the slow, seductive, ostinato beat allows the female to generate a strong erotic presence. As this couple leaves the dance area, another pair enters, two or three couples sometimes dancing simultaneously.

At some point in the performance, one of the attendants or masqueraders presents a large calabash containing a carved baby painted dark brown and covered with gold costume jewelry from the head to its exposed breasts. The rest of the carving is wrapped in fine cloth. Each time the carving or *bankelu* is placed before a spectator, that person places a donation in the calabash or on a fan held by an attendant. This elaborately jeweled carving, wrapped in beautiful cloth, epitomizes the fancy aesthetic of the Freetown Gelede societies.

The fancy aesthetic is also traditionally a part of the Egungun masked presentation. Houlberg, Thompson, and Drewal have often commented on the importance of beautiful cloth in Egungun masquerades. Moreover, they have stressed that beauty is found primarily in the materials and not in the carved headpieces. (See plate 2.)

Egungun masquerades are of many kinds. The classification of costumes is a troublesome exercise, and not all students of Egungun make the same distinctions.[7] What appears to be constant, however, is the observation by most scholars that the costumes range from ensembles with elaborate cloth to ensembles with little or no cloth, some of which may include different parts of animals. This dichotomy is evident in the many masquerades of Sierra Leone, which include fancy Egungun costumes of the *okosha, alabukun, aredé,* and *ojofoembo* types. Fancy costumes are considered by the Egungun to have less spiritual importance than their fierce counterparts. They serve to entertain the crowds with their beauty and with their pantomime of the more serious spirits.

The okosha costume consists of a long gown attached to a board that projects on top of the dancer's head. The gown is made of colorful cloth patterns interrupted by a brightly striped fabric extending from top to bottom at the back of the gown. This striped part, called *alabala,* is found in most Egungun entertainment costumes. The okosha devil carries a switch in each hand as it sings and dances for the audience. Its interference with the ancestor masqueraders, at times making fun of their movements, never fails to please the crowd. Shouting at the spectators in the deep trill voice of the ancestors, much as cheerleaders do at American sporting events, okosha pushes the audience to high levels of excitement. It sometimes exhibits eroticism in pantomimes of lovemaking to the earth or to someone in the audience. If the erotic act "appears fine," elder women join in the dance, and others pitch money around the masquerader's feet.

The aredé is a more elaborately dressed entertainer than okosha. Usually three or four aredé dance at a celebration. Unlike okosha, the masked aredé players sit on chairs to avoid soiling their costumes. The aredé does not relate to the spectators as the okosha does; rather, it appears between the dances of the ancestral devils to provide relief from the more studied steps of the ancestor dancers.

The costume of aredé, like that of okosha, consists of a cloth covering that hangs from a concealed board which extends over the forehead. To this board, which is somewhat smaller than that of the okosha, are attached a front cloth panel of one pattern and a back panel of another pattern. Both panels join at the side, and the seams are often covered with lace or fringe. Additional cloth panels hang from the waist of the dancer and extend to the ankle. Aredé carries two horsetail fly whisks. Its slow and stately dancing presents a marked contrast to the crude, awkward motions effected by okosha.

Aredé waits, seated quietly in a chair, until an escort leads it to the center of the dance arena. There it slowly leans and sways to the music. As the beat quickens, the masquerader's arms stretch outward from the sides, causing the panels to spin about the body. Accenting this movement, the dancer touches the ground with the fly whisks, stirring the dust dramatically. As the dance speeds up, the spread panels open further to transform the devil into an abstraction of pure motion. This rotation may well exceed the dancer's abilities, in which case the attendants and drummers must slow down the music.

The most elaborate of the Egungun fancy costumes is the *alabukun,* sometimes called *aludibe* (see figure 40 and plate 3). The alabukun usually features a carved headpiece and the most costly materials. It has more yardage than any other Egungun costume. The cloth alone might cost $200, and with the headpiece added, many of these costumes sell for over $300.

The Navy Ojé Egungun Society of Freetown was originally formed by seamen and longshoremen who earned large incomes by working overtime during World War II. They established their society to express their brotherhood and newfound wealth. Navy became famous for its fancy Egungun creations; but as work at the docks declined in the postwar years and the society leaders died, it ran into financial difficulty and ceased to perform. It was revived by one of the original members and several younger men. For the society's reappearance on Republican Day in 1978 they chose as their uniform costume Muslim white gowns, loose-fitting pants, and white slippers with pointed toes.

To reestablish their reputation, they commissioned one of the most popular alabukun costumes presented that year. (See figure 41). The costume was similar in construction to other Egungun entertainment costumes. It had a flat headboard over which were hung attached cloth panels. The face was covered with a veil of cowrie shells, wool strands,

FIGURE 40   This Yoruba Egungun headpiece or eri from Nigeria is a prototype of the headpieces made in Sierra Leone. Photo credit: Margaret Thompson Drewal

FIGURE 41 An alabukun masquerade devil from the Navy Ojé Society of Freetown.
Photo credit: John Nunley

and synthetic materials in a variety of colors. The gown was made of a material called canopy, which was then popular in Freetown for bed-covers. At the front and back of the gown hung a print of maroon background with light blue and white flowers. Fringe and plastic flowers were placed along the edge of the headboard. At the center of the top of the costume was a small platform, to which was attached a carving of a navy man. (See figure 42.) The carved figure had a full beard and wore a paper collar and a navy cap with lace and tassles. The Navy alabukun walked in the procession but did not dance. The weight and considerable length of its garment would have made rhythmical move-ment exceedingly difficult. Its dazzling appearance captivated the public.

The alabukun is most likely intended to be looked at in the context of street processions or as it is seated behind the Egungun play. Its attraction is in the richness of the costume itself and not in the context of motion. Perhaps fear of soiling the costume in dancing has restricted its use. A similar fear extends to the Ode-lay societies, which no longer cover their masqueraders with a medicine made from palm oil and local herbs. Society members once complained that their personal dress could be ruined if they should accidentally be brushed by a masquerader doused with such a mixture.

The Fierce Aesthetic

As the Ode-lay fancy aesthetic has been shown to derive from the earlier Egungun and Gelede and later Arishola and Ambas Geda societies, the fierce aesthetic may also be shown to derive in a similar manner. The fierce aesthetic is equally compelling to the members of the urban youth societies and their audiences. Fierceness is an emotional response evoked by the masqueraders' representations of Ogun and the ancestors.

Feelings toward the ancestors are ambivalent. Ancestors are feared and respected; yet, as Dennis Duerden points out, it is a relief to be rid of them.[8] In the African context, this means the ancestors must reside in a separate world of spirits where they cannot harm the living. Ancestors are both a source of protection and a source of personal affliction. They may bring good fortune or, without warning, disease, poverty, and child-lessness. This ambivalence toward the ancestors is a primary source of the fierce aesthetic.[9]

Before discussing the origins of the fierce aesthetic, we should caution that the terms *fierce* and *fancy* should not be confused with *beastly* or *bad* and *beautiful* or *good*. This may be explained by citing a commu-nication problem white and black Americans experience when using the word *bad*. For the black *bad* means *good*, as in That is a bad dude, i.e, That is a good man; whereas to a Euro-American the likely interpretation

FIGURE 42   Detail of headpiece of Navy masquerade devil. Photo credit: John Nunley

might be That is an evil man. In a similar context, Thompson notes that Yoruba *alakoro* masks broke all aesthetic canons so as to terrorize neighboring enemies.[10] In this sense, for the Yoruba, bad sculpture is good. In Freetown, likewise, *bad* means *good*; and in this light, fierceness or fearfulness is considered to be a good and powerful thing.

Fierceness made an early appearance in the colony with the Hunting societies and costumes called *odé* or *alankoba*. In the Yoruba pantheon, the central force in the hunter's worship is Ogun. In each hunting shrine in Sierra Leone, the head of a ram or dog is buried in honor of this deity. The power of the Hunting masqueraders in medicine, Ogun, and wisdom is believed to be superior to that of the Egungun. Egungun spirits are thought to be erratic in temperament, deploying harmful medicines haphazardly. Hunting spirits, it is claimed, exercise patience before striking; but once they strike, their blows are irreversible. Ogun is associated with lightning and fire, which are attributes of both the smithy and gunpowder. In this respect Ogun may be related to Shango, the Yoruba god of thunder.

Shango also is considered a sacred deity; the center of his cult of worship is located at Mountain Cut. Peterson found several archival references that point to the existence of shrines and sacred images of this deity.[11] In conversation with several Freetown elders it was clear that few people recognize the term *Shango.* It is possible, perhaps, that over the years Shango as a spiritual concept has become amalgamated into the worship of Ogun. The gun, a current symbol of Ogun, spits fire and makes a noise like thunder while projecting iron from its barrel. Thus, the fire (lightning) and thunder of Shango and the iron of Ogun may have become one.

The first Hunting costumes, the alankoba, did not exhibit carved headpieces; instead one or two horns projected from the top of the headcover.[12] (See figure 43.) The materials currently used for these constructions are animal and vegetable parts that are obtained from the bush, as were their prototypes. In contrast, the fancy costumes are made entirely of manufactured goods. *Alankoba* costumes have three parts: the headpiece or *eri,* the shirt and pants or *asho,* and the vestlike *hampa.* The headpiece is a hat, decorated with cowrie shells, to which horns are attached. The shirt and pants are tailored of country cloth woven in narrow strips and sewn together. The hampa hangs in vest fashion from the shoulders to a little below the waist. (See figure 44.)

At the top of the hampa are attached horns, which project vertically if the garment is balanced carefully across the shoulders. An imbalance results in the horns pointing to one side. The materials of the hampa include wooden spoons or *ibako,* which symbolize the power of women. This power is expressed in the saying *Women we born pikin no bad, lek una de sock bobi dem na comra,* which means, Women who have children are not bad, for they let everyone suckle. These utensils are a reminder that the Hunting devil, like a mother, can be warm and protective.

Also on the hampa are small gourds from which project porcupine quills; it is believed that these quills help to defend the masked spirit against witches. In older versions of the costumes, the quills were placed only on the head so that in case of danger the masquerader could lower his head offensively in the direction of escape. (See figure 45). Quills are thought to be beautiful as in the sense of bad: *De quills dehm mak en bado,* i.e., The quills made them good. The foundation of the sea porcupine is the hampa. The sea porcupine (puffer fish), which is bought from fishermen who occasionally catch them in their nets, is gutted, stuffed with leaves to maintain its shape, dried, and filled with medicine. Costume makers explain that the sea porcupine gives shape to the hampa, allowing it to last up to fifteen years.

FIGURE 43 Early descriptions of Freetown Hunting Society masqueraders suggest a costume with a single horn projecting from top of the head. Drawing by Linda Horsley-Nunley.

FIGURE 44   A Hunting costume featuring the headpiece and medicine smock or hampa. Drawing by Linda Horsley-Nunley.

FIGURE 45   A Seaside Firestone bush-devil, made by John Goba, surrounded by officers and attendants with quill headpieces. Photo credit: John Nunley

On the front or back of the hampa are attached a few tortoise shells or *trokiback*. These symbolize the invincibility of the devil, for it is said that an animal which carries its own house is well protected. Also sometimes attached are mirrors, in which the bila and soweh men can see the reflection of witches as they come *to poil* (to destroy physically or metaphysically) the devil. Horns of bushbuck, which are filled with medicines, and land snail shells are dipped in poison and hung from the vest in memory of Adada, who, according to many hunters, founded their association. A variety of animal skins, including civet, baboon, and bush antelope hang from the front and back of the hampa. (See figure 46.) Combs and a cartridge belt filled with empty casings complete this part of the costume.[13] (See figure 44.)

The Hunting costume has recently undergone two major changes. (1) The horned headpiece has been replaced by a brightly painted, carved head of an antelope or sheep. (2) The porcupine quills formerly reserved for the head are now placed in gourds that are attached over the entire hampa. The new interest of hunters in the carved headpieces most likely stems from their appearance in Alikali costumes. Men like Eku Williams, a carver from Mountain Cut, and the late Pa Decker introduced these carvings to improve the fierce bush-style devil and to compete with other societies. Early examples were covered with animal skins, but later carvings were painted in bright enamel colors. (See figure 47.)

The aesthetic of fierceness is not the exclusive property of Hunting devils; it is also characteristic of a special Egungun costume called *agbaru agbadu*, which means *black snake*. Rather than perform in the play area, this masquerader appears at cemeteries on Easter Monday, when all the ancestors of the societies are presented sacrifices. He also appears on the morning before the yearly celebration of each Egungun branch. The agbaru agbadu informs the people of the underworld that a play is to be held in their honor. This masquerader's costume includes a small back hampa, with land snail shells, cowries, and a few quills, which gives it an appearance similar to that of the Hunting devil. Another feature it shares with the Hunting costumes is the single horn that projects from the top of the head. Unlike the early Hunting garments, the Egungun version is encircled with several tree branches. Occasionally one or more knives or cutlasses are stuck illusionistically through the dancer. The blades are placed at the head or stomach, which is covered by cloth, so they appear to pass through the body. The appearance of this devil is frightful indeed.

The horn projection at the top of the agbaru agbadu costume is a sign of a spirituality that Freetown celebrants associate with fear and ferocity. A similar projection was noted among the Ohori Yoruba of Nigeria in a costume called egun elegba.[14] (See figure 48.) Both costumes have a ragged, patched quality. An illustration of the Ohori Yoruba costume shows a masquerader with three wooden rods in one hand;

FIGURE 46   Headpiece and hampa of a Hunting costume. Photo credit: Jerry Kobylecky

FIGURE 47   A carved Hunting headpiece or eri. Photo credit: John Nunley

these rods are reminiscent of the blades in the costume of agbaru agbadu. It has been claimed that the significance of the horn in the Yoruba masks is in its mediating ability, that is, in its ability to establish contact between man and the supernatural. The horn, which is the property of messengers, informs man of his destiny and the status quo in the spiritual realm.[15]

Both the one-horned agbaru agbadu and alankoba of the Egungun and Hunting societies are, likewise, mediators between man and the supernatural. The masquerading Egungun devil emerges from the cemetery, the divine world of the dead, to announce to the world of the living that all is right in the underworld, that the sacrifices have been accepted by the "living dead," and that the Egungun spirits are ready to perform.[16] The Hunting devil plays the role of communicator between these two worlds in a similar manner. At the death of a society member, this character emerges from the bush, the home of many hostile spirits, and processes through the town, signaling that the spirits of the society have agreed to perform for the deceased. Thus both Freetown fierce devils are intermediaries between the world of the living and the "other" world; in this capacity they inspire fear. An Egungun member gave the following description:

> Of the *agbaru agbadu* some are brown and others are black, the material can be country cloth or flour sack. The devil may carry an axe or a hammer in one hand. The hands are covered with the longsleeves of the *asho*, which are folded back and tied to conceal the hands. The devil is the focus for a medicine that is taken to the cemetery. On the back of this devil is a civet skin with a bell attached to the tail. It appears that this devil has a *hampa*, but actually it only has a few conch shells and the bell.[17]

FIGURE 48   A single-horn headpiece from Nigeria. *African Arts* 11, no. 1 (1977): 45.
Photo credit: Margaret Thompson Drewal

Another well-known masquerader of the fierce genre is called *aladigo* and belongs to the Gelede society. This character may have its counterpart in the Nigerian Gelede mask known as the Great Mother of Gelede. Both costumes have projections on the top.[18] The aladigo's movements are far less rhythmical than those of the other Freetown Gelede masqueraders. It propells itself in straight marching steps, which terminate in sharp right-angle turns. This masquerader performs alone in the streets near the assigned play area, patrolling and "smelling out" enemy medicine men and witches. The crowds are anxious about this devil, and even the children sense impending danger in its presence. On one occasion an aladigo entered the dance area and, while searching the crowd, suddenly turned in front of several women and children who were seated on a bench. The velocity of the unexpected move and the threatening appearance of the devil caught the spectators by surprise, causing them to recoil and fall backward off the bench. On another occasion, at a late evening presentation, an aladigo "smelled" a witch and charged into the crowd after it. This caused great confusion among the spectators, many of whom fled into the streets, which, in addition, resulted in long lines of traffic. Thus, the aladigo can change the music-inspired celebrants into tense and enervated individuals.

The aladigo is more masculine in figure than are the other Gelede characters. It does not have carved breasts, it does not have a bustle to exaggerate buttocks and hips, and its angular appearance and movements suggest maleness. An interesting feature of the mask is its unique two-faced form. It has an upper face that represents a sheep or a ram and a lower face that is the face of Gelede, with two snakes extending from the ears to the mouth, where the snake heads meet. This is the only Gelede mask that has carved rams horns projecting from the top. Since the ram is the symbol of Ogun and the Hunting society, it may be argued that the Gelede aladigo found some of its inspiration in the fierce aesthetic of the Hunting costumes, which also have ram horns. The two heads, which give the Gelede masquerader four eyes, is another element to be feared, for only witches and persons who control the power of such malcontents are said to have four eyes. The aladigo carries a concealed medicine called *ouwu* to protect itself from evildoers. In this respect it resembles the agbadu agbaru and the Hunting devil. Horns, concealed medicine, and the ability to contact the supernatural realm define as fearful the Hunting devil, the aladigo and the agbadu agbaru. Each of these characters parades through the streets, whereas their fancy counterparts are confined to the security of the play area.

Another fierce witch-hunting devil said to be of Yoruba origin is the *ayogbo*. Few examples of this mask type are found in Freetown today, but in the early part of this century many such masqueraders formed part of the Egungun celebrations and rituals. The Temne in the Port

Loko region (see map 1) have incorporated this devil into their Egungun societies.[19] Currently Freetown persons seeking the services of the spirit make the trip to Port Loko or visit a man in Mountain Cut who owns such a costume. The appearance of the ayogbo costume is similar to the Hunting costume in that it has several medicines and a bell attached to the head. It consists of several horns, porcupine quills, and charms, which are attached to a mud-packed mound at the center of the mask. Perched horizontally over the head, it purportedly points in the direction of a suspected witch.

The Fancy/Fierce Opposition

A myth of creation in the Hunting and Egungun societies explains the origins of the fancy and fierce aesthetic opposition.

The Story of the White Triplets and
the Beginning of Hunting and Ojé[20]

There were three twins [triplets], two male and one female.
The female one was Kaende.
One of the males was Adada; today some people look like him, for he was a hunter with dredlocks.
Adeboro was the other male, he did work for the house, brought wood and gathered fruit.
His brother brought home the meat.
Kaende kept the house in order.
One day Adeboro went to get some fruit, and he come across a guava tree.
He was carrying a knife on his side on that day, when he decided to climb the guava tree.
As he climbed the guava, his knife scraped along the cover of the tree; and as part of the cover (bark) was pulled away, water the color of blood came out.
This fell on the head of Adeboro.
So when he returned home his brother and sister saw the red lines on his white body.
Adada saw Adebora and his stripes and he became the first ojé devil.
He became Ajofoembe [Ajofoyembo].
Adada became the Hunting devil.
Kaende became the beautiful head of the alabukun [the Egungun with the carved headpiece].
The three were happy and there was no trouble in the house.[21]

The symbolism in this story sheds light, not only on the meaning of the fancy/fierce–aesthetic opposition, but also on the origins of the Hunting and Egungun masquerades. One informant interpreted the hunter Adada as being the stronger of the two males. It is claimed that he had the ability to sit in the bush night after night waiting patiently for the anticipated prey, and he seldom relied on medicine for protection. On the other hand, Adeboro, the founder of the Egungun, was a man of little patience. For example, he could not wait for his own trees to produce fruit, so he stole from others. It is said that the medicine alé, which was introduced by hunters, was stolen by members of the Egungun. It appeared that the founder of Egungun borrowed or stole; whereas his brother, the hunter, acted more independently. The acquisitive nature of Egungun was used to explain why the society borrowed from other masking traditions.

It has been suggested that the Yoruba Hunting cults originated with hunting and gathering peoples who migrated to present-day Yorubaland. These wanderers married into families of settled agriculturalists of the region who had established the agrarian cult of the ancestors as manifested in the Egungun masquerades.[22] In this respect we recall from the story of the white triplets that the founder of the Egungun society was sedentary, lived in the house, gathered wood, and harvested fruit. His actions, unlike those of his brother Adada, were characterized as feminine. Here fanciness is equated with femininity, and fierceness is equated with masculinity. This aesthetic dichotomy is also expressed in other conceptual pairs of opposites, as further discussion of the Ode-lay masquerades will demonstrate.

The Masquerades

The high-spirited Ode-lay street processions are far different from the privately held, meticulously planned ceremonies of the Egungun and Hunting societies. This does not discount the fact that the Ode-lay presentations have their roots in the traditional societies. The masquerade carol of hunters and certain Egungun celebrations have served as models for Ode-lay mask presentations, especially the masquerades that feature fast, propelling movements, portable instruments, uniform costumes, participation of women, and competition between rival groups which results from devil confrontation. Although the young men have adapted the internal organization of the older groups and, to some extent, the styles and materials of traditional devil building, it may be said that the urban environment has been a much stronger stimulus in the development of the Ode-lay mask presentation. The parent Yoruba societies have also undergone modifications that stem from the impact of the city.

Seemingly the most removed influence on the Ode-lay would be the carefully planned and well-studied choreography of the Egungun plays, which are mostly confined to private residences or vacant lots. The plan of an Egungun masquerade seldom varies. (See figure 49.) At one end of the play area are situated three drums and their players. The smallest

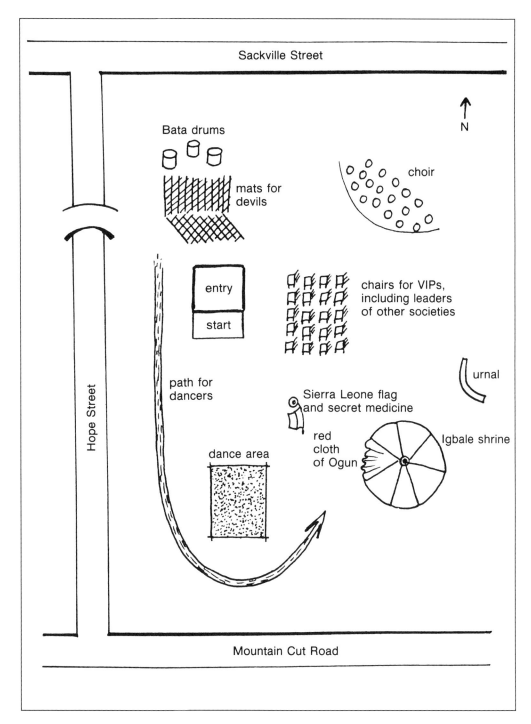

FIGURE 49   Layout for an Egungun dance procession in a private lot. Diagram by Ryntha Johnson.

drum or *aku* directs the dancers with its sharp high tones played in rhythmic sequences that are understood by the dancers and other society members. This instrument is played by the best musician, and on it depends the success of the play. I once saw, in an *Awodie* Egungun celebration, one of the cloth-covered dancers briefly exposed. This would have constituted a violation of the principle of invisibility of the spirit; however, the aku drummer noticed the mishap before most of the observers did and with a quick staccato warning signaled the dancer to disappear. The devil quickly moved behind a wall of concrete blocks at the back of the lot and was later escorted to the shrine house. This interaction between drummer and masquerader typifies the relationship between mailo jazz musicians and Ode-lay masqueraders. It is the young men's consensus, like that of the Egungun elders, that the beat of their ensembles determine superior masquerading and correct dancing.

The Egungun plan continues with a chorus led by the vocalist or *awoko,* who stands next to the drummers. This leader, together with the musicians, selects the traditional songs used and sings the leading lines, to which the chorus responds. Choir members often beat the time of rhythmically complex songs with hand-held sticks. They sometimes charge across the play area with raised sticks ready to strike someone sitting nearby. As they lower the sticks over the intended victims, the violent swings give way to gentle taps on the victims' shoulders. Such aggressive display occurs throughout the play.

The ordinary cloth devils are seated on cane mats opposite to, or sometimes in front of, the Egungun drummers. Behind them, seated on chairs, are the fancy devils, including *aredé, alaribe,* and *alabukun.* These fancy masqueraders are the first and last to perform. In between their dancing, the cloth masqueraders perform individually, while the others rest on the mats. In an outstanding performance, members of the audience move to a spot before the dancer and toss coins that bounce off his shoulders onto the ground; these coins are gathered by the group's treasurer. For a particularly superb dance, as many as fifty spectators may respond in this way, urging the devil to dance faster. At every play one man carries a sack of one-cent pieces wrapped in rolls of ten or twenty; these rolls are exchanged for currency. It is preferable that coins and no currency be tossed at the masquerader. One suspects that their luminosity, weight, and sound as they hit the ground add more than paper to the sensuality of the performance.

Chairs for guests, patrons, and friends of the society are placed around the perimeter of the play area. If the celebration is very large (involving a thousand or more), a VIP section is added. A flagpole is sometimes planted at the center of the arena, and lights are strung from it to the walls of nearby houses in anticipation of night performances. Medicines may also be attached to the pole. On the side farthest from the spectators, a temporary shelter of cane mats provides the masqueraders with a place to change. The dancing commences at about six in the evening and continues until nine or ten o'clock, sometimes even until early the next morning. If the audience is well-behaved, the celebration ends with members, their wives, and their girlfriends dancing in what is called *jubilee*.

Egungun masquerades, like those of the Ode-lay societies, have been influenced by the urban environment. This is partly because in Freetown a shift in membership has occurred from primarily Yoruba descendents to migrants of Limba, Temne, and Mende origin (see map 1). As the number of migrants has increased, their lack of knowledge of Yoruba tradition and exposure to the city have affected presentation of the plays. An example of such change was seen in May 1978, in the celebrations of the Limba Ojé Number One, which were held at a large clearing between Mountain Cut Road and Sackville Street in Sierra Leone. Everyone agreed that the Limba plays were successful. One factor singled out for their success was the order and planning of the dancing.

For this event a streetlike pattern was marked on the ground to indicate the positions, stations, and directions of movement of the masqueraders. White chalk lines about six inches wide represented the lanes of traffic. Box number one was the first dancing station. As the dancer in this spot moved to the next box, another took a position in the first box. When the second dancer advanced to the next position, yet another one entered the arena. (See figure 49.) After the performance, the masqueraders moved along a curved arrow, which pointed in the direction of the shelter. By utilizing one-way traffic, lane markers, and parking areas (places where the dancers could rest) most of the confusion that marks large festivals was avoided, and the society was able to retain the attention of the audience. This ability to capture and keep the attention of the audience often determines the peacefulness of the play. In mediocre performances the disappointment of the crowd may end in heated arguments and fighting. The adoption of urban street-planning (Freetown traffic is directed on one-way streets) to effect order and discipline in the presentation of ancestor masquerades shows the extent of the environmental impact on devil presentations.

Hunting performances, which feature loud marching cadences, street processions, interaction between masqueraders and spectators, style of costume, and fierce aesthetic, have been a primary source of inspiration for the Ode-lay societies. Hunting celebrations are held at the forty-day death ceremony, after a hunt, for weddings, and occasionally on national holidays. Hunting presentations are of two kinds: (1) the play, in which masqueraders and musicians perform at a given location; and (2) the street procession, in which hand-carried instruments are sounded as the masquerader moves through the traffic and neighborhoods of the city.

A Hunting Society performance I observed one evening in November

1977 was held to celebrate a wedding at Mountain Cut. In Freetown weddings are held on Thursday, the day associated with the Islamic tradition, or on Saturday. For this event the men of the society wore white pants, blue smocks or *rappa,* and raffia hats or *oku arbor.* Pieces of raffia were attached to the buttonholes of the smocks. The women wore full-length, blue gara-cloth gowns of local manufacture. The Hunting drum ensemble, like that of the Egungun, consisted of three instruments: the *agereh, arkor,* and *afaray.* The agereh player maintained the tempo for the ensemble, while a flute player called the devil with his instrument. Most of the female members of the group were seated in the play area adjacent to the street.

The first masquerader appeared from a nearby house wearing the traditional garb of animal skins, shells, brown sack-dress, and wooden headpiece. As he moved quickly down the street and out of sight, the crowd became still. The flutist then called the dancer in high-speechlike tones. Eventually the masquerader returned, stopping just short of the play area, then retreating once more. This teasing created tension and expectation in the audience. Each time the devil approached the rumblings and noise of the onlookers increased, and each time the sound quieted as he withdrew. The drumming and singing simply overpowered the performer as he finally danced into the arena. This ear-splitting crescendo signified the crowd's approval.

Fifteen minutes after this masquerader returned to the dressing room, another dancer appeared in the same costume. This masquerader moved to and from the play area in a manner similar to his predecessor's, again exciting the spectators. The medicine man stood by holding a calabash of soweh, at the bottom of which was a shotgun cartridge. An attendant dipped a small handbroom into the mixture and splashed it on the dancer. Then a member of the society poured drinks of bottled liquor for the participants and guests. Invited guests offered coins to members of the wedding party, who accepted them in their mouths. This "eating" of wealth is common to all Freetown Yoruba-descended societies. By 1:00 A.M. the wedding celebration was over. All characteristic parts of this Hunting ritual have been adapted by the Ode-lay: the uniform dress or ashoebi, the medicine, the bush devils, and the interplay between crowd and masqueraders.

The most important contribution the Hunting societies have made to the development of the Ode-lay is the street processions, which are held in the morning before weddings and upon return of hunters from the bush. These morning processions, called carols, include a number of persons dressed in the ashoebi, a masquerader, a bila man, and a flute player. The members strike bamboo slats or wooden spoons to establish the beat for the dancer, while the flutist leads the procession from a position of about forty feet ahead. The processions begin at about 10:00

A.M. and last until noon or until a particular section of the city has been covered. The colors of the uniforms communicate to the onlookers which society will perform in the evening. The expertise of the dancers, the excellence of the music, and the richness of the costumes are meant to attract large crowds for the evening's entertainment. In adopting this strategy to announce their celebrations, the Ode-lay groups, unlike the Hunting societies, use a fancy devil for their morning processions.

During the carol both Hunting and Ode-lay society members collect funds for the evening supplies of food and drink. As the masqueraders perform at street intersections, large traffic jams often result, which allow members to move about the lines of vehicles with collection plates in hand. The carols begin in the area where the evening celebrations are to be held. They proceed to the center of the city, turn at Circular Road, and then return to the starting point. The principal thoroughfare for these processions is Circular Road, a place of intergroup fighting, which police have designated a problem area. (See map 5.)

The street processions of Hunting societies, especially those that mark a return from the hunt, generate much enthusiasm among drivers and pedestrians. Such a procession on Kroo Town Road included a flutist wearing a policelike uniform and a blue beret. Following him were sixteen men in pairs, each pair carrying, on a pole hoisted between their shoulders, a bushbuck tied by the feet. Behind them danced a two-horned alankoba masquerader with hand brooms. Next came the general membership dressed in paramilitary garb consisting of khaki uniforms, belts with canteens, and other military gear. Many participants played the bamboo sticks or wooden spoons. Near the devil was the bila man, who in this instance carried a real rifle rather than a carved replica. Were it not for the absence of mailo jazz and costumes reflecting the fancy aesthetic, this procession might well have been mistaken for an Ode-lay event.

Although the Ode-lay societies have drawn their costumes and masquerade format from Yoruba traditions, they have created a unique masquerade that has adapted to the urban environment. The fancy aesthetic documented early in the life of the colony by the missionaries was found in the Gelede and Egungun societies as well as in the colonial fancy-dress balls. Cloth merchants imported prodigious quantities of fabric for the balls and for masquerade costumes. The fierce aesthetic, too, which ultimately derives from Hunting costumes inspired by the warlike god of iron, Ogun, has been adapted by the Ode-lay societies. Early descriptions of the one- and two-horned headpieces and of the carved antelope head confirm the origin of the Ode-lay fierce style. Another adaptation from the hunting costume is the hampa, with its skulls, shotgun casings, medicine packets, sea porcupine, land snails, and quills.[23] Armed with these objects, the masquerader becomes a human missile of Ogun. Whereas hunters use horns and skin-covered carved headpieces for their costume construction, Ode-lay artists make elaborate zoomorphic double- and triple-headed forms, which they color with high-effect brush and spray paints (see plate 4). The overall effect has been to add beauty to the costume while simultaneously preserving its fierce character. By this combination of fancy and fierce in a single masquerade, the Ode-lay associations have broadened the appeal of their mask performances.

Because the young men perform in the streets, their performances are more closely identified with those of the Hunting societies than with the Egungun. Most Egungun ceremonies are held in vacant lots and on private property. In one Egungun example a streetlike pathway was created within a closed area. A primary inspiration of the Ode-lay has been the returning hunters' parade in the streets with their prey and masquerader. The fast, propelling beat of the drums, the antics of the bila man, and the threatening nature of the devil have all been incorporated into the Ode-lay masking ceremony. The morning caroling of the hunters has also been adapted. Where urban toughness is a requirement of survival in Freetown, Ogun and his artistic accoutrements have been readily transformed in the Ode-lay experience.[24]

6

The Ode-lay Artist

Dis na fine debil play, e day pass all we play Delco beat is a common Freetown expression uttered in response to certain masquerades. Translated it means This is a fine devil play, one far superior to masquerades that falter in rhythm and beauty of costume.[1] In this context *Delco* refers to a now abandoned battery factory that was known for its incessant noise and sputtering machinery, which to the Africans sounded like poorly played drums. The goal of Ode-lay societies is aesthetic praise, and to this end they commission the best artists and musicians.

The Artistic Personality

Any examination of the role of the Ode-lay artist must take into consideration personality, social milieu, technique, and mode of artistic presentation, as well as function of the artistic creation.[2] It has been argued that the artist in African society is less a creator in the Western sense than a person who readily responds to the needs of his people. The artist is, then, a well-adjusted individual who understands his society and works in harmony with it. The artist in Western society, on the contrary, is often seen as a misfit, a neurotic person who is at odds with his society. This view has some validity. Although artists in traditional cultures play a central role in society, they sometimes also serve as instruments of cultural change and in this respect may be at odds with their peers.

Artistic and cultural change may be affected by individuals who are not satisfied with their status and who therefore seek alternative structures and behaviors to accommodate their needs. In so doing, these individuals effect innovation. In Freetown, as well as in northern Ghana, not all artists were, as this view claims, well integrated into the scheme of things.

However, their inability to integrate smoothly was a source of their artistic energy.

In the Sisala area of northern Ghana, for example, the artist Semani Wisituwo was not raised with his agnatic kin as was customary. After his father died he was taken by his mother to her natal village. This left young Wisituwo without the strong patrilineal ties that are pivotal in a young man's achievement of manhood in Sisala. Without these ties he lacked rights to the land and the proper relationship with the ancestors; the former depended upon the latter.

Through the years Wisituwo adopted as his religion a spirit cult that revolved around the *kantomung* or bush spirits, who—it was believed— aid carvers. However, the Sisala community was opposed to such spirits, for they saw them as antithetical to the ancestral spirits. Farming and the ancestors were intimately linked.[3] As Wisituwo increased his carving activities, he became more involved with the kantomung and less involved with farming and the ancestors. Consequently, he was often accused of witchcraft. Although his twin-figure carvings were part of his culture, his other sculptures were for the benefit of the bush spirits. The problem was that there was little demand for twin sculpture. The extent to which Wisituwo could create a market for bush-spirit art was the measure of his success in changing Sisala culture.

Semani Wisituwo demonstrates that an examination of an artist's particular culture and unique social circumstances adds to an understanding of his creative abilities. The artist's experience and the dialectic between himself and his sociocultural setting should be considered. In Freetown the response of the participants of the societies—spectators, general audience, press, and government—also figures in this dialectic.

In comparison with work in Freetown, work in Ghana was relatively easy, because in Sisala society fewer variables affect the lifestyle. It was simple to plot how far an artist had deviated from the Sisala way, i.e., the way of the ancestors, farming, and manhood. In Freetown the problem of differentiating normal from deviant personality is compounded by the fact that there is no single path to manhood in that city. Multiethnic situations, contractual arrangements, and the function of occupation in determining status all make it extremely difficult to measure the degree to which Freetown artists are unusual or unique. Artists differ from other people, not only by the special skills they develop, but also by their personalities.

The elusive variable in artistic behavior is motivation. Positive response from peers, pecuniary benefits, status, personal satisfaction in the development of a skill, the aesthetic of creation, and involvement with a society's philosophical and religious worldview as expressed by art are without doubt important factors in the makeup of every artist. It is difficult to sort these motivations and to assign priorities to them. Given the available rewards, why do a small number of people become artists and the remainder choose to pursue other fields of activity? Is there an independent variable that can explain artistic behavior? A characteristic that seems common to artists, whether in Freetown, Ghana, or the United States, seems to be a love of doing something in the sensual realm to make an aesthetic statement.

In Freetown, artistic creativity is concentrated in the Mountain Cut area behind Foulah Town. Within a radius of a quarter of a mile live three of the city's most celebrated artists. This is not by chance. Mountain Cut is the home of the first mosque in Freetown; and nearby, at Oke Mori, is the home of the early Hunting and Egungun societies. Mountain Cut is also the location for the Gelede and Egunugu masquerades. The two most effective traditional doctors of the city also live in the area. In brief, Mountain Cut plays a major role in the cultural life of the city. It has been noted that the activities of the Egungun are heavily concentrated in that neighborhood.[4] With this rich cultural underpinning, it is not surprising that many artists are located at Mountain Cut.

The Artists

The first artist of note in the area was Morlai Bebe, who was active before World War I. To him is credited the making of the first Jolly mask in the city and the tutelage of Saidu Kalley, who specialized in creating carved headpieces for the Egungun societies. Kalley seems to have been an innovative builder; to him Mustapha Kargbo, another Mountain Cut artist, credited the first carved antelope headpiece for the Hunting devil.

Kalley's first daughter married Eku Williams, who through his marriage apprenticed himself to his father-in-law. Mustapha Kargbo disclosed that Williams liked to drink rum most of the time and that, when drunk, he would retire to the latrine and grind his teeth to the great annoyance of his neighbors. Williams also smoked great quantities of marijuana. He established a reputation for carvings that he sold to Hausa traders and for his Hunting, Gelede, Bundu, and Gongoli masks. Williams also played the guitar in a renowned band that made maringa music popular in Freetown. His reliance upon a diet of oysters, drink, and "sleep rice" (a food eaten to cure a hangover) may have shortened his life span. Some said his death was a result of witchcraft, for he died with a swollen belly. For this reason no other artists attended his funeral.[5]

MUSTAPHA KARGBO

Mustapha Kargbo was born in Freetown to Tonka Limba parents from Medina in northern Sierra Leone (see map 1). Soon after Kargbo was born, his father died. Kargbo's birth was considered to be distinguished by "special circumstances," because he was preceded by triplets and was born with *dada* or dreadlocks, which were considered a sign of spiritual enlightenment. He was nicknamed Dow, the Limba name customarily given to children who follow triplets.

As a youngster Kargbo made frequent trips to his parents' natal town of Medina, where he met his father's elder brother, a master carver for the Gbagbani, the Limba men's secret society. From his uncle he learned to carve, first simple objects like mortars, pestles, and spoons, then more difficult objects like twin figures, Bundu masks, and staffs of the Limba women's society.

While still a student in a Muslim primary institution at Oke Mori, Kargbo went to work for Eku Williams. The two were neighbors in Mountain Cut. Kargbo's apprenticeship under Williams began by sanding pieces carved by the master. Later he carved bowls and horns. His first commissioned work in Freetown was a tourist mask. Through observation and learning by trial and error, Kargbo became the best sculptor in Freetown, where he makes objects for all societies.

Kargbo also established a thriving tourist business, which requires the assistance of two apprentices to help collect wood and do simple carving. His commerical work includes chairs, tables, masks, and doors, all of which are decorated with traditional motifs and innovative forms based on his own experience. His tourist and local commissions make Kargbo the only full-time artist in Freetown.[6] Kargbo's yard is always covered with layers of fresh chips and numerous logs placed in direct sunlight or near the hearth to dry.

The working day for Mustapha Kargbo begins with a couple of marijuana sticks and one or two small cups of locally distilled gin. After these drugs take effect, he starts work, usually making masks. In carving a mask the first step is to secure materials. This is difficult in the city, but the problem is overcome by obtaining large pieces of cottonwood, sometimes illegally, from public land. The cottonwood tree, Kargbo claims, is best suited for carving, because it is light in weight and crack resistant. To calm the wrathful spirit of the log, he provides rum and kola nut for sacrifices to the tree from which the wood is obtained. Kola-nut halves are tossed on the ground to divine the wish of the ancestors in matters of carving. Halves appearing face down or up in even patterns reveal the ancestors' consent to the work. Afterward some rum is poured on the ground to thank the spirits. With the wood properly prepared, the artist is ready to work.

The carving of masks is the concern not only of the artist, but of the commissioning society as well. Consequently leaders of the various groups often provide sketches of the masks they desire. In one instance a Jolly society gave Kargbo two photo prints of East Indian gods and spirits, whose divine expressions he was to capture in mask carvings. (See figure 50.) The calm gaze of these Eastern spirits, the group's leaders said, would well represent them. This society, Kofi Jolly National, was named after a location in Mountain Cut called Kofi that is notorious for marijuana traffic. The serene smiles of the Hindu and Buddha principals, the young men maintained, were not unlike the look one has while contemplating with the aid of this easily obtained drug. Kofi Jolly, which staged a week-long celebration in Mountain Cut, was highly acclaimed for its peaceful conduct and brilliant masquerades. Word of its reputation had spread throughout the city and to the vice-president of Sierra Leone, who invited the group to perform at his residence. For this occasion Kofi leaders selected Kargbo to prepare the king and queen masks they wished to use. Although the task of carving the masks was given to Kargbo, the added decoration and painting were left to other artists and members of the Jolly society.

In carving a mask the first step is described as the "layout." With an adze the artist outlines the general contours of the sculpture. Kargbo explained that he does not draw the outline on the log because his hand is not too steady. He prefers to work directly with the adze. Next he carves the details with a penknife and lets an apprentice sand the piece. Upon completion of a carving, society leaders may either paint it them-selves or give the task to another artist.

A mask of the Jolly type can be made in one day at a cost of about twenty dollars. Of this amount four dollars covers the cost of the log and sacrifice and another four feeding of the apprentices. This gives Kargbo a profit of about twelve dollars, most of which he spends on marijuana and gin.

Kargbo, like the artist of Ghana, protects himself with carving med-icines. One protective device consists of a powder stored in the white horns of a small bushbuck. A stone called *kamato* represents the spirit of the medicine. Kargbo explained that, as he was walking one day, he came upon this stone three times before he finally picked it up. The spirit of this object appeared to him that night in a dream and told him that soon he would have a commission. Now he consults the stone for advice in carving.

Although Kargbo is at times unstable and never predictable, he is very lucid on the subjects of carving and secret societies in general. He is sensitive to the spiritual realm but can clearly and analytically explain how his creations are constructed. He provides accurate and useful information but on occasion lapses into a noncommunicative state, mut-tering to himself. In his more communicative moments, he understands questions and even anticipates others. His loss of control causes con-siderable hardship and physical affliction. Once, after having drunk several cups of *omoli*, he entered into an argument with a neighbor, which ended in a fight. Because of his drunken condition his adversary was able to bite through his upper lip and tongue, causing a major infection.

FIGURE 50   Mustapha Kargbo (standing) with chromoliths showing serene expression to be duplicated on Jolly masks and with sculptures made for local use and export. Photo credit: John Nunley

Kargbo has six children to feed, clothe, and educate. He and his wife are constantly at odds in financial matters, because his personal spending habits are not reconcilable with the family budget. He earns as much as $200 a month, but his home shows little sign of the affluence such a sum might effect in Freetown. His wife complains of his trips to Medina, which often involve stays of up to six months. Suddenly and without announcement he might leave for his hometown, where he finds ample employment making art objects for the Limba rural secret societies. But acquaintances know that when the food, work, and hospitality there are curtailed and the hard work of farming begins, he will return to Freetown.

AJANI

Abdul Aziz Lasisi Alayode Mukhtarr, better known as Ajani, best fits the description of the *bricouleur*-handyman artist noted by Levi-Strauss. As a tinsmith, locksmith, lantern builder, sculptor, tailor, hunter, song-writer, drummer, and dancer, Ajani moves through all realms of secret-society life.[7]

Ajani was born in Freetown about 1935. His father, Abdullah Eberunke Mukhtarr, was of Creole descent; his mother, Kosnatu Ebelola Mukhtarr, was of Temne descent. His great-grandfather, Pa Musa, introduced the Egunugu society to Freetown and was the most powerful society man in the neighborhood. Ajani patterned his own life after him. The artist's father, who was a security guard for the Sierra Leone Shipping Company, showed little interest in the intricacies of secret-society life.

Ajani considered the circumstances of his birth special. He explained: "I am a child who has returned and came back circumcised. My younger brother also died and came back with a long mark on his back drawn with hot coals or fire. His name is Ousman Nuraine. My sister Madina also came the same way and she was also marked on her toes. She came back with the marks."[8] These circumstances of birth reveal Yoruba in-fluence on notions concerning children who are born to stay only a brief time in this world and then return to the dead. These infants (*abiku*) are considered to be "born to die," and they are often marked in some way to prevent their return to the mother's womb, where they might die again at rebirth.[9]

Ajani was educated at the Amarai, Islamia, and Muslim Association collegiate schools. He obtained a British Form III education, equivalent to junior or senior status in an American high school. He ended his formal education in 1957 to begin preapprentice training at the Technical Institute in the western end of Freetown. At the institute he became proficient in metalwork, blacksmithing, locksmithing, and carpentry. With these skills he became involved in lantern building. As a young man at Mountain Cut he joined the Black Arrow Society, which was famous for its prize-winning lanterns. He eventually built these constructions for the society and won several prizes. His abilities have attracted to him several other young builders, who themselves have gone on to become famous lantern artists.

Ajani joined the Oke Mori Egungun society at Mountain Cut and learned the music and dances of the society. His knowledge of these arts caused some resentment on the part of the general membership. He explained:

> For my wide brain in this line, I was hated by some older members of the society, so they planned to pass me off by a poisoned rum. I saw and heard them making the plan from up a berry tree situated at the side of *egballeh* [ojé shrine house]. Because I saw and heard, they missed me. I revealed the exercise in a general meeting and left the society. It was because of this incident that I won the title *Ajaniokay,* [a Yoruba term] meaning *a flying dog.* This name has been so popular that people do not know the rest of my names.[10]

Flying Dog is a title well deserved by this remarkable artist and personality.

In 1978 Ajani lived a few blocks north of the Firestone settlement on Mountain Cut Road, onto Doherty Street, halfway up the hill, in house number seven. I first saw him sitting on a verandah facing the sea; he was a man of early middle-age, medium height, and strong build. A handshake revealed the power in his short fingers and the roughness of palms, which had sustained nicks and cuts during many years in the metal trades. He introduced himself as Mr. Lasisi and bade me step inside his room.

The first impression conveyed by the interior of Ajani's house was that here, like the home of Semani Wisituwo, the Sisala carver of northern Ghana, lived a major artist of the community. Lasisi's room, however, reflected a culture more complex and urbane than that of his Sisala counterpart. Whereas Wisituwo's small compound was filled with freshly carved wooden figures and various medicine shrines, Ajani's space reflected the influence of the media. Wall decorations included pin-up girls from magazines, the queen of England, the prince of Wales, as well as photographs of Ajani, his family, and friends. From the upper part of the walls hung several large movie posters, among them a Chinese action film, Count Dracula, and *Terminal Island.*

The walls were painted with blue enamels. On one side of the room hung a curtain of blue, pink, and white polka-dot material, which contrasted brilliantly with the blue walls. The same cloth pattern covered the parlor chairs. On the curtain-covered wall hung a photograph of the artist, his father, and his mother framed in an elaborate wood carving painted cream and red. Above the picture the word *Ajaniokay* was printed in dark blue letters; below it the inscription *Long live Ajani* was printed in white. Around the wall space, framed by a pair of curtains, was a large painting of an American Indian maiden with her long hair in braids.

Above this work a public-address speaker was attached to the wall and plugged into a small but powerful transistor radio.

The artist had arranged his sculpture and pictures in nichelike spaces. Sections for posters, photographs, and sculpture were located in different parts of the room. Above the suspended ceiling was a storage space where masquerade costumes were kept. Several sculptures, including a Mammy Wata mermaid motif, were placed on a table. Another Mammy Wata figure served as a centerpiece.[11] The base of this carving was attached to an electric-light fixture that resembled a chandelier. Also on the table were figure sculptures and headpieces for Egungun costumes in various stages of completion. Two Gelede masks hung on the corners of the east wall, and on the west wall was a small fancy-devil mask called Sugar Daddy after a male character whose great wealth could support many young women in a luxurious manner.

By July 1979 Ajani had married and moved to a new location. His living quarters had been redesigned by a painter friend, and the focal point of his studio was a portrait of a woman clad in wet drapery in the classical Greek tradition, the animal at her side revealing an Eastern influence.[12] (See figure 51.)

Ajani is a member of Egungun, Hunting, Egunugu, Jolly, Ode-lay and Arishola societies. In addition to his membership in particular branches of these societies, he is also commissioned to make costumes and to dance for other groups. It was he who in 1978 reestablished the Navy Egungun Society, for which he recruited many young people of the Central One constituency, along with some of the group's original members.[13] He established other societies as well. Apart from his duties as a locksmith at a hospital, he is dedicated to the arts of the Freetown secret societies.

Artistic education began for Ajani with his membership in Black Arrow, where he learned lantern building. As a lantern builder he worked with wire, cane, and wood in making the substructures and frames for costumes. As a founding member of the Arishola fancy-devil society, he learned to sew and tailor costumes. Thus wire-working and sewing were his first acquired artistic skills. As Ode-lay groups increased in number and artists with carving abilities received many commissions, Ajani decided, rather late in life, to apprentice himself to Mustapha Kargbo, who lived about a hundred yards away. Since the completion of his apprenticeship with Kargbo, Ajani has received carving commissions from Ode-lay fancy-devil and Egungun groups; however, the bulk of his work is still in cloth and wire. Several times a week he may be found at home working with wire in the preparation of new designs for fancy costumes. (See plate 5.) These creations are made either on commission or in hope of selling them to a future client. Although Ajani is best known for his cloth costumes, he is fast becoming known as a competent carver. When he experienced difficulty in making a carved face mask or Egungun

FIGURE 51   Ajani's studio in 1979 reflected his changing attitude toward life and art.
Photo credit: Hans Schaal

headpiece, he often paid Kargbo to finish the piece for him. He himself
has helped other artists complete fancy costumes and even occasionally
carved some masks for them.

Ajani is widely respected for his talents. Two lines of a poem written
on a wall reflect his sense of importance to the community: *Da bright
star we God gee / Ajaniokay,* which translates to "The bright star which
God gives is Ajaniokay." Ajani's most coveted honor was his appointment
by the national government to represent Freetown artists at the Nigerian
Pan-African Festival, Festac 77, for which he built many fancy costumes.
Walking through the city after work, he is frequently stopped by well-
wishers who congratulate him on his most recent success or talk with
him about particular problems and triumphs of the secret societies.

Despite the money derived from his artistic pursuits and the salary he receives from locksmithing at the Ministry of Works, Ajani always needs money. He has nine children, who add to his financial difficulties. However, the dances and thrills of artistic presentation absorb these problems and add quality to his life. Before a performance Ajani often appears on his verandah dressed in fashionable attire. He has a bottle of rum or beer available for those persons who stop by before the evening festivities. At these times Ajani is often found dancing and singing the old society songs. These lighter moments are as frequently counterbalanced by quiet, introspective moods, which result in several days' absence from work.

JOHN GOBA

The terms that describe John Goba best are quiet, purposeful, and deliberate. Goba, who is in many ways the opposite of Ajani, lives about a half mile from both Ajani and Kargbo. He was born in 1944, in the district of Bonthe, of a Sherbro mother and a Mende father. His father was employed at the Ministry of Works and was a member of the Free Masons. His great-grandfather was an herbalist in Bonthe and was renowned for his ability to perform miracles. Making devils appear and disappear were his most popular feats; he could call a Bundu devil out of the water. As a member of the Mende Poro Society, John Goba learned the secrets of his ancestor's miracles and also the secrets of Poro medicines, which he uses to protect himself in his work as an artist.

Goba obtained several certificates in auto mechanics while working for the Rural Transport Department and in that capacity receives a monthly salary greater than that of all other Freetown artists. He also contracts mechanical work outside the department and for this reason is difficult to locate. He rents a two-room apartment in a modern concrete-block house north of Mountain Cut Road. In 1978 the house was painted crimson on the outside and electric blue on the inside. Scattered throughout the yard were automobile-frame and engine parts, signs of his past moonlighting activities.

Goba's parlor or receiving room was well kept. Whereas Ajani's quarters were filled with artifacts placed in temporary arrangements, Goba's contained a more or less permanent, uncluttered display. His auto-mechanic certificates, a large photograph of himself with his sculpture for the Mexico City Ode-lay Society (of Freetown), tourist Gelede masks, elaborately painted calabashes, and a red-and-white pair of Jolly masks hung on the walls. (See figure 52.) On a coffee table that stood opposite a small couch were several Ode-lay headpieces. The blue enamel walls contrasted well with the glittering string of decorations suspended from the central light fixture to the corners of the ceiling.

While attending primary school in Mountain Cut, Goba became friendly

FIGURE 52   A Gelede face mask (right) and tourist pieces carved by Goba. Photo credit: John Nunley

with Bramah Sesey, who later became one of the founders of Firestone. After school young Goba would watch Sesey make lanterns and carve headpieces for devil costumes. He would also watch Bgobgosorro (the alias of an artist for Black Arrow, the main neighborhood young men's society before Firestone) make hampas and eris. In 1961 Goba began to make costume parts for Black Arrow and continued to do so until the society collapsed in 1967. In addition to learning from Black Arrow artists, Goba took instruction from Mustapha Kargbo, with whom he occasionally works on large commissions. Goba often sends difficult parts of carving to Kargbo, who in turn leaves the finished pieces for his former student to paint. It is difficult to distinguish who does what in these collaborations, for each artist claims the entire piece. Generally, Mountain Cut artists are selected to make art according to their special abilities. Goba is known for his painting and for complex carving designs, Kargbo for carving skills, and Ajani for tailoring and wire building. With these skills the three controlled the majority of Ode-lay commissions in Freetown in 1978.

Goba is the most popular Ode-lay headpiece and costume builder and has sold his work throughout the country. He has been commissioned by groups as far removed as Kono (see map 1) to personally supervise the assembly of his work. His carvings include alligators, dragons, antelope, sheep, angels, human skulls, snakes, Mammy Wata images,[14] unicorns, leopards, and human faces. He receives as much as $200 for a complete costume. During the wet season many groups arrive with drawings, upon which they ask him to pattern their headpieces. (See figure 53.) Three apprentices assist with sanding and carving simple parts of sculptures.

Goba's reputation is based on the success of masquerade presentations that display his art. In 1978 Kono Tenda (Kono Thunder), a prestigious Ode-lay society in the Kono District, became acquainted with his work through a neighboring society, which had purchased a Goba crocodile carving that had been first sold in 1972 to members of the Mexico City Society in Freetown. Kono Tenda leaders came to Freetown and asked Goba to create a zoomorphic sculpture combining lion, snake, and rabbit forms in a headpiece about two feet high.[15] They also commissioned a hampa and an asho, for which all the necessary materials were provided. When the three parts were completed, the executive committee of the society returned to Freetown to escort the artist to Kono to assemble the parts for a Republican Day celebration.

The Ode-lay artist, unlike the Western artist, plays an active role with respect to the persons who commission him. Whereas art patrons of the West seldom meet art producers or meet them only in a gallery context, African buyers carry on a dialog with the artist from the beginning of the work to its final installation or presentation. For example, during a commission for Seaside Firestone Ode-lay in Godrich, a village located a few miles west of Freetown (see map 4), Goba taught the group various Ode-lay sacrifices and how to dance with the costume he created. The group hired Goba's apprentices to masquerade in the costume. (See figure 54.) The young men of Seaside Firestone, who resided mainly in one part of the town, wished to demonstrate superiority over their counterparts in another section of the town. For this reason their leader, who was called Alfonso, came to Goba for advice concerning the establishment of a society. Alfonso, who was a lorry driver, and other young men from Godrich brought calabashes, mirrors, colored threads, baskets, land snail and cowrie shells, fans, liquid glue, and animal (baboon, monkey, antelope, and porcupine) skins for the artist to use in building a costume for the 1978 New Year holiday.

The headpiece of the Seaside Firestone costume represented a mustached Mexican bandit with dark brown skin and red cheeks. This sunburned villain commemorated the group's leader, Alfonso, who wore a large Mexican sombrero in the masquerade. Attached to the top of the carved face was a sheep's head, from which projected two horns in honor of the Hunting societies from which the Ode-lay had evolved, and also two snake heads. The aesthetic of this head was fierceness. To complete the piece, three carved calabashes painted red and studded with porcupine quills were mounted on the horns.

John Goba usually works on his mask projects late at night, after most

FIGURE 53   Sketch for an Ode-lay headpiece given to John Goba for execution.
Photo credit: John Nunley

FIGURE 54   The Seaside Firestone Ode-lay costume created by John Goba and his
apprentices. Photo credit: John Nunley

other Freetown residents are asleep. Upon his return from work at the
Rural Transport Department, he bathes and changes into short pants for
his mask work. (See figure 55.) His atelier is well ordered, with an
assortment of chisels, adzes, hammers, knives, sandpaper, and pieces of
wood. Cigarettes, rum, and kola are on hand to aid him during the long
hours that are required to complete a carving by a designated deadline.
Goba likes to work alone, either in his room or in a small clearing a
few yards away from the house, an area that is protected by several trees
and a wall. This seclusion respects the Africans' traditional reverence for
devil costumes. Although Ode-lay costumes have less of an association
with the ancestors than do Egungun costumes, they, too, are regarded
as spirits, and they are not to be seen by the public except in the dance
presentation.

EDMUND COKER AND ABDUL KARIM SILLA

Edmund Coker, who was in 1978 the youngest carver in Freetown, is
another student of Mustapha Kargbo. He was born in 1950 at Campbell

Street on the west side of Freetown. The yard in front of the old Creole house in which he was born retains the farmlike character of the original settlement. Coker's father, who was a Sherbro Mende, met his mother in Zaire while working for the merchant marine. They were married and returned to Freetown. Edmund Coker attended the primary school at Fergusson Street for seven years and there excelled in art. In 1968 young Coker joined the Bloody Mary Society and made sculptures and costumes for them. In addition to carving for the Ode-lay societies, he has also been commissioned to make Bundu masks and figurative sculptures for the tourist market.

As a young man without a family or a steady job in 1978, Coker was free to travel to outlying districts to make Ode-lay carvings. He spent two months in the Kono District working with the Masaanday and Rainbow groups, the latter a branch of the Freetown society of the same name. The Masaanday costume was made in Kono at the request of the group's leader, Agba Fode, who escorted Coker from Freetown to Kono. The carving consisted of two skulls, one in front, the other in back, with porcupine quills covering the entire piece. The star-shaped hampa was made of foam rubber, which lightened the load of the dancer. The carving also displayed a small face-mask in the Senufo style at the top of the double head, and a small Poro-style carving at the back. Three snakes, one on each side and one at the top, completed the sculpture. The artist explained that the Medusa pattern was inspired by a film entitled *Calypso* and that the Senufo mask idea came from an illustration in an African art book.[16] The costume for the Rainbow Society of Kono featured a fierce tiger headpiece, which was balanced by a fancy hampa with angel wings and Christmas-tree decorations.

Abdul Karim Silla was born in November 1949 to Susu parents. His father, a trader, was still alive in 1978; his mother was deceased. Silla rented a room in a Creole house near Edmund Coker and lived with his wife and two children. He was educated at Saint Anthony and Saint Ellena secondary schools, but in spite of his formal education eventually converted to Islam. While in primary school he built small trucks, cars, and bicycles out of wire. He was later to use this wire technique in building devil costumes. In 1963 Silla joined the Limba Ojé Society Two in Mountain Cut, where he began making Egungun costumes. He was fourteen years old at the time; but in the newer, less tradition-bound Egungun branches, age restrictions had been loosened.

Silla's teacher, Mr. Sori, had built fancy-devil costumes for the Abanshola and Ajo societies. His cloth and hampa work had won him commissions in the outlying towns of Bo, Kenema, Lunsar, and Makeni (see map 1); and he had also worked for a branch of Firestone in Monrovia, Liberia. His Ode-lay commissions in Freetown came from the Texas, Masaanday, Domingo, Russia, and Lebanon societies.

FIGURE 55   John Goba at work. Photo credit: John Nunley

Silla and Coker had created one costume jointly. It was commissioned by the Juju Wata Ode-lay Society for a performance on Easter Monday, 27 March 1978. Parts of the hampa and asho were assembled at Silla's home in Freetown. Since Silla, unlike the other artists, did not carve, the carvings were completed at Coker's residence a block away. The week preceding the holiday, Silla's room was crowded with assembled costume parts. So the neighbors would not suspect what was going on inside, the curtains were kept drawn. Materials were purchased at a large department store and were brought home, carefully wrapped, by taxi.

The headpiece of the costume was made of wood, wire, and cloth. At the center of this piece was a Janus-faced crocodile with spitting tongues. This part of the costume was supported by a wire substructure. A three-quarter-length carving of a nude female angel was set on top of the crocodile figure. The wire substructure of the hampa was constructed of bedsprings, which were lined with foam rubber for the comfort of the masquerader. The front of the hampa supported one projecting spring, to which was attached a Jolly mask, which moved in rhythm with the steps of the dancer.

The room was filled with various unfinished parts of the wire structure, cloth materials, Christmas tree ornaments, and tools for construction of the costume. One week before the celebration, the parts were taken by taxi late at night to a house in Hastings, where the parts were to be assembled. The house, owned by a society sponsor who belonged to the Internal Security Unit police, was a newly constructed concrete-block structure. Its complete set of contemporary furnishings and high-fidelity sound system reflected the affluence of its owner.

The costume was kept in a small room on one side of the veranda. The shutters in the room were closed, and the room was very dark and hot. On the walls hung photographs of Fidel Castro, Che Guevera, and other revolutionary figures. In this small space Silla and Coker lived and worked for several days, complaining about the crowded conditions and the heat. The smell of perspiration betrayed their hard work and discomfort. In the tradition of secrecy, the builders were not allowed to go out into the town; however, they were given ample food, drink, and female companionship to offset these adverse circumstances.

The front part of the hampa included three carved face-masks arranged in a single vertical tier. The bottom mask, named Sali Motto, described a prominent leader of the Gelede society from Ibadan. This image was decorated with an African coiffure made of wire coils that were wrapped with thread and adorned with feathers. The center mask, named Binti Sudan, referred to a beautiful Fulani woman—the kind who appears in men's dreams. The curling black lines down the sides of this mask represented a Sudanic woman's hairstyle; Christmas tree decorations at the sides added to her fanciness. The top mask, which also represented

FIGURE 56 Juju Wata costume, front view, showing masks and beaded veil.
Photo credit: John Nunley

a character from Ibadan, was called Injiana National after a juju man. The herbalist facemask was covered with a beaded veil; it thus bore an astonishing resemblance to the costumes of diviners and royal Yoruba personages. Like the veil of Yoruba kings, the veil of this masquerade character was suspended from the front of a crown. (See figure 56.) The wire and cloth projections of the hampa with attached mirrors were symbolic of feminine beauty; the glass reflectors were likened to a woman's vanity pack.[17]

Prospective for Ode-lay Art

The artists of the Ode-lay societies are not content with historical sources for inspiration; they are also greatly influenced by contemporary media. Ajani and John Goba best exemplify the use of these new sources. In 1978 Ajani's room reflected the degree to which the media had gained a foothold in the West African city. While it displayed several traditional Jolly, Gelede, and Egungun masks, it also displayed—along with photographs of British royalty—scenes from films and centerfold poses of women. The film posters, representing two American films and one Chinese film, were in prominent positions on the walls. The outstretched arms of Dracula in one of the American film posters echoed a standard position taken by Egungun masquerades as illustrated by Ajani.

Ajani's selection of a poster to meet his own aesthetic standards of costume presentation, as taught in Egungun performance, is indicative of the manner in which most elements of the media are adapted by the people of Freetown. Aspects of the media are selected in accordance with local aesthetic needs and are incorporated in a traditional structure.[18] Likewise, elaborate fancy devils of the Arishola Society, with Christmas-tree ornaments made by Ajani, are fitted within three parts derived from traditional Yoruba costume construction. As the artist sews Egungun ancestral costumes or works on his newest creations at night, he listens to a transistor radio rigged to a conventional public-address system. It plays BBC world news and musical works ranging from the classics to current hits.

As the media spreads from Freetown to the rest of the country, its impact will become even more graphically in evidence than it is in Ajani's studio and workshop. Television, newspapers, sound recordings, photography, and film will all play a part. To the casual observer the influence of the media on traditional culture appears at first to be simply imitative. One must, however, carefully observe the manner in which elements of the media are accommodated by traditional artists. In this way the extent of change in the process, not the product, of creativity may be appreciated.

See, for example, the photograph of artist John Goba with his apprentices and his work (plate 6). What is striking about this is the surrealistic mood that is effected by the artist, his props, and his assistants. Their poses are completely self-conscious and directed toward a certain effect. Goba has been photographed many times, and with this experience he has become aware of the power of this medium to create an image. In this particular instance, it was his intention that the picture convey the image of an intense and mystical artist. Behind this obvious yet affective part of the artist's work is his authentication of foreign elements within the traditional structure of the Yoruba-rooted Hunting masquerades.

The large devil costume in the foreground of the illustration was inspired by a film entitled *Who Can Replace a Man?* The theme, taken from a Brian Aldiss science-fiction short story, features insectlike animated creatures moving with machinelike precision across the high horizon of a Boschian landscape. Stimulated by the rich source of imagery in the film, Goba produced a masquerade costume that reflected his own conception of a robot. The arrangement of porcupine quills at the top of the costume, palm-frond skirt, calabash head, mirrors, and plastic waist piece may all be seen as parts of an automaton. To one cognizant of the three parts of the Hunting costume, however, it is clear that the robot has been assembled in the manner of a traditional Yoruba costume. Moreover, the attendant with the enameled pan on his head, carrying a carved gun, represents the bila man of the Hunting society who protects the masquerader and at times feigns the hunter. The enameled helmet, which is a transformation of the traditional straw hat or *oku arbor*, is in keeping with Goba's interpretation of the film. The bila man is seen turning away from the central costume while aiming his weapon as if to shoot; he thus lends to the scene a sense of action and drama that is a common feature of the Hunting masquerade. Through metaphor the artist has transformed the photograph into a "moving" picture that emphasizes the interrelationship between art, music, and drama.

7

Music of the Freetown Societies

The popular music of the Freetown urban associations first developed during the 1920s and 1930s. The fierce rivalries and political character of its musical forms were to be reflected later in the mailo jazz music of the 1960s and 1970s and in the masquerades accompanied by the groups who played this music.

The music of the Geda branches, which were based in part on an ethnic society composed of Mandinka migrants who arrived in Freetown in the 1920s, clearly points to a political role for music. The first of these Mandinka groups, called *Yankadde* (*here is sweet*), was named after a popular tune played in French Guinea after World War I.[1] A Mandinka tribal head in Freetown brought Mandinka musicians or *jelibas* to the city to play the song. A number of young men learned the song, and it soon spread throughout the town. These youths organized the Yankadde Society, collected funds, and proclaimed that the mission of the society was to entertain and help each other in times of stress.[2] Thus the Mandinka societies were the first to provide an expressive and instrumental association for migrants.

When the Yankadde Society first appeared, it was extremely unpopular with the native-born citizens of Freetown. Even its own followers became dissatisfied with it, and some of them formed a new group called Tarancis, which, unlike the parent group, drew many members from among peoples other than the Temne.[3] The musical style and rhythms of the Tarancis Society were less complex than those of the Yankadde and had greater appeal for non-Mandinka groups. Eventually what was originally a Mandinka-inspired phenomenon became a Temne-dominated activity with widespread appeal.

Music and dance presentation were, once again, key factors in the development and success of the new Tarancis associations. Tarancis adapted Yankadde organizational features but added to the original one-drum music two additional drums, an accordion, and shakepans made of metal plates with rings attached around the rim.[4] With this more stylish ensemble, the group attracted followers from every quarter of the city. The Temne, in organizing groups like the Ambas Geda and Tarancis, were the first of the rural migrants to adjust to the urban environment.

The motivation for the establishment of these groups stemmed in part from the youths' alienation from their elders: "The problem was made more difficult as the leaders of the Temne community were not educated and most of them were of limited means. Their appeals to the youths were ineffective."[5] Music was used to express these generational conflicts, even as Ode-lay youths still use it today to criticize their leaders and call them tangaist. Early Ambas Geda lyrics expressing such conflict have been recorded:

> Ah, look what is being said,
> Look what is being done!
> How they envy our play.
> Ah, I do believe (in the play)
> As the old folk envy the geda
> Let them just go on envying!
>
> I've been done a bad turn, why?
> Though not knowing me, they've
> done me a bad turn; why?
>
> The old folk have nothing but bad turns
> up their sleeves. Hear me, Allah!
>
> Oh look! The moriman leaves his prayers
> And calls a curse on our play!
> If God takes him tomorrow, pity him!
> For he may go to hell. Our play is blessed.[6]

Lantern Music

In the presentation of the visual arts, popular music like mailo jazz finds a precedent in the music of the early lantern festivals. Lanterns, which celebrate the beginning of Ramadan or Eid-ul-Fitry are similar in construction and appearance to the American floats displayed, for example, in the Rose Bowl Parade at Pasadena, California. (See figure 57.) Lantern building was introduced to Freetown by Daddy Maggay from Banjul, where the Catholic fathers used hand-held lanterns in Easter processions. The Muslims of Freetown adopted lantern displays for the celebration of the twenty-sixth day of Ramadan, the day the Koran was sent down

FIGURE 57   This lantern, made by Yaskey in the late 1960s, includes a Moslem knight (left) playing a rokee or trumpet like that used by Daddy Maggay and his Bobo group in the 1930s. Photo credit: Mrs. Yaskey

by Allah. This day is called *Lai-Lai-Tu-Gadri* or the Day of Light. The early hand-held lanterns consisted of small paper-box enclosures mounted on sticks.[7]

The first lantern celebrations were small and peaceful, but a musical innovation of Daddy Maggay's group soon unexpectedly attracted large crowds. As the reputation of Maggay's wife for home-cooked corn or *kpa* and couscous or *ogi kpa* spread, more people joined the celebrations, and the crowds occasionally got out of control, which resulted in injury to some lantern carriers. This prompted Maggay and his followers to wear heavy boots for protection. But the boots had the unexpected effect of drawing even larger and more unruly crowds. Drums may not be used in lantern celebrations because the Koran bans them. In their adoption of the heavy marching boots, however, Maggay and his followers discovered that they now had a means of coordinating their steps into rhythmical patterns. They introduced a marching beat called Bobo, a name by which the group later came to be known. Then professional musicians and a bugle player were hired to complement the marching beat. The addition of the trumpet or *rokee,* which was very popular, stimulated the appearance of lantern groups at Waterloo, Kosso Town, Magazine Cut, and Foulah Town. (See figure 57.) Thus the Freetown celebration evolved from processions using simple hand-held lanterns to parades of large floatlike constructions made of bamboo and wire frames covered with layers of fine fabrics and paper. A contributing factor in the proliferation of the festival was its intimate relation to popular music, with its percussive marching beat, which was not unlike the beat of the bass box in mailo jazz.

The competition in lantern celebrations became extremely intense, at times ending in violence.[8] This prompted the elders of the Fourah Bay Muslim community to change the date of the procession from the twenty-sixth day of Ramadan to the thirtieth out of respect for those Muslims who wished to observe the holiday in peace.

In the 1950s, when the Ode-lay boys began to build lanterns, the competition reached a peak. New groups with names like Beetles, Ashanti, and Super Combo reflected the style-consciousness of the youth who had taken charge of the festival. At this time the original Bobo group disbanded; its members were too old for such rigorous competition.

Several features that emerged in the development of lantern music and celebration have found their way also into Ode-lay music and masquerades, where the use of music is strikingly similar. The boot rhythms and bugle playing of the lantern celebrations constituted a new musical style which boosted the popularity of the lantern processions. Mailo jazz groups had a parallel impact on the Ode-lay celebrations. These groups also adapted the bugle. The complexity of lantern forms, sparked by intergroup competition, was reflected also in the elaboration of Ode-lay costumes. In fact, many Ode-lay costume builders were also lantern builders.

Competition in both forms of celebration has played a major role in grassroots politics. The lantern songs of the 1930s celebrated the great labor organizer Wallace Johnson, his affairs in court, and his West African Youth League. In 1968 many of the songs dealt with the change in leadership and with the ascendancy of the All Peoples Congress party. The lantern associations, functioning in the political context, used the mediums of sculpture, music, and street procession, and in this respect foreshadowed the Ode-lay presentations. What is remarkable about the lantern presentations is the inevitable use of traditional African mediums to reinforce the solidarity of city neighborhoods while simultaneously expressing social change. The music, dance, and artistic display that lie at the heart of African aesthetic sensibility thus become integral components in the intergroup rivalries and confrontations of the traditional societies.

Mailo Jazz

Without doubt the most important musical form in Freetown is mailo jazz. The musicians of the mailo jazz bands are treated with great respect in Sierra Leone. The precision of their rhythms and the originality of their song texts may determine the success or failure of an Ode-lay presentation. Before the introduction of mailo jazz, Ode-lay musicians played the hand clappers and horns of the Hunting societies; but these instruments were ill-suited to noisy Ode-lay street processions.

During the late 1960s Olufumbe Cole (whose first name means *Gift from God*) was strongly affected by Congo music, which was played in all the pubs and record shops in town. When not at his job with the Ministry of Tourism and Cultural Affairs, Cole often relaxed at home to the deep-bass sound of the rhythms from his hi-fi and smoked marijuana. He said of his enjoyment of these private moments, "When a man lives alone he can think."

Cole, who is commonly known as Dr. Olu, drew upon this experience to create the music called mailo jazz. With the intention of imitating the Congo bass sound, he created the bass box, an instrument built on the principle of the reflexive speaker box. The top of the box he constructed of inch-thick plywood and the sides of house siding. He cut a hole in the top of the box to serve as a baffle, like that of a high fidelity speaker. The new instrument measured two feet square and nine inches deep, about the size of the speaker cabinets of his home sound system. (See figure 58.) When Dr. Olu showed the instrument to members of the Lord Have Mercy Ode-lay Society, they were impressed by its sound and wanted to use it for their devil processions. To his new sound Dr. Olu added three *sangbai* drums, which were similar in shape to the three drums used by the Hunting societies; and, like the Hunting instruments, each had a different pitch. (See figure 59.)

Then he added tin cups similar to those used by the hunters to effect a mid-range metallic sound. Cole modified the instruments, however, by joining two tin cups of different pitches to make the first double gong or *agoogoo*. When the instrument proved too flimsy for street use, he took the cups to a blacksmith at Tengba Town on the west side of Freetown. The smith attached the cups to opposite ends of an iron bracket and added a center metal extension that projected at a perpendicular angle from the bracket so the musician could attach the T-shaped instrument to a belt. (See figure 58.)

Next were added the Limba-wood slit gong or *keling* and a trumpet. The keling, which is used by the Limba men's Gbagbani initiation society, obtains a height of five feet and is often carved at one end in the likeness of a human head. The Freetown version of the slit gong is sparingly

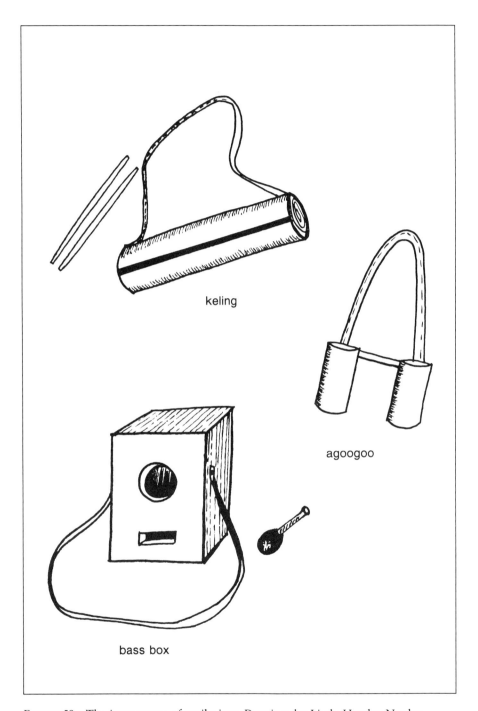

keling

agoogoo

bass box

FIGURE 58   The instruments of mailo jazz. Drawings by Linda Horsley-Nunley.

FIGURE 59   The sangbai drums essential to mailo jazz ensembles. Photo credit: John
Nunley

carved, with only the form essential to effect the sound. The gong player
produces a rapid, forceful beat, which is expressed by a large number
of sharp and discrete sounds per second. When a devil dances in front
of a house or in a small area on the street, the keling tempo is reduced
to slow the masquerader. When the keling tempo is accelerated, the
procession abruptly shifts to a fast-paced march. The staccato sound of
this instrument cracks the air and stirs excitement in the crowds.

Dr. Olu held the first practice sessions using his new instruments at
his home. The musicians first listened to Congo records; then they imitated the sound. The group did not immediately succeed with their new
musical medium. They practiced four months before they were finally
hired. Cole recalled:

> We started playing about ten years ago. We went to a party where they
> were cooking *mailo* [homemade gin]. This woman, who brought us to that
> business, gave us some beer and stout; but we said we needed something
> warm to keep us lively. She said, "What is the name of the thing you need?"
> We said, "Mailo." And she replied, "So you people love this thing? You
> mailo boys."[9]

This same woman, who was known as Koni, later hired the group to
play for a birthday party, where their music was well received. When

Koni's guests asked what the group called itself, Dr. Olu replied, "We are mailo jazz men." Word about the new sound spread through the town. The group then received invitations from well-placed individuals to play at wedding and Christmas celebrations, and eventually they came to play for the Ode-lay societies.

In 1978 Dr. Olu and his mailo jazz band played at Port Loko, where the president and first vice-president of the All Peoples Congress party opened their annual rally. Seaside Firestone—an Ode-lay group—a Hunting group, a fancy devil from Bo, and masqueraders of a local Egungun society appeared there also. Dr. Olu, who in 1978 was in his forties, said he seldom plays in public himself any more, because the street processions of the Ode-lay societies are too "heavy" for him. He appears only at special request performances for the government.

Currently there are numerous mailo jazz groups in Freetown, and the number in rural areas is growing. (See figure 60.) Most ensembles include a bass box, two or three agoogoo, the sangbai drums, keling, and—in a few cases—a trumpet. The groups that have been formed by the young men of Freetown satisfy the Ode-lay demand for mailo jazz.

The mailo jazz sound is unique to Sierra Leone, where its popularity has reached every district and major town. For many members of the lower class it provides a way to make a living. The bands earn as much as one hundred leones (U.S. equivalent $100 in 1978) for each occasion. The musicians often live on the outskirts of the city in pan-bodi settlements. The group Bantus, for example, resides at the mouth of the Congo River, next to the city garbage dump. This location, at the foot of a steep embankment, is a drain field for the Congo Cross area. Many Bantus members also have steady jobs; but they never have enough money for gambling, women, and alcohol.

The striking feature of the mailo jazz sound is that it is a product of the urban environment. It derived its primary inspiration from the baffle-box speaker and high-fidelity recordings. The portability of the instruments was, likewise, influenced by the urban environment. These instruments were designed to be carried by jazz groups marching in city-street processions. The cadences of the drums and the ripping sounds of the keling and agoogoo are well designed to compete with the noise of city traffic and the hum of conversations issuing from apartments adjoining the streets. Finally, the lyrics of mailo jazz songs reflect contemporary urban life, in contrast to those of Hunting and Egungun songs, which express traditional themes in the natural environment.

Songs, Traditional and Modern

A comparison may be made between the lyrics of traditional Yoruba-descended songs and those of modern genres. One characteristic theme

FIGURE 60   A mailo jazz group in the countryside, with (left to right) bass box, drums, shake shake, and metal gongs. Photo credit: Nancy Minett

of the traditional Egungun and Hunting lyrics is the forest, which no doubt cradled these societies. Each of the following lyrics, for example, relies on a forest metaphor:

EGUNGUN

1. *Da secon big tick way cover the bush dae whistle.*

   The second largest tree that shades the forest is whistling.

2. *Chief of God sidom saful, mor fet for de nor in close, listen me lek wild beast na bush en falla me go no di dance place.*

   Chief or Almighty God always sit peacefully, fight for the devil, listen to my voice as the wild creatures of the forest and follow me to the dancing place.

3. *Da mammy way born plenty pekin or da tick way get plenty han dem for feed the han dem or the pikin den one by one.*

   The mother that gives birth to many children or a big tree that has many branches must feed the children or branches one by one.

4. *God in tick cam quick cam save we from the tick trouble Ramanu.*

   Tree of God come and save us from Ramanu, the tree of trouble, without delay.

HUNTING

1. *Tick wae breeze dae blow kin fresh you nor go able understand any secret pass you join the society.*

   A tree that is always exposed to the wind is always fresh. Look at it, look at it. You will never understand the secret until you are a member.

2. *We de bush pekin dem dae ask Miniru the tick of trouble for save we society from Wahala.*

   We are asking for forgiveness, we the sons of the bush Miniru tree of trouble. We pray you, save our society from destruction.

In the Egungun and Hunting lyrics, trees are seen as spiritual entities and are sometimes likened to ancestral costumes. The Freetown aredé or tall-devil costume with cowrie-shell veil is sometimes called *Miniru,* the tree of trouble. This costume has an equivalent in the Freetown Egunugu devil, which society members claim originated in the Nupe country, north of Yorubaland (see map 2). Egunugu members whip each other with tree branches as they dance around this "tall debil," which represents a tree spirit.

The mailo jazz or Ode-lay songs seldom express forest imagery; rather, they reflect an urban orientation. As an example, a popular mailo song, *Put am na mi wiz,* is translated Shove It! Another song that is concerned with Ode-lay medicine falls within the Western context of the doctor:

An docta so me an tal, kin but, kin retien, kin re foe, that is, The doctor gave me medicine, one in the morning, one in the afternoon, and one at night.

Other Egungun and Hunting songs are concerned with death and the ancestors, for example:

EGUNGUN

1. *Wan by wan we goo we patrol but no wae papa cam.*

   One by one we shall continue our journey, immediately our father comes.

2. *Any body way layon na im belleh na die man, no for bring am na do.*

   Whosoever is lying on his or her stomach is dead. Let us bring the dead outside.

3. *Dance lek spirit na graveyard.*

   Dance as you used to dance in the underworld.

4. *An go na grun lek wae blood dae waka na bodi.*

   I went underground as easy as how blood flows in the body.

5. *Una carin an go me dead bodi wit di juju and cova em wit di juju close.*

   Take my dead body away with the juju and cover me with the torn clothes of the medicine.

HUNTING

1. *Remelekunis also here to listen to the sounds. Whose kine ceremony dis? Na for dem die man, who sic we day go? We dae go who sic we able reach. Leh dem die man tinap en listen to the sweet music way de Afaray day pull. Remelekun sef don cam for yerri.*

   What is this ceremony for, for the underworld people. Where are we going to, we are going to anywhere that our journey can take us to. Let the dead stay back and listen to the happy sounds of the Afaray [whistle or flute of the Hunting society].[10]

The Ode-lay songs recorded for this study did not focus upon matters relating to the ancestors, the people of the underworld. Even though each society has a juweni man, whose function is to contact the spirits of the deceased, the songs do not reflect this aspect of society's ritual.

Where the songs of the traditional societies and the Ode-lay groups do correspond is in their relationship to the masquerade presentation, the philosophy of toughness, and societal unity and obedience. The Egungun song *Nor Fraid You Load,* which means you should not fear your daily responsibilities, found its descendant in the Ode-lay song *All Man Cam For Fen E Yone,* which translates to One Must Fight for His Bread. lyrics are:

All man cam for fen E-yone
Ah Mama Ah
All man cam for fen E-yone
The world don change O-O
Mama
The world don change O-O
Mama
Yeah yeah O-O
Yeah lay lay O-O
Yeah-lay-lay-O-----O

In brief, the song proclaims that each person is responsible for his own survival in a world that is moving fast. This theme is echoed in the popular Freetown expression E lef pan yu, which means it is your responsibility to make the decision.

Egungun songs also call people to join in the masquerade and enjoy the beauty of the devils. *Look na door and join we pan di dance* (Look outside and join us in happiness) is one such invitation. Mailo groups have similar invitational songs with lyrics that are affected by the media. A lyric by Matembe, the leader of the Bantus group, shows such influence:

If you como Liverpool
    Cam na ya so

If you como Sierra Leone
    Show yu sef O

If you como America
    Cam na ya so

If you como Sierra Leone
    Show yu sef O.

Here Matembe alludes to the English rock group, the Beatles, with the use of the word Liverpool, the birthplace of that group. "If you Como" implores its listeners, wherever they are, to show themselves as they really are and join in the celebration of the devil and the mailo jazz.

Another Matembe mailo jazz song inviting people to join the mask celebrations opens with the following lines:

How are yu don kam
Let we dance sam mo
A haw are yu don cam
So so liba liba O-O.

How are yu
Let's dance some more
How are yu
Is your mind ready for dancing?

Implicit in the Matembe lyrics above is an awareness and appreciation of dress styles and of the way people carry themselves from country to country. The acceptance of individuality derived from fashionable dress expresses the aesthetic of fanciness. This aesthetic is also expressed in Egungun songs. One such song asks a participant why he has taken money; he replies, "To buy the whiteman's cloths." Asked what kind of cloths, he responds, "Cloths the color of a frog." "Why?" he is asked; and he replies, "Because it attracts everyone's attention." Here again the fanciness of brilliant color is emphasized.[11]

Other fancy-dress masquerades included the Juju Wata celebration at Hastings during Easter of 1978. The mailo jazz group hired for the occasion opened with an invitational song with the following lyrics:

> Oh yes A feelin fine
> Oh yes A taken my time
> Oh yes A drinkin fine
> Oh yes A drinkin wine.[12]

The band used for this celebration, unlike the mailo jazz bands that accompany the fierce Ode-lay masquerades, played smoother, more syncopated rhythms, omitting the crisp, militant marching sounds of fierce mailo music. The Juju group was led by a whistle player who, like the flute player of the Hunting society and the whistle player of the Ambas Geda, signaled a change in the beat with his instrument.

Another theme common to traditional music and mailo jazz is the principle of fierceness. Egungun society members are asked to brave the appearance of the devils and to stand with courage for the protection of the society. The Krio song *How You See Me So Ah Nor Day Frade None Neff* (As You See Me I Don't Fear Any Knife) invokes Egungun members not to fear the medicines of other societies. A similar idea is expressed in *Omo Jessa Leh We Go Who Na Nor Frade Natin,* which translates to Omo Jessa [a Hunting society] Let Us Go, Fear Nothing. The mailo jazz song *Shove It!* expresses the same defiant attitude.

The Back to Power Society's fierce masquerade in 1977, which celebrated the association between the god of iron (Ogun) and President Siaka Stevens, was accompanied by mailo jazz music of threatening, militant character. Unlike the emphasis of fancy music on lyrics, the emphasis of mailo jazz is on the beat. Music for the opening of the masquerade sounded like a British fife and drum ensemble with a rolling mailo beat in the background. Throughout the masquerade the agoogoo was struck very hard at the downbeat of each measure of time. The double gongs of that instrument were tuned about one half an interval apart (on the diatonic scale). This resulted in a harsh, dissonant sound, which amplified the militancy of the music. A bugle was heard in the background, reminiscent of the bugle or rokee introduced by the Bobo lantern group to reinforce the aggressive sound of marching combat boots.

Given the severe conditions of life in Freetown, some mailo bands have adapted the song *Mama Do Yu Wone Yu Pekin Dem?* Like the existential expression E lef pan yu, this song asks the why of existence.

Mama do yu wone yu grand pekin dem
Mama do yu wone yu grand pekin dem
Some man dae enjoy ti-day
Na mammy en daddy born dem
Na mammy en daddy born dem
Watin do?

Mama do yu wone yu grand pekin dem
Mama do yu wone yu grand pekin dem
The life ti-day na life way dae na we had
How yu sel yu sef
Na so den go buy
Som man dae enjoy ti-day
Na mammy en daddy born dem
Watin do?

In essence this song asks an elder woman to warn her grandchildren about the pitfalls of simply enjoying the minute and the consequence of having unwanted children. It ends with the question "Watin do?" (Why?) being asked by the unwanted children.

Reggae

In recent years a new form of popular music has found its way to western Africa and Freetown. This music can be heard on record players and radios in all the local discotheques, bars, and homes. It is music with a hypnotic, low, slowly rocking beat verging on an adagio tempo. It was originated in Jamaica by the Rastafarians. Reggae is the Caribbean blues; its message is usually political or utopian. Based on the Rastafarian creed, which claims that the new world and second coming of the savior, Haile Selassi (the last monarch of Ethiopia), will bring everlasting peace and will unburden the black man, reggae combines spirituality, politics, and lifestyle. Rastas, by accepting the Rastafarian creed, adhere to a vegetarian diet and smoke marijuana daily out of religious conviction. They espouse a nonviolent point of view.

There has been much controversy about the rasta man and reggae in Freetown. The convergence of marijuana smoking and the common urban blight shared by Jamaicans and the lower classes of Freetown has helped this music find roots in Sierra Leone. (See figure 61.) Unlike the popular music described above, reggae most likely will remain outside the masquerade. Its musical character is better suited to individual dancing or "lying back" and listening. Reggae is a music of contemplation rather

FIGURE 61   Painting of the late Bob Marley, Jamaican reggae star, in a Ghanaian bar. Courtesy of Charles D. Miller III, Long Island, N.Y.

than arousal. Its songs, such as *Equal Rights, Pressure Drop* (pressure of the future revolution), and *Many Rivers to Cross* (before a new and free society can be established), convey utopian and political messages.

In contrast to the Jamaican and Freetown adoption of reggae is the resistance of Caribbean countries like Trinidad and Tobago. In the capital of Port of Spain the grand carnival masquerades move through the streets some 200,000 strong, all dancing and masquerading to the samba, soca, and calypsonian beat. While many of the songs are political, their wit, satire, and catchy beat are uplifting. With its lively enthusiasm for life, this music reflects the high standard of living of Trinidadians by comparison with their Caribbean neighbors and African brothers. Although calypsonian bands may criticize the queen of England or local parliamentarians, songs like *Party Party, Push Push Push*, and *Feelin Nice Now* return the dancers' thoughts to the sensual realm where life is strictly for enjoyment. In such a cultural climate reggae is out of place. It may be heard with consistency, significantly, only in sections of the city that resemble some of the poorer sections of Freetown.

As reggae rises in popularity in Freetown, one wonders what its impact will be on mailo jazz. Will aspects of this new music be assimilated by the jazz leaders as aspects of the visual arts have been assimilated by the local artists? Is it possible that reggae may replace mailo jazz as the representative form of musical expression of the young? If the mailo jazz ensembles should disappear, what kind of musical ensembles will replace them in the Ode-lay masquerades? Any change in the jazz format of Freetown is likely to influence the Ode-lay mask performances. Ultimately, the central role played by music in the masquerades suggests a need for continued observation and research in this area.

8

A Theory of Art and Performance

Ode-lay plastic arts cannot be considered without a separate study of the public celebrations for which they were intended. Ode-lay creations, unlike Western art, are made to touch, smell, cover with medicines, as well as to inspire fear, revenge, danger, pollution, and purity. They emphasize the ideals and taboos of their creators and participants. For this reason the analysis of the artist and description of his work are only half the artistry picture.

Ode-lay art is performance; it is the orchestration of visual arts, drama, music, dance, and extemporaneous behavior. It is a complex phenomenon. How the masquerades work and why they are successful are examined in this chapter. Masquerades of the Seaside Firestone, Juju Wata, and Freetown Firestone societies are here analyzed and compared. The fact that the Freetown Firestone event was unsuccessful gives an opportunity to compare it with the two successful events of the other societies, thus allowing us to identify the factors that are part of the successful masquerade. By breaking down each performance into what Roger Abrahams calls enactments or what this author calls frames, key or quintessential frames of masking behavior are discovered.

A good masquerade results in ecstatic behavior on the part of the membership, as a result of which participants become one with the society and one with Ogun. Part of the explanation for this achievement is found in the notion of medicine broadly defined.[1] Society members are ritually joined through medicine that is internalized by eating. That medicine must be protected from violation by opposing medicine men and other secret societies. Mary Douglas's writings on purity and pollution help explain the importance of particular frames and society medicine. Medicine, according to her theory, should be classified as a purifying substance.

Purity is defined by what is considered impure or what is considered polluted. Without pollution, purity is meaningless and, as will be demonstrated, the key frames in a successful masquerade presents the opportunity to cope with pollution.

A striking characteristic of Ode-lay life and of masquerading is its fierce or aggressive trait. Throughout Ode-lay existence, violence has been part of the celebrations. How does this violence erupt, and how does it elevate the experience of the participants? Gregory Bateson's work on communication is of considerable use in answering these questions. Ode-lay performance, gestures, and signals are, in his terms, equivocal. What may appear to be "play" at times may be interpreted as the real thing, or what appears to be a nip may at times be read as a bite. The confusion of play and fantasy with real, fierce behavior in particular Ode-lay performance frames contributes to successful masquerading.

Two Successful Performances

Seaside Firestone Ode-lay Society takes its name from its location in Godrich, which overlooks the ocean, and from the rock-covered cliff upon which it perches. (See map 2.) In the evening the rocks reflect the sunlight, giving them the appearance of "fire stones." The name also was selected to honor the Firestone group at 101 Red Pump in Freetown.

For this successful masquerade, members of Seaside Firestone elected to pull their devil on 2 January 1978. Before the mask presentation the costume was placed on a large oil drum for last minute adjustments. The carving consisted of a double-faced image with a carved human head that was flanked by two snakes and topped by a ram with projecting horns.[2] A black Jolly face-mask was placed at the center front of the hampa. The skulls of two dogs, which had been sacrificed earlier during preparation of the costume, were positioned at the sides, and the body of a sea porcupine was also attached to the center front of the hampa. A wire crocodile tail extended from the back of the costume, giving it a dragonlike appearance.

After most people had left the shrine, a dancer was fitted with the costume. Members waiting outside were tense with expectation. Then, without notice, the devil knocked down a mat wall of the shrine house and presented itself to the society. The society leader, Alfonso, quickly summoned the Bantus Mailo Jazz Band, which had been playing songs for members waiting at a local bar. The group met the masquerader and proceeded down the main street of the town, followed by more than a thousand supporters, including children (see figure 62), members, elders, and market women. A delegation from the Bloody Mary Society was there to evaluate the performance.

A half hour after the appearance of the masked dancer, he stopped at a member's house. There he was replaced by a second dancer, who emerged from the dressing room just as an Egungun Society parade passed by. Out of respect for the Egungun spirits, the mailo jazz band stopped playing immediately and the devil withdrew. With careful timing and an alert bila man and masquerader, Seaside Firestone thus avoided a masquerade confrontation. The fear and anxiety associated with such confrontations, however, heightened the aesthetic intensity of the event.

The procession then moved to the house of the town's headman, who congratulated the society for its fine presentation and orderly conduct and for attracting outsiders to Godrich. The group then proceeded east to Lumely Beach (see map 4), a distance of five miles. It returned to Godrich at about 6:00 that evening.

The 1978 masquerade of Juju Wata, held on Easter Monday at Hastings (see map 4), was another successful Ode-lay celebration. Sometime during the preceding night the costume parts were moved from the sponsor's house to the square enclosure constructed of bamboo and mat walls and palm fronds behind the society's headman's house.[3] (See figure 63.) Inside the enclosure a sacrifice of uncooked rice in a bowl of water, a bottle of rum, and a 45 RPM record still in its paper sleeve, which was meant to symbolize the record-breaking beauty of the devil, were spread before the assembled costume. The shrine was separated from the leader's house by an old rail bed, where some of the members had slept to protect the devil. Early the next morning, sacrifices were performed while members drank rum from a glass offered by the mammy queen. Afterward several persons returned to the house of a wealthy sponsor of the society, drank rum and ginger beer, and danced to Congolese and reggae music played on a phonograph.

At 8:30 A.M. a bush devil, which had been used the previous year, caroled through the town to announce the procession of the Juju Wata devil. The bush-devil costume was decorated with porcupine quills and hunter's raffia. The headpiece was much more elaborate than the deer flat-top of the Hunting society; but like the hunters' costume, it displayed few fancy materials. (See figure 64.) The caroling procession moved from house to house until noon to the accompaniment of snapping sounds of rhythm sticks similar to those used by the Hunting societies.

By 1:00 P.M. most members of the Juju Wata Society and their girlfriends had gathered around the house of the society leader. The women wore long uniform dresses or ashoebi of brown print; their hair was decorated with cowrie shells to complement the fancy masquerade. A flag carrier paraded up and down the road with a town crier, who rang an assembly bell to announce the procession. The men of the society wore jeans and printed T-shirts that bore the name of the group along with a variety of designs and slogans. The air was charged with excitement.

FIGURE 62 Young Seaside Firestone followers with a clothed figure sculpture. Photo credit: John Nunley

FIGURE 63   The masquerade costume is prepared for sacrifice. Photo credit: John
Nunley

At the shrine enclosure several members in ashoebi and tennis shoes and
the mammy queen, dressed in black satin pants and blouse, served portions of rum in the bottlecap. Other members carried phonograph records
in honor of the event. Several broken 78 RPM phonograph discs hung
from a flagpole. The group's sponsors paced back and forth waiting for
the performance to begin.

Expectation and tension mounted as word spread that the Bantus
Mailo Jazz Band would not play until it received a cash advance. This
method of guaranteeing payment was often employed by these groups.
After a compromise was reached, the Juju Wata leader signaled the jazz
group that the devil was prepared to dance. As the band struck up the
first notes, the masquerader crashed through the mat enclosure. He
danced for a few moments and then was carefully led down a hill and
across a rocky path of the old rail bed. The journey was difficult for the
devil because of the limited visibility afforded by the costume and the
danger of soiling the materials. On the opposite side of the rail bed,
women, flag carriers, Bantus, and society members moved to a point
where they could meet the devil. The excitement of the music and singing
climbed to higher and higher levels as the crowd and masquerade party
converged.

FIGURE 64   A previously used Mammy Wata headpiece of the Juju Wata Society at Hastings. Photo credit: John Nunley

After the two groups met, the procession turned toward the home of the society's financial sponsor, where the devil danced for several minutes. Then the group departed for the homes of other important members of the society and residents of the town. At 2:00 P.M. the party made its way to the village headman's house and performed there for fifteen minutes. The headman presented a contribution to the society and gave a speech lauding the beauty of the procession and the restraint with which the group conducted the celebration. The procession then returned to the agba's house to change dancers and refresh the musicians. An hour later Juju Wata was prepared to play until the late evening. By 10:00 P.M. the mailo jazz band and society members were exhausted. They returned to the agba's residence for rice, meat sauce, and drink. (See figure 65.) The band joined with some society members who played mouth organ, triangle, and *mbira* (the so-called African thumb piano) in a jam session or what the group called "back off," which continued through the early morning.

This Juju Wata performance met the expectations of its members and, indeed, of all Hastings. The village headman requested that he be considered a grand patron for the society's next masquerade. As the celebration was a "record breaker," the agba smashed numerous discs at several points along the procession route (see plate 7). The standard bearer broke records at Bethlehem junction, the market, Egba Town, and Kosso Town. Each time a record was smashed, soweh medicine was doused on the scattered plastic fragments. The music of the mailo jazz band and the beauty of the fancy costume caught the attention of one of the heads of the local Bundu Society, who later requested that the band and the devil perform for her society over Easter vacation. The fancy aesthetic in masquerade had affirmed the reputation of the society.

An Unsuccessful Performance

Because the government rejected Ode-lay requests for public mask permits in 1977, the Firestone Society of Freetown selected the first week of December in that year for a private presentation of the devils it had constructed before the cancellation. The members explained that this was so the time and money spent in preparation for the Eid-ul-Adha festival should not have been wasted. Furthermore, that year was the society's tenth anniversary.

The masquerade was held at the society's headquarters at 101 Red Pump and Mountain Cut Road. In compliance with city ordinances, the devils did not range far from the neighborhood and for the most part stayed away from public roads. At about 6:00 P.M. the masks of *yamamah* and *garboi,* two devils of Mende origin, made their way from the set-

FIGURE 65   Juju Wata women prepare food for the night's celebration. Photo credit: John Nunley

tlement down Owen Street to Mountain Cut Road. These masqueraders clowned with children and called everyone to the play. Some of the Firestone members attended these characters and took up a collection with cups. One of these dancers was the Ode-lay artist who introduced rural masquerades to Freetown and integrated them with the Ode-lay mask dancers. He also was the first to use country devils as motifs in lantern building. His appreciation for Mende costumes had been gained at the Kenema Art Fair, which was held annually in December.[4] The incorporation of rural elements into the city cults is indicative of the broad cultural base represented by the Ode-lay societies. It explains, in part, the present success of the one-party state, which has a broadly based constituency.

After the clown devils returned to the Firestone settlement, two bush devils (as the Ode-lay members call their fierce Hunting-style costumes) appeared. One costume is illustrated in plate 8; the other consisted of a double-face mask, a pair of angel wings, and the body of an antelope projecting from the back of the dancer. The top of the headpiece was crowned with a half-length figure of Mammy Wata.[5] The bare breasts of this seductive image loomed above the crowd.

While the devils performed, the mailo jazz ensemble played in a cleared area adjacent to a sprawling garbage dump off Mountain Cut Road. The audience stood or sat on palm fronds on the ground. Members of Bloody Mary and Paddle were present to honor the anniversary of Firestone. Two other masked performances were taking place at the same time: (1) just south of Firestone an Egungun fancy devil was performing for a wedding, and (2) a few blocks west, at Fort Street, a Hunting celebration was in progress. A comparison of the three concurrent performances readily evidenced the low position held by the Ode-lay in Freetown's social stratum. Along the roadside near the celebrations of the traditional societies were parked the cars belonging to the membership; near the Firestone celebration not a single vehicle was parked.

Even society members admitted that the masquerade was not very exciting. Ode-lay masquerades have evolved in the urban setting of streets and alleys, where songs such as *Gutter Ase, Pole to Pole,* and *Banga Banga* reflect urban situations. The strong marching cadence established by the bass box and keling of the jazz ensembles propels the dancers and their numerous followers through traffic-snarled streets. The explosive music and masquerade dancing are not intended for a confined, private area. Thus, the Firestone performance did not reach its potential aesthetic intensity. Although the society leadership had arranged for performances on three consecutive nights, the general failure of the first play caused them to shorten the engagement by one day.

Although this masquerade did not impress the adult spectators, it nevertheless had a striking effect on the children. Several hundred Mountain Cut children ignored the two concurrent festivities to watch this one. The studied rhythms of traditional Yoruba drumming and the intricate steps of the fancy-devil dancers in the other performances held less attraction for them than did the powerful blasts of the mailo jazz and the fierce Firestone devils. The Ode-lay masquerade as a form of cultural expression is a major part of the enculturation of the large number of children who live on the streets of Freetown and other similar cities of Sierra Leone. (See figure 66.)[6]

A Theory of Performance

The obvious success and aesthetic achievements of the Juju Wata and Seaside Firestone celebrations prompted their plans for future masquerades. In contrast, the failure of Firestone's celebration at Red Pump was so disappointing to the members and participants that one of the remaining two days scheduled for the celebration was canceled. What was responsible for the success or failure of these groups? Were the differences in costume, sculpture, direction, and context of the celebrations accountable for the outcome? Perhaps the major difference between the

FIGURE 66   A young masquerader in the city of Bo imitating a Firestone fancy devil.
Photo credit: Jeanne Cannizzo

successful and unsuccessful masquerades was their locations. In the Juju Wata and Seaside Firestone events the costumed dancers and participants paraded in the streets, whereas in the Freetown Firestone celebration the masqueraders and participants were confined by law to private property. In short, Freetown Firestone could not *take it to the streets.*

Roger Abrahams's theory of enactment helps explain what went wrong with the Freetown Firestone celebration.[7] Abrahams defines *enactment* as any cultural event that brings people together to employ multivocal and polyvalent signs and symbols to heighten the experience. Enactments include performances, games, rituals, and festivities. These four components are interpenetrating, as, for example, the coin-toss and national anthem *rituals* in the *game* of football. In Ode-lay enactments the *performance* of a masquerader may be interrupted by the *play* of a character called the *kaka* or shit devil, who mocks the real performance. Overlap is also evidenced in the postmasquerade feast (*festivity*), during which members *play* in kung fu reenactments.

Abrahams notes that these four components are highly stylized forms of behavior, each *marked* (or what this author calls *framed*) to foreground form and movement of the participants of the enactment.[8] Given the appropriate number of frames and their most effective editing, the organizers of Ode-lay enactments, according to this theory, have at their convenience a mechanism for structuring masquerades to heighten the experience of the individuals, raising that experience above the quotidian within the body politic.

By listing the number of frames of an Ode-lay enactment and by assigning affective significance to each one, an ideal and successful enactment may be compared with an unsuccessful enactment. Drawing upon several successful Ode-lay enactments, it is possible to develop a primary list of frames. These include, in sequence:

1. Society officers gather to select the day of the event.

2. A permit to masquerade in the streets is requested from the police.

3. A meeting of the general membership is called to collect funds and select an artist to make the costume.

4. Officers approach the artist to request a particular costume style and iconographic system.

5. Official visits are made to the artist as he works on the commission.

6. Collection of artifacts from the artist in late evening a week or so before public display.

7. Selection of mailo jazz band.

8. A flyer is sent to announce the society program and credit the organizers.

9. Sacrifices are made to the dead at the local cemetery on the

morning of the masquerade; and sacrifices of kola nut, rum, and uncooked rice to the mask and costume are perched on a mortar (symbol of Shango) inside a mat enclosure or the society shrine or igbale.

10. The morning parade or carol of a fancy masquerader takes place on the day of the enactment.

11. Women prepare food for the event.

12. Members dress in uniform fashion: batiked long skirts, blouses, special hairstyles for women; blue jeans, stenciled T-shirts for men.

13. Alcohol is drunk, marijuana smoked.

14. Soweh medicine is prepared and applied to the costume by the soweh man.

15. Reception of the mailo jazz band, usually involving heated debate over the amount and method of payment.

16. Masquerader and members are doused with soweh from this point throughout the enactment.

17. Mailo jazz music commences, and the masquerader breaks through the walled enclosure into the street.

18. The three or four changes of masked dancers are considered dangerous times for costume and dancers, because stripped of their "covers" they are susceptible to malevolent acts of diviners and competing societies.

19. Encounter and confrontation with competing groups, representatives of other societies, and police.

20. The masquerader retires to the society settlement.

21. After-parade feasting, at which the day's events are recounted.

22. Press coverage is monitored throughout the following week.

23. Confiscated costumes are retrieved, and offending members may be jailed for disorderly conduct and vandalism.

In comparison with the above scenario, the unsuccessful Freetown Firestone celebration was lacking in frames 16 to 19 and 21 to 23. What intrinsic qualities of these frames, otherwise included, would have heightened the experience of the participants? Just as missing notes in a song or unexpected gaps in melody leave listeners questioning the legitimacy of the song, missing frames of the Freetown Firestone masquerade left participants unconvinced of this enactment or performance as performance.

Clearly, each of the omitted frames contains intrinsic qualities that account for the affective failure of the Freetown Firestone event. These inherent features are best explained by Mary Douglas in her work on purity, danger, and social pollution and by Gregory Bateson in his study on play and fantasy.[9]

Douglas introduces as a primary assumption that "rituals work upon the body politic through the symbolic medium of the physical body."[10]

In this analysis it will be shown that the symbolic notions expressed by ritual formed intrinsically valuable parts of the missing frames and therefore were not made manifest in the Freetown Firestone masquerade or its body politic and vice versa. The lack of this reverberating process precluded the heightened experience sought by the society.

Douglas identifies four types of social pollution that inspire body ritual: (1) pollution that presses on external boundaries, (2) pollution that transgresses internal lines of a system, (3) danger in the margin of lines, (4) danger from internal contradiction, i.e., basic postulates that are denied by others.[11] Both Ode-lay and Hunting members express fear and anxiety, especially over the first two kinds of pollution. These shared anxieties are expressed in individual body ritual, projected onto the masquerader, and passed on to the body politic. Hunting and Ode-lay members fear harmful medicines or *fangay,* which cause skin rashes, scabs, and other skin disorders on what Douglas calls the external boundaries. Skin pollution is counteracted by the use of soweh. They also fear medicine that penetrates the stomach—in Douglas's terms, the internal boundaries.

Stories and practices related to the stomach and medicine abound. From the day an initiate joins a society, he must take the medicine or oogun of his group and swear to maintain its secret. Should he reveal the secret, his belly will swell and kill him seven days after his induction. Related to this stomach anxiety are stories in the newspapers and in neighborhood gossip pointing to lethal stomach poisoning by witches. It is recalled that one of the most powerful Yoruba-descended diviners in Sierra Leone, Ajagunsi, described how the repatriated slaves carried medicines in their stomachs on the ship. Hunters and Ode-lay members believe the stomach is vulnerable: although it contains the purity of the society medicine, it can swell and eventually kill its carrier if he should pollute it by revealing its secret or by taking another medicine.[12] In summary, body rituals in the urban secret societies of Freetown pertain to purity and pollution of the skin and the stomach.

The soweh man applies medicine on members' skin for protection against fangay pollution. His use of the broom applicator is remarkable, as if by analogy it sweeps clean the polluting agent. Hats, shoes, and long pants also protect the skin of the participants. To safeguard the stomach and the purity of its medicine, members eat and drink the sacrifices prior to the masquerade.

These body rituals, if provided the proper framing, are projected onto the masquerader, especially through the parts of the masquerade costume: the asho, eri, and hampa. The asho covers the entire body, with the exception of the head, which is protected by the horned eri. As an additional layer, the asho protects the skin.[13] The most powerful part of the costume, the hampa, contains medicines that protect the stomach area of the dancer. Like newly initiated members who consume the medicine of the society and forever carry it in their stomachs, the masked dancer likewise carries the medicine in his hampa. The masqueraders' skin and stomach must be inviolate to impurities inflicted by outside sources. The empty shells, sea-porcupine bodies, skulls, tortoise shells, shotgun casings, horns, and small sacks that make up the Seaside Firestone costume are filled with medicine. These components, like the stomach, serve as medicine containers. Masqueraders and society members are homologically served from these containers with carved ladles, which are hung on the back of the hampa.

Only two of the eight frames missing in the Firestone celebration—the morning parade and the postmortem news reports—were not directly related to concerns about pollution. Street processions provide both masquerader and members with an opportunity to apply medicines for protection against malevolent diviners and members of competing societies; but the government's refusal to grant a procession permit to the Freetown Firestone celebration preempted this option, which if realized would have added to the intensity of the masquerade, helping it to achieve what Abrahams calls the heightened experience.

Although societies abhor pollution, they are bound to it by paradox. Purity cannot be defined without knowing impurity, in the same way that a feast cannot be appreciated unless the daily menu of a particular society is known.[14] In rituals, games, performances, and festivities, participants can attain the purity of heightened experience only by becoming susceptible to pollution. Taking the masquerade to the streets provides the necessary susceptibility.

Another problem with the unsuccessful Firestone masquerade was in its orchestration. When a member eats the medicine during the masquerade initiation, he is prepared to reexperience the sense of mystery and brotherhood felt when he first ate it at his original initiation into the society. The denial of the opportunity to partake of medicine during the street procession eliminates the opportunity for that reenactment and the dangers it represents. Thus improper sequencing and missing frames do not accord with the aesthetic expectation of the participants.

In spite of the pitfalls of overly structured analyses, let us for the moment suspend doubt and pursue the concept of individual pollution and its projection onto the masquerader and presently onto the body politic. A diagram of the Ode-lay procession suggests an anthropomorphic formation that expresses individual fear of the two pollutions. At the head of the procession the flutist directs the masquerader through the streets. He is the eyes and ears of the dancer. Next is the bila man who, with carved gun in hand, protects the masked dancer. He is the hands of the dancer. The masked spirit itself symbolizes the stomach of the procession with the large, medicine-filled hampa. Members protect the stomach or hampa by forming a semicircle around the masquerader.

These participants are fully dressed in ashoebi or uniform dress. Collectively this dress constitutes the social skin of the body politic inside which lies the "stomach" of this social body represented by the hampa.

Denied the occasion to form the body politic in the streets, Firestone members could not project their personal concerns about pollution and its dialectical partner, purity, onto the group or the masquerader. Thus the aesthetic experience, which accelerates as it moves from body to masquerader to body politic in a reverberating motion, was truncated.

One explanation for the participants' inability to identify with the Firestone masquerade has to do with the types of communication available *off the streets*. Gregory Bateson describes and discriminates between three types of communication: (1) the denotative (This is a ball); (2) the metalinguistic, where the subject of discourse is the language itself (*Jerry* rhymes with *sherry*); and (3) the metacommunicative, where the subject of discourse is the relationship between the speakers (We are Firestone; who are you?). Bateson notes that an important evolutionary step in communication is the recognition by both parties that signals are signals which can be trusted, distrusted, denied, corrected, and otherwise modified. In addition, higher forms of communication involve the understanding by the parties that the message, of whatever kind, does not consist of the objects it denotes. "The word 'cat' cannot scratch us" is used to illustrate this point. Bateson continues, "Rather language bears to the objects which it denotes a relationship comparable to that which a map bears to a territory. Play implies the map-territory distinction. Play denotes 'not play'; it stands for things other than itself."[15]

Play, threat, and histrionic behavior are based on the participants' ability to recognize signals as signals and map-territory relationships. Rituals are also predicated by these behaviors, Bateson adds; but occasionally during these periods humans cannot or do not recognize signals as signals and map-territory distinctions. When this happens play changes to mood-sign behavior and nip becomes bite. Bateson concludes:

> The discrimination between map and territory is always liable to break down and (for example) the ritual blows of peace-making (among the Andaman Islanders) are always liable to be mistaken for the "real" blows of combat. In this event, the peace-making ceremony becomes a battle.[16]

Ritual may be mistaken for the real thing, and with the real thing another kind of heightened experience is obtained by the participants.

In the region where art, magic, and religion overlap, humans have evolved *the metaphor that is meant*. To appreciate the metaphor-that-is-meant and how it comes into play, Bateson provides a useful classification of messages. One kind of message is called the mood-sign. During this message-sending phase the parties are nonreflective; if they exhibit biting behavior face to face, they take real action and bite. Here the map and territory are the same. The second kind of message *simulates* the mood-sign; and by exhibiting a set of behaviors called play, the nip results instead of the bite. The remaining type of message allows the receiver to discriminate or equate mood-signs and those that resemble them. The third message asks the question Is this play? The equivocation introduced by this question allows the Ode-lay participants, in this case, to confirm the metaphor-that-is-meant and its resultant potent experience.[17]

It has been suggested that Ode-lay masqueraders are militant. Members often wear military costumes and carry carved or real guns. In the Education Society, for example, members carry knives in textbooks while masquerading. On the level of play, moreover, the participants perform martial-arts games with each other or with members of competing societies. At times the playful behavior may turn to the mood-sign; then nip will become bite and people will get hurt. The confusion of nip and bite is seen in the relationship of these groups to the police. Where members may parade with a coffin in front of police, playfully warning them not to interfere with the procession, the playful taunting may result in the law enforcers using tear gas or some other form of force to stop the play. In this instance the police equate map and territory. In the unsuccessful Firestone event, the absence of particular frames preempted the third type of message. Without it, map and territory could not be equated; therefore, the real metaphor and the heightened experience that results from it were denied.[18]

The labile nature of Ode-lay signaling or message sending during street processions is the axis on which its affective success turns. The metaphor-that-is-meant creates excitement and a nonanalytical Gestalt perception of the enactment. In successful Ode-lay masquerades, each member becomes the masked spirit, and the spirit becomes the membership: the spirit is the medicine, is the membership, is the masquerader. The achieved aesthetic diminishes the participant's sense of being separate. "We are Ogun," "We are the god of iron," "We are inviolate" are all pronouncements expressing that collectivity, as if to say, "Our external and internal boundaries are pure and protected in the collective purity of the body politic." At this juncture Bateson's words are appropriate, "Here we can recognize an attempt to deny the difference between map and territory, and to get back to the absolute innocence of communication by means of pure mood-signs."[19]

The Juju Wata and Seaside Firestone masqueraders were able to take it to the streets and, in so doing, risked the spiritual and physical pollution of masquerader, member, and group, i.e., in the words of Mary Douglas, the body politic. By experiencing this list, these groups achieved ritual purity. The excitement generated by the masked dancers breaking through the mat enclosures onto the public streets, sacrificing along the routes, the vulnerability of changing dancers, and performing before important personages en route all added to the ritual intensity of the event. These successful celebrations did not take place in Freetown, however; thus, they were denied the tougher urban environment of that city, where, in confrontations like those between Bloody Mary and the eastern groups and between Civili and Rainbow,[20] for example, the confusion of play and bite could result in the metaphor-that-is-meant and foster a highly charged aesthetic environment.

9

Conflict as a Factor of Society Life

The existential ring of the popular Ode-lay expression E lef pan yu (It is left to you) emphasizes individual decision-making as a guide to ordering one's life. The same can be said for each Ode-lay society that on its own has sought the course of action most beneficial to its membership. In this process conflicts between leadership and members, different societies, and societies and government have often erupted. Violent at times and always culturally expressive, these conflicts have been indispensable to the development of a local and national cultural base. One can neither predict the result of these conflicts nor be certain of their effect on the welfare of the state. Clearly, though, their demonstrations have gained for the Ode-lay societies opportunities and privileges that could not otherwise be had.

The nightly gatherings, devil processions, and aesthetic competitions fulfill expressive needs of the Ode-lay membership. Open conflict serves as a release valve for the expression of frustration that has resulted from long-term disappointment. The music and celebration reaffirm basic assumptions about traditional African culture, while their transformation in the urban masquerades helps to make social and economic hardships more tolerable. The carefully written constitutions of the societies teach young members the rights and obligations of contractual behavior, which are worlds apart from traditional expectations of behavior in rural areas, where status, age, and sex determine actions. Violation of this written code is a primary source of intragroup conflict.

Intragroup Conflict

Perhaps one of the most important factors to consider in the Ode-lay prognosis is the internal stability of the groups. All Freetown masquerade associations have some internal dissension. Many disagreements concern members who lose control during celebrations. Conflict also stems from the leadership's mismanagement of society funds, particularly in the making of private loans. (One wonders if Sergeant Potts faced similar conflicts over dispersal of asusu funds in the first years of the colony.) On the positive side, conflict at this level gives members an opportunity to raise their voices and also sets the stage for the creation of new societies.

One source of conflict that has its roots in the traditional Freetown groups, including the relatively peaceful Hunting societies, is the competition for leadership among members. According to one of the city's most noted society men, the Hunting society called *Ajakabiloke* (we are going up the hill from Oke Mori) came of just such a power struggle. John (Pa) Thompson, one of Freetown's leading herbalists, taught the secret medicines of the hunters to Eku Williams. With this knowledge Williams became the ashigba of Thompson's society and used his power for personal ends.[1] Thompson challenged him, and the two fought with medicine. Thompson won and Williams was forced to leave the society. Williams then organized his own branch just a few blocks up the mountain. A few years later Williams became very thin, his belly "turned on him," and he died at the age of thirty-six. Many people believed Pa Thompson had caused his death.

Another source of conflict in the traditional societies is the internal disruption that often occurs at the transition of power or at the death of a society leader or principal agent. In such a case at Ginger Hall in east Freetown, a new Bundu society was formed. According to the former tribal headwoman of the community, the first Bundu of the Mende people of Freetown was established at the turn of this century by Mama Njama. Her designated heir, Madam Ngombui, was to receive the deceased leader's shrine and its medicine. A dispute developed, however, between Madam Ngombui and another leading member of the society; and, as a result, the second woman, called Naalie, secured her own shrine and established a second Bundu society.

Group customs, also, are a source of conflict. Mrs. Martin, one of Freetown's most powerful medicine women, was a member of both the Egunugu and the Autta Gelede Society. On the day of her daughter's marriage, she invited members of the Gelede to watch as the Egunugu masqueraders prepared for their presentation. Several of the Egunugu members protested, claiming that outsiders were prohibited from witnessing the society's sacred rites. The general membership of the Gelede agreed with the Egunugu leaders and penalized Martin and the persons who had watched the preparations. As a result, the reprimanded individuals resigned from the Gelede and formed their own society. The group commissioned a carver to make masks for the new society, but they did not obtain the proper medicine and consequently disbanded.

In another dispute Egunugu members claimed that Martin had misused her power by allowing women to join the dancing. She allowed women, like the men of Egunugu, to carry whips that were used to lash other dancers during the performances. The men claimed that in Nigeria, where the society originated, women were excluded from the dancing. Again the dissenters formed their own group.

The stories of fighting within the traditional societies suggest that the principal sources of instability are to be found in disputes over money, medicine, succession, and custom. These are the same issues that cause conflict within the Ode-lay groups.

One incident involving the youngbloods and older members of Firestone well exemplifies an Ode-lay conflict over money and its repercussions. In 1977 the older members of Firestone, including the officers, built a devil costume at a cost of about $150 with funds collected from the general membership. When the government refused to give the society a permit for public procession on Eid-ul-Adha, the costume was used for a celebration at the society shrine at 101 Red Pump.[2] Soon afterward the costume was sold to a group outside the city.

Because the money from the sale of the costume was not returned to the treasury, bitter feelings were aroused among the youngbloods of the society. In fashionable revolutionary rhetoric, the youngbloods criticized their elders. One person explained on behalf of the younger members: "The youngbloods wanted to secede from Firestone because they felt the society had lost its prestige as a result of the rule of the *tangaise* [the old boys]." One of the younger members called an older member a tangaise man, poking fun at his unstylish dress, not-with-the-times attitude, and slow-mindedness. The tension within Firestone gave way to violence as members turned on each other. Eventually one faction burned the settlement, destroying its three shelters.

The youngbloods then decided to relocate farther up the hill and to call themselves Mau Mau. They later returned to Red Pump, however, and constructed temporary shelters there. Night gambling, drinking, and smoking resumed. Then the police raided the settlement, allegedly because one of the members involved in the sale of the costume informed the authorities of the society's illicit traffic in drugs. The use of drugs by the younger society members was another area of conflict between them and the older members. A newspaper report of the incident gives clear insight into activities at the rebuilt society headquarters:

Some Drama at 'Red Pump'

The name 'Fire Stone' has been made popular by the mass following masked-devil Society in the East end of Freetown.

But the name also goes for a hide-out at Red-pump where, for years, youths have mustered in the evening to smoke diamba and drug off with 'cloud nine' capsules.

The area is well known to police personnel who have raided it on occasions.

Wednesday evening was the time for drama, this week.

The usual junkies were at their hide-out when a tall man in a 'Muslim Lapel' attire with cap to match joined them. Moving directly to the 'pusher man' who was squating on a rock under a breadfruit tree, the tall man requested a parcel of diamba, producing a bundle of leone notes.

The money did the trick and the marijuana appeared.

The tall man then left for a nearby Fullah-shop while a teenage girl with an exceptionally high afro hair do and who lives at Doherty street got so high on the drugs that she collapsed, helpless, by her boyfriend.

The tall man then made a signal to hidden friends who materialised like magic.

They turned out to be detectives who whisked the helpless girl, her boyfriend the pusherman and six others to the CID [Central Intelligence Department] headquarters.[3]

There are remarkable parallels between the disputes in Firestone and those in the Oke Mori Hunting Society. Both groups are located at the base of the hills of Mountain Cut; both have suffered internal conflict that led to the location of a branch society farther up the hill. In both disputes, lifestyle and generational differences were sources of conflict. The dispute between Pa Thompson and Eku Williams centered on both lifestyle and medicine. Thompson represented the proper Creole in religion, dress, and moderate manner; Williams overextended himself in drink, marijuana, and medicine. Williams, who was described as a broad man with shining skin and red eyes, drank great amounts of locally distilled gin. His excesses did not agree with Thompson's reserved demeanor.[4] Their conflicting attitudes and lifestyles may be compared with the later conflicts between the youngbloods and the tangaise men.

After fire destroyed the Firestone settlement at 101 Red Pump, the young faction of the society decided to employ the traditional practice of divination to identify who was responsible. When their attempt to hire a witch-hunting *ayogbo* masquerader from Lungi to find the culprit proved too expensive, they instead hired a licensed diviner named Diamond to find the arsonist. A Firestone member was expected to bring several small stones from the settlement to the diviner. The diviner would then recite passages from the Koran while running the stones through his fingers. If he was successful, stones the culprits had walked on would provide clues to their identification. In the event this ritual was not successful, the so-called Jinna (or Jina) Musa technique would be used. In this method the spirit of Musa appears to the diviner in a mirror and identifies the persons who have committed crimes, and sometimes even the image of the guilty party appears. To summon this spirit the diviner holds a *tasbeer* or rosary in his right hand while reciting from the Koran.[5]

When the guilty party has been identified by name, the diviner places a
fly whisk covered with medicine on the mirror. Afterward the spirit of
Jinna Musa and the offender appear. The diviner then touches the image,
first with the fly whisk, then with a red cloth if the offended party wants
the offender hurt or with a white cloth if he wants him killed.

Crime in the Ode-lay societies, as in the older Yoruba organizations,
is based on tradition. Crime and intragroup conflict, it is maintained,
have their origin in the supernatural realm, where spirits of evil persons
and medicines are at play. In one instance a member of the Bantus Mailo
Jazz Band, who was also a member of Bloody Mary, died suddenly of
what appeared to be a swollen stomach. Bloody Mary members were
convinced that the young man had died of witchcraft perpetrated by a
jealous lover, who was a member of the female side of the society.
Allegedly someone had aimed a small witch-gun in the direction of the
deceased's house to effect the illness. This alleged source of personal
affliction was widespread in Freetown and received much attention in
the press. (See figures 12 and 67.)[6]

The internal conflicts of traditional secret associations over power and
medicine sometimes lead to bodily injury and even death. This is true,
also, for Ode-lay societies, except that in their case the conflicts are
generally larger in scale and more violent. The tensions that result from
long-term unemployment, involvement in illegal practices, and the excitement of nightly entertainment all contribute to sudden and violent
outbursts.

Intergroup Conflict

Another form of conflict in which the Ode-lay societies participate is
intergroup rivalry. The confrontations of this nature are often manifested
in the masquerade competitions. In this context a person may feel free
to confront competitors with criticism on the bases of aesthetics and
performance rather than with bottles, knives, and guns. Here, too, the
Ode-lay aesthetic rivalry finds its origins in the parent Yoruba societies.
A few competitions of the Yoruba associations described below add
historical perspective to the mask competitions of the Ode-lay societies.

In the 1940s the Egunugu devil made its first appearance in Freetown
at a wedding celebration in which the blue costume obtained a height
of twenty-two feet. (See figure 68.) At Savage Square in Fourah Bay the
Egunugu masquerade encountered the old, prestigious Egungun devils
of Awodie. A fight ensued, not in the *bonical* or physical sense, as a
participant recalled, but in the herbal or spiritual sense. The juweni men
of each society fought an invisible battle that tested the medicine of
each. Eventually, when a curious member of Awodie tore a hole in this

Witch-gun death: now herbalist is docked !

THE witch-gun sage allegedly surrounding the death of the Personnel Manager of Seaboard West Africa Limited—the flour mill at Cline Town—thirty one year-old Mr. Mohamed B. Bangura, last Friday resulted in a "medicine man" being docked at the Freetown, Magistrate's Court No. 1 on a charge of manslaughter

Herbalist Santigie Kamalaneh Sesay, 31, of Mapagbo village, Mambolo Chiefdom, is alleged to have unlawfully killed Mohamed Bangura at Mapagbo village, on Friday, September 22, this year.

The case for the persecution is being conducted by State Counsel Mr. O.V. Robbin Mason.

No plea was taken on Friday, and hearing was adjourned to November 20.

A submission by the per-

Contd on page 2

Whitch-gun

Contd from page 1
secution that bail should not be allowed, on the grounds that the case is a very serious one and that the accused might likely interfere with prosecution witnesses, was overruled by Principal Magistrate Mr. L.E.K. Daramy.

FIGURE 67   Source: *Sunday We Yone*, 12 November 1978

heretofore unseen Egunugu costume, reportedly nothing was underneath the garment but a small cane. After the incident several Awodie members died of an unidentified sickness. In all, twenty-four persons succumbed mysteriously in groups of three. Leading members of the Egungun society went to Mountain Cut to plead with Pa Musa, the head of Egunugu, to end the "bad juju."

Behind this conflict was the Fourah Bay community's objection to the formation of the Egunugu and their encouragement of the Egungun to challenge the new devil. In response Pa Musa marched his followers into Awodie territory to prove to the community that his medicine and devil were stronger than those of the Egungun group. Such territorial conflicts are a major source of frustration for the police, who must carefully plan the routes of Ode-lay processions so the devils do not confront one another. (See appendix 2.)

A narrative written by a member of Bloody Mary reveals many of the important social and aesthetic themes in Ode-lay intergroups rivalry:

> OSS117 Mission Bloody Mary Operation Lotus Flower
> The reason for establishing the devil by the name of Bloody Mary was because of some misunderstanding between some devils in the East by the name of Rainbow and Firestone. Like, for example, on one occasion, Easter Monday, we [members of an Ode-lay called Yoncolma] were masquerading along Mountain Cut when suddenly some members of Rainbow group came down on us and rushed our expensive and one of the most fantastic devils in the whole of Freetown by the name of Yoncolma. Those particular devils cost more than 180 pounds or so and our intention was not to fight because of our expensive devil. During the festival the attack was cause of jealousy due to some members, i.e., James Kortulu and some others. Those particular members are here a lot. They don't give a damn about their cares. What they feel like doing is what they gonna do. Before the incident they were at liberty; after the incident they were some of the people who died in a riot in the Pademba Roads Prisons in the 1970s. So after returning home that evening with our devil we . . . decided to get a meeting and the meeting was for taking revenge on those bitches and we decided to introduce the most outstanding and fantastic devil by the name of OSS117 Mission Bloody Mary Operation Lotus Flower. The star of the film was Ken Klarke [sic]. A brother by the name of Johnny Shaft gave the devil this name from the movie he witnessed a day or two before the meeting was called, and the name was supported by Mr. Bond. The reason for giving that name to the devil was because of the movie, which was thrilling and filled with suspense and action. . . . It just reminded me of how we were to get revenge on those bitches. With our own means and strong ways we decided on the day for the pulling of the marvelous devil, that day was 17 November 1972, on the celebration of the Muslim holiday, Eid-ul-Adha. On this day we met a group on the way called Paddle. We made them to understand that we are great and we are out for revenge. It was a day not to be forgotten for you to see this fantastic devil displaying on the outskirts of Freetown. From that previous day to this day our devil was one of the best devils in the whole of Freetown. The devil on this occasion was a special bush devil just at the price of about 45 Leones [$45], just to revenge; and it was built by a brother called Edmund and Mr. Bond. It was fearful, dreadful, and outstanding, because of the way it was built and prepared in that rough way and without even taking care of the making of it. Like the porcupine, jege [cowrie shells], the head, which was a skull obtained for us by the juweni man from Heaven City, and some other items.[7]

In this incident Yoncolma did not fight its attackers directly because its first priority was the protection of its fancy devil. Instead, members of the group formed another society with a fierce bush devil that was modeled on Hunting costumes. The Hunting devil would lead them in a reprisal against the eastern societies. The Bloody Mary bush devil was appropriately selected to head this revenge mission, thus linking the formal aesthetic of fierceness and a matching social action. The root of the fierce aesthetic was in Ogun, the Yoruba god of war and hunting.

Ode-lay rivalries also sometimes reflect the various political conflicts at the grassroots. An incident between Civilian Rule and Rainbow is a good example. On 19 April 1978, Independence Day, several groups, including Civilian Rule, paraded. This was a special occasion, since on the previous Eid-ul-Adha the Ode-lay groups had been refused permits. (See appendix 3.) In preparation for the celebration, the head of Civilian Rule screened off part of his Kroo Town drinking establishment for the assembly of the costumes. With the employment of four mailo jazz bands, the society was prepared to outperform its old enemy, Rainbow.

The Civili masqueraders left the shrine at 1:00 P.M., making their way to Campbell Street, where they met a government vehicle, a Mercedes-Benz with national and party flags withdrawn. The car was occupied by a woman and the chauffeur of one of Sierra Leone's prominent politicians. The chauffeur, who was drunk, forced his way through the Civili procession and ran down (*banga banga*) a musician. The leader of Civilian Rule claimed to have heard the woman exclaim to the driver, "Get the hell out of here!" The head of Civili admonished the man for his impatience and lack of respect for the devil procession and asked him to take the injured man to the hospital. The driver again attempted to pass through the procession, but the leader of Civili lay down in front of the car to block escape. The police arrived, interrogated the parties, and marked locations of the principal characters in the incident for possible later use as evidence in the event of a trial.

Word of the matter reached the employer of the driver. That afternoon, with the Internal Security Unit, he intercepted the masquerade procession and arrested its leader. At the jail the Civili leader telephoned a relative who was assistant commissioner of police and with his aid was transferred to police headquarters, where he was later freed. The Civili devil, however, performed until dark and then returned to the shrine, where activities continued until early morning. The factor underlying the celebration and conflict in this incident was the superiority of the Civili Society's masquerade aesthetic over that of the Rainbow Society.

This incident underlines the problem inherent in having several agencies police the city. The various agencies are similar to the competing mask societies in that each organization is patronized by a different set of politicians. In this case Civili's leader was transferred to the Central

FIGURE 68 Igunugu dance costumes of Nigeria, which are identical to those displayed by the Egunugu in Freetown. *African Arts* 4, no. 4 (1971): 61. Photo credit: Jola Ogunlusi

Intelligence Department so his relatives could have him released. At the ISU headquarters he might have had a more difficult time, considering that that agency was patronized by the same individual who sponsored Rainbow, Civili's crosstown rival.

At the root of this incident was the rivalry between the groups' sponsors, whose reputations were affected by the degree of success each group's masquerade obtained. Patrons were actively involved with their groups. On the morning of the Rainbow celebration, the Internal Security Unit and the grand patron drove in a cavalcade to the edge of the wharf and proceeded on foot to the sacred shrine for sacrifices. It was rumored that the gifts for these sacrifices were not as expensive as those the Civili sponsors had presented and that Rainbow had not received enough support to build a fancy devil or hire several mailo jazz bands. Word also spread through town that the Rainbow group had performed poorly. The driver of Rainbow's sponsor had been instructed, therefore, to find the Civili procession and assess its performance. The backer of Rainbow was, indeed, jealous of the display of Civili and, accordingly, was sufficiently aroused to have its leading member arrested, an action he hoped would stop the rival performance and thus ruin it.

Conflict has characterized the Ode-lay societies from the beginning. The causes of intragroup fighting have involved the misuse of society funds, competition for leadership, and competition for power through the use of traditional medicine. At the base of many conflicts is the violation of the constitutions adopted by the new societies. Though fighting is disruptive and can lead to the breakup of a group, the release of tensions in conflicts helps to stabilize the groups and to calm their members.

The newspapers, encouraged by public outcries against the masquerade performances have frequently criticized the celebrations. The intergroup conflicts accompanying the masquerades have occasionally ended in full-pitched battles, with guns, knives, and bottles. The groups enjoy their reputations for roughness, which is part of the traditional fierce aesthetic.

Rivalry of an aesthetic as well as physical nature is not a new feature in secret-society life. Stories of clashes between early Hunting, Egungun, and Egunugu societies abound. Such conflicts result when one group attempts to destroy another through the medicine of its juweni men or through witchcraft. In some cases the devils themselves are attacked. Ode-lay conflicts, intragroup and intergroup, are similar to and are rooted in conflicts that beset the older traditional societies.

10

The Politicization of
Urban Secret Societies

From the time of their establishment in Freetown, the Yoruba-descended
secret societies were political. They served as pressure groups, defying
or otherwise modifying attempts by the Church and government to
control their activities. Thus political activities of masquerade societies
in Freetown did not originate in the twentieth century. However, the
mixing of the Yoruba descendants and the rural migrants to Freetown
in the new Creolized urban masking societies constituted a broader
network of peoples, whose impact on government was far greater than
that of the original Yoruba groups. Cutting across tribal and geographical
boundaries, these societies brought their needs and demands to the
attention of the national government.

In the Ode-lay bid for unity, the government recognizes the necessity
of securing the support of these groups. At the same time the government
(the All Peoples Congress party) understands that such a widespread
network based on cooperation rather than conflict might also pose a
threat to the aspirations of the party. Thus the government looks with
ambivalence upon the Ode-lay attempts to unify. But the government
believes it can maintain control of these groups by controlling their
masquerades.

The Traditional Societies and Politics

Groups such as the Ambas Geda were among the first migrant-controlled
associations in Freetown to create political pressure. The Ambas Geda
Society was founded by an illiterate goldsmith, whose intention was to
organize the Temne youth in the hope of bringing their needs to the

attention of the national government. He provided a room to serve as a meeting place for the young men. Because of their infamous reputation, he did not want to be directly associated with them, so he convinced a young Arabic teacher to lead them instead.[1] The new society had two objectives: (1) to entertain by means of dance and music and (2) to provide mutual benefit for members in time of stress.

The political leverage offered by groups like the Ambas Geda must have been recognized by Sierra Leone's present leadership. With a tightly knit system of urban associations and a platform built on generational differences and Islam, support was available to outsiders who aspired to political office. The ability of the youth organizations to support political candidates was exercised in one World War II election that involved the Ambas Geda. Whereas the elders supported a candidate of their generation, the youths, who wanted a literate representative from their own ranks, chose instead the schoolmaster who had led the original Ambas Geda. To run an open campaign against the elders' candidate, the schoolmaster withdrew from the society; but he nevertheless kept in close contact with the network of Temne groups.

From the Temne groups the candidate received financial contributions and general support to convince the electorate of his political talents. On election day society supporters and members of other groups that had sprung up in the rural areas demonstrated on his behalf. They paraded, carried banners, and danced through the city. Outlying societies brought four thousand pinflags out of concealment and fastened them to their clothing. Chartered lorries arrived with individuals who were anxious to vote, even though many were not qualified to do so. Thus the young schoolmaster transformed the young men's associations into the most effective party machinery Freetown had ever known.[2]

At the time of the Ambas Geda demonstrations, the first vice-president of Sierra Leone under the one-party state was about fifteen years old. As a Temne he may well have been associated with one of the societies. He must have also realized the potential for such a political machine at the national level. The schoolmaster may well have served as his model. After his election, the former schoolteacher transformed his office into one of great power. Through his control of the associations he enlisted broadly based support, both urban and rural. He would appeal to these same constituencies again in his bid for national power. He was later selected as treasurer for the Sierra Leone Peoples party.[3]

The All Peoples Congress party adopted similar political tactics and applied them to the referendum on the one-party state. The APC victory in this matter was celebrated by Ode-lay and Egungun societies from Port Loko, which chartered lorries from that Temne region, decorated them with flags and banners of the APC, and moved in a large motorcade through the town. The success of the APC was based on the early exportation of the Ode-lay society from Freetown to other parts of Sierra Leone, including Port Loko. (See map 1.) In some areas it was mandatory for a male of a certain age to join these groups.[4] The implanting of the Ode-lay in the Mende and Kono districts was crucial for the party's success. The key factor in organizing political demonstrations was the leadership's patronage system, through which politicians were in close communication with their particular groups.

The Ode-lay societies have long admired the patronage system of the Hunting societies, which have elevated their own status to a level upon which they now are able to compete with the Free Masons. Their success has encouraged some Ode-lay leaders to form an amalgamated society like the hunters'. The annual Thanksgiving ceremonies of the Hunting societies held during the spring show the effectiveness of the patronage system.

One such ceremony was held in 1978, in the large and historically important town of Waterloo, a few miles outside Freetown.[5] For the occasion, the society members wore black suit-jackets with a mono-grammed badge featuring the initials of the Hunting society. A blade of grass was looped through a buttonhole of the jacket. Their trousers varied in pattern and color. Wives and members wore white dresses and straw hats with green bands and decorated their hair with yellow ribbons.

The church in which the ceremony was held was a fine example of nineteenth-century wooden construction in colonial Gothic architecture. The wonderfully carved rafters and furniture gave the interior a light, airy feeling. Some of the ranking women of the society were seated facing the congregation; others distributed the collection plates. This latter custom is reflected in the function of the Ode-lay mammy queen who also collects contributions. The Hunting society women took the offer-ings and placed them in the hands of the priest before the altar.

The sermon on this occasion dealt with reconciliation of the cultural forces of Christianity and traditional African religion. The topical ques-tion was Can Christianity tolerate African culture? The speaker stated that African masquerades in the form of Hunting devils are compatible with Church doctrine, since both the Church and the Hunting associ-ations worshiped one God. The former worshiped in church; the latter worshiped in the context of dance and costume. The speaker cited the Festival of African Culture (FESTAC), which had been held in Nigeria the previous year, as an expression of African culture that also served in the worship of God. The representation of Sierra Leone at the Nigerian festival with Hunting devils, lanterns, and fancy and Ode-lay devils had portrayed a country firmly in control of its destiny, with one foot sup-ported by African tradition and the other stepping bravely into the world of the twentieth century. The Christian God and Ogun, the god of iron, were manifestations of the same spiritual essence.

After the sermon special patrons moved to the front of the church to make their offerings. The priest then recited a long list of past or deceased members of the society, calling them by their society names. The use of alias names is also common in Ode-lay practice. In the case of youth in the Ode-lay, the society names reflect an interest in contemporary film rather than in older Yoruba culture. The hunters, however, chose Yoruba names, stressing the protracted history of their traditions. Next, a general collection was taken. When the priest gave a final blessing to the society, he stated its motto of Unity. This is also the word most commonly used to describe the objectives of the Ode-lay societies.

The choir band, which consisted of brass, woodwinds, and drums, had played Christian hymns inside the church and now moved outside to prepare for the march through town. Once outside, the director, by a costume change, became a drum major, and the music took on a militant flare. The drum major blew the whistle to signal the start of the procession; then, with high-marching steps, the band moved ahead. The whistle-blowing major is reminiscent of the flute player of the Hunting masquerades. Behind the musicians followed the political dignitaries, who waved to the crowds, taking advantage of the publicity. Behind them were members of the Hunting association and other persons who had attended the church service.

The procession wound through the town for an hour on its way to the sacred shrine of the hunters, where presumably the head of a ram or dog was buried in commemoration of Ogun. The shrine was connected to a temporary cluster of shelters made of large bamboo posts with cane-mat roofs. Under the shelters, chairs and dining tables had been arranged for the guests. As society members and guests were seated, the olukortu or officer in charge of food and drink and his attendants distributed drinks, while women passed trays of sandwiches and fried pastries. The table of the grand chief patron was elaborately decorated with flowers and laden with bottles of Captain Morgan rum—the favorite libation of the hunters—Remy Martin, Courvoisier, Star and Heineken beer, and palm wine. First everyone drank a glass of palm wine in honor of the society; then each chose beverages suited to personal taste. The musicians, who had changed from military dress to T-shirts and rolled-up sleeves, now gathered in a circle and became a jazz band.

The music started slowly with a few tunes featuring Willie Pratt, the country's most famous trumpet player. Then followed a speech by the grand chief patron, whose gift for oratory inspired guests and members to higher levels of excitement. The speech pointed to the accomplishments of the APC and to some of its chief officers. It specifically commented on the importance of the Hunting society to the country and its growing influence as compared with that of the Free Masons, "that other organization," which had enjoyed a near monopoly of political influence until the 1960s. The audience cheered in thunderous applause as the speaker ended his presentation by offering a large cash gift to the society. In expression of its approval, the band played *When the Saints Go Marching In.* At 9:00 P.M. the grand patrons and other guests departed; but the Hunting society members stayed until the early morning hours.

The Ode-lay Societies and Politics

Politics at the secret-society level have worked well for members of the All Peoples Congress party. In addition to the hunters, politicians have also patronized the youthful element of the population, which is represented by the Ode-lay societies. Records of the Paddle Society demonstrate how this occurred. Until 1968 Paddle enjoyed the success of expensive presentations without a need to register; but the society finally registered under the Friendly Society Acts in 1968 to secure political patronage. Around 1968 Paddle attracted aspiring Freetown politicians who, like the schoolmaster of the Ambas Geda, sought a political following. Ode-lay support was class-based, consisting of Christians and Muslims, and rural and urban peoples. The APC, which was a relatively young political party, whose ranks were filled with aggressive new talent anxious to depose the Sierra Leone Peoples party (SLPP), saw in the Ode-lay societies an important base of support.

The Paddle Society minutes show the names of politicians, some of them prominent in national politics in 1978, who sought membership in return for support. The minutes are interesting in their seemingly objective comments about each of the politicians who applied for membership. In some instances applicants for membership were turned down, but no record was kept of the specific reasons for that action. These rejections were often the result of another politician's desire to block or prevent the opposition from enlisting Ode-lay support. Where a politically strong individual supported an Ode-lay society, as long as that society remained under his patronage, it was closed to any other politician. The patronage system was an integral part of nominations and elections in Freetown. By the medium of devil presentations and—at times—more physical tactics, Ode-lay societies helped insure the success of their candidate.

In one section of the Paddle minutes, members debated the possibility of electing outsiders to office. These prospective officials ranked high in the political system. On one side of the debate were those individuals who believed the interests of Paddle were best served by government officials who were not necessarily from the Magazine Cut area (so named because it had once been a storage place for explosives). On the other side were those who felt that officers should be "Magazine born," in other words born and raised in that neighborhood. "We must not allow people from afar to lead us; this is our society." In this respect members of the society were unsettled about the scope of their activities and involvement with the various political parties. The advocates of outside participation made the point that with such support it would be easier to obtain masking permits. The issue was not resolved at this meeting.

At the end of this session, discussion turned to the use of government property for society headquarters. From this point of view Paddle needed a political ally. Since Ode-lay groups like Paddle do not own land, settlement by squatting is a constant source of insecurity. Members decided to tighten their claim to the property surrounding the Devil Hole by obtaining a notice of acquisition, which would be attached to the front of the cave. It was also agreed that a number of mats would be obtained so all members could be seated inside the hole for meetings. An APC member helped the group secure its territory and presented a donation for the general improvement of the society's headquarters.

The winning of the masquerade competitions by a particular Ode-lay group reflects the quality of its sponsorship. Political leaders have as much to lose in these competitions as do the societies themselves. This political and aesthetic rivalry aggravates ill feelings among the various groups, as the Paddle minutes of 1976 indicate. The minutes record that Bloody Mary threatened to attack Paddle at the next celebration. When some Paddle officials suggested that a committee be appointed to negotiate with Bloody Mary to arrive at a peaceful settlement, members claimed that this would amount to an admission of fear of the other group. An alternative put forward by a political supporter was that some officers meet with the commissioner of police to convince him not to give a masking permit to Bloody Mary. In the previous years, permit granting had become a political issue; now it has also become a tool used by government patrons to control the societies. Because of the efforts of its own patron, however, Bloody Mary did receive a permit on that occasion.

Patronage of the Ode-lay societies in Freetown is also the means by which Chernor Maju, a special parliamentary assistant to the president of Sierra Leone, sought to elevate his position. In the East One Ward he was a popular figure among the youth. This area near the docks was a major source of crime. To alleviate this condition and show his leadership capabilities to the party, Maju amalgamated the Mau Mau, Island, Gladiators, Datsun, and Zaire Ode-lay groups into a new society called Back to Power or National. Since the new group's establishment in 1975, the group had performed with its devil three times up to 1978. Because the special assistant is ethnically a Foulah, the group has attracted many persons from northern rural areas, as well as Guineans who found Sekou Touré's regime too pressed by inflation and a shortage of consumer goods. Most of the Back-to-Power members belonged to the APC Youth League, which held its meetings in the East One constituency at party headquarters on Fourah Bay Road.

The success of this amalgamated group came to the attention of party leaders, who wished to use its masquerade elsewhere in the country. An occasion for this arose at the 1977 Kenema Fair. Kenema, in the heart of Mendeland, had been a constant problem for the APC. The party had always enjoyed a northern base of support, consisting of Limba, Susu, and Temne. To the south, however, the Mende had traditionally reserved their allegiance for the Sierra Leone Peoples party. This north-south split occurred because of religious, educational, and economic differences between the two areas. The Mende traditionally have had greater access to privileges offered by the British during the colonial period.[6] Mendeland, an important mining area south of Kono, felt the crunch of the northern migration of youths who came to work in the diamondiferous areas. These youths formed gangs of between 1,000 and 1,500 to dig pits, wash, sift, and extract finds illegally in a single night. This exacerbated relations between the Mende who backed the SLPP and the northern groups who supported the APC.[7]

Elections at Kenema reflected the intensity of the conflict between the APC and the SLPP. Strong-arm tactics were not ruled out in the struggle. In 1968, the year Siaka Stevens came to power under the APC banner, that party established its largest branch in the Kenema District. (See figure 69.) In response the SLPP attempted to run a Poro secret-society campaign in which all males of the district would be forced into initiation. This, it was believed, would have the effect of expelling strangers, especially those persons who backed the APC. In a quick response to the situation, the government declared a state of emergency and postponed a special election for that year. The Poro campaign might have succeeded, but SLPP activists were placed in detention and the campaign was abandoned. Relations between the northern migrants and the Mende remain bitter.

The year before the 1977 Kenema Fair, the elections were once again characterized by violence. In the attempt to stabilize the region and establish support for the referendum election calling for a one-party state, the APC stepped up its activities in the Kenema Youth League. As part of this strategy, the league invited the Power devil to perform at the fair, which would attract thousands of people from the district. It was hoped that, by staging a peaceful celebration with emphasis on the theme of unity, the one-party state would gather more support. The events that lead to this celebration reveal clearly the ties between the Ode-lay societies and the APC. At the party youth-center, one room contained parts of old bush and fancy devils, together with several mailo jazz instruments. There the printing press, mimeograph and teletype machines, and telephone usually associated with campaign headquarters in developed countries were here replaced by an essentially African media.

FIGURE 69   The All Peoples Congress party headquarters in Kenema, where Power members met and prepared for the masquerade. Photo credit: John Nunley

On the day of the Back-to-Power parade, the Internal Security Unit and the Sierra Leone police were out in full force. The red caps of the ISU troops appeared over thick clouds of dust stirred up by military transport trucks. As the Back-to-Power devil passed these troops, they gave the stiff arm salute to affirm their support of the Ode-lay. (See figures 70, 71, and 72.) A song on everyone's lips praised the devil:

> *Hey Power A like you Power.*
> *We get de Power We get de Power.*
> *Nyah bon de sia mi people.*
> *Dunie dunie Power de go lay me carran go.*

> Hey Power I like you.
> We have the Power we have the Power.
> I was born to see my Mende people.
> I beg you I beg you Power take me with you.

The Back-to-Power devil, like its Yoruba prototype, was constructed in three pieces: headpiece, vest, and undergarment. The costume stood about ten feet high, with wings spreading to a distance of between seven and eight feet. The construction represented a zoomorphic creature, an

FIGURE 70 Side view of Power devil with APC flag. Photo credit: John Nunley

FIGURE 71 Deer-top headdress of Power devil with photograph of President Siaka Stevens. Photo credit: John Nunley

FIGURE 72 Back view of Power devil with photographs of Vice-President S. I. Koroma and Chenor Maju, a member of Parliament. Photo credit: John Nunley

antelope-headed bird. The wings and body were made of wire substructures covered with paper and cloth, the technique used in lantern building. The movable parts were controlled by guide-wires that were operated by the person inside the costume. Lanterns also are operated in this manner. Although other Ode-lay devils are made in this fashion, the Back-to-Power devil was unusual in that it displayed photographs of President Siaka Stevens on top of the antelope head, First Vice-President S. I. Koroma on the wings, and Chernor Maju on the body of the costume. The image of Maju was lined with cowrie shells, denoting the power of the parliamentarian's traditional medicine. Thus the effect of presslike photography, coupled with the tradition of the masquerade with its reference to the spiritual world, provided the political elite with a volatile medium with which to build a patronage system at the grassroots level.

In an adverse example of patronage, Bloody Mary supported a parliamentary nominee for the West Two Constituency in 1978, when a vacancy occurred at the death of J. T. Kanu, the previous officer. This occasion afforded an opportunity to witness the patronage system at the grassroots. As the West Two position was theoretically open to all parties, it seemed that an opposition party might put forth a nomination. The APC had previously given its symbol to a young engineering student who had recently returned from West Germany. This young man was given a post in one of the country's leading export industries. Since the deceased parliamentarian had become "minister of the cemetery," as his Ode-lay supporters expressed his death, it was time for a new man to take power. The APC candidate had once been a member of Yoncolma and was, by succession, a member of Bloody Mary. The group made plans for their campaign in mid-January, about two weeks before the special election. One of the leaders of the group declared that since Marcada (the candidate's society name) had been out of the country for a long time and would not be readily recognized by the people, and since he had been given "the heavy hand of the party," it was the responsibility of Bloody Mary to see that the people understood him. The group therefore planned a devil procession, with the Bantus Mailo Jazz Band, for nomination day.

Nominations were held at the Technical School near Congo Cross in the western part of the city. On the evening before nominations were made, Bloody Mary and the mailo jazz group posted themselves at the school, along with the army and the ISU. They drank, smoked, and gambled through the night. Many members sniffed bottles of stencil blotter to bolster their highs. By the afternoon of the next day, the opposition had not contested the nominations, thus assuring an APC victory. In the atmosphere of impending victory, the question remained whether the devil would be allowed to demonstrate for the candidate.

By late afternoon permission still had not been granted and the jubilant

FIGURE 73   An Ode-lay bush devil in an unidentified location in the countryside indicates the spread of the Ode-lay phenomenon. Photo credit: Nancy Minett

atmosphere subsided. Bloody Mary members were hungry. They were generously provided with drink and other "food" for the mind (drugs); but, except for hard and green mangoes, they had had nothing to eat. Some members had long since lost consciousness by the side of the driveway. Others insisted that the devil would parade to the president's house on King Harmon Road, then to Campbell Street, and on to the main west-side streets.

It eventually became clear that the devil permit would not be granted. One member rationalized the government's refusal: "So it's just the Bantus Mailo Jazz Band the government does not mind paying for. For some reason mailo just does not attract the attention where a devil lets the whole city in on it and causes some pretty unexplainable panic and chaos. So no devil positively no devil. *What tin wi foh do?* [What are we to do?]" At about 7:00 P.M. Bloody Mary and the mailo jazz band left the school in procession through the western part of the city. Dressed in red shirts, hunting hats, and party symbols, they moved south on Campbell Street. Many of the respectable members of the Egungun associations joined them, but the Bloody Mary devil was conspicuously absent.

The following morning Johnny Shaft and the rest of the Bloody Mary membership resumed their drinking and smoking. After thirty hours of demonstration and little sleep they were exhausted. Resentment was expressed toward the party leadership. "I'm not happy because I'm being suppressed," one person complained. "It is our right to play with the debil. We should not have to ask for permits. Debils are a part of our culture."

The government was as aware as the Ode-lay of the excitement and reactions the devil processions effected on crowds. The combination of music, uniform costume, masquerader, and audience participation account for this intensity. Though these performances are judged on aesthetic merit, a spiritual element is communicated through the fancy and fierce media. Both the sacrifices to the ancestors before processions and the passing of the "invisible" into the devil elevate the performances to a realm beyond the strictly political. The identification of audience with the masqueraders moves participants in a way in which roles and status cannot. As a consequence, the political system ceases to be at the center of focus and is thus left unprotected. Unless the leadership is secure, it is bound to look upon such cultic expression equivocally, depending upon it for support, yet mistrusting the intensity of its expressive aims.

The Ode-lay associations are involved in a patronage system similar to that of the earlier Ambas Geda. The registration of these groups in 1968 was related to the ascendancy of the APC party. As a primary source of APC support, it was important that the Ode-lay be legally invested. Demonstrations for the one-party state during the national referendum in 1978 revealed the close ties between the government and the youth organizations. Like the earlier schoolteacher leader of the Ambas Geda, officials of the APC recognized the potential of exploiting an urban-based society that could establish branches and thereby enlist the support of youth in the rural areas. (See figure 73.) The participation of Bloody Mary in a western ward's special election indicates how close the ties between the Ode-lay and party officials could be. Politicians did not, however, exclude other more traditional groups from patronage, as was indicated by the Hunting society's Thanksgiving service held in honor of a high APC official.

11

Unity and Control

The Ode-lay societies offer a way of development that combines traditional culture and modern technology, two elements that in the future might be combined by gifted leadership. The tendency of postcolonial African elites, however, has been to remove themselves from the grassroots and to consolidate their position with strong-arm methods.[1] Though one-party states are common in Africa, the trend does not need to go hand in hand with the increased deployment of force. A one-party state does not mutually exclude individual rights. Whether the All Peoples Congress party currently in power and Sierra Leone's secret societies will converge in a mutually supportive patronage context to work for the benefit of all remains open to question. There is little evidence to support an answer either way at the present time.

One may point optimistically to the Beni dances of East Africa, where musical companies of the colonial period played a role similar to that today of the Ode-lay. Beni associations expressed their aesthetic inclinations in costume and transformed African rhythms in crosstown rivalries in a manner similar to those of the Ode-lay, Hunting, and Egungun societies. For sixty years or so, the Beni companies added quality to the lives of individuals under foreign hegemony.[2]

But why, one may ask, did these companies fall from popularity during the postcolonial period? Were the Beni societies merely products of pressures brought about by the confrontation of European and African powers, or were the societies in fact rooted in precontact traditions? It has been concluded that the Beni associations were part of a base culture of East African origin, with roots in Swahili and indigenous rural traditions.[3] The cultural configuration of Beni in this respect resembles the Ode-lay with its Creole and indigenous cultural layers.

The question remains: If Beni declined during the development of an

African state, why have the Ode-lay societies not experienced a similar decline? Perhaps the strength of Yoruba culture has affected the adaptability of the Ode-lay associations. Freetown's Yoruba-based traditions have survived the postindependence transition and have widened their sphere of influence to include most of the larger towns of Sierra Leone. At present they are viable and, indeed, vigorous institutions. The future of the Ode-lay hinges on such unpredictable factors as economic prospects, form of government, town planning, and development projects. Recognizing the great political force of the Ode-lay societies, the All Peoples Congress has supported such groups while striving to maintain control of them.

The Permit Issue

The issue of masquerade permits (see appendix 2) best illustrates the dialectical relationship between the government and the Ode-lay. The dramatic events leading to the celebration of Eid-ul-Adha in 1977 reveal the ambiguities of that relationship. In anticipation of this Islamic event, Bloody Mary, Firestone, and Paddle all applied for permits. Although Islam is theoretically opposed to the display of images, it has shown remarkable tolerance toward the Africans' use of images in traditional practices. Islamic doctrine itself leaves room for belief in spirits in its reference to the existence of *jinna* spirits.[4]

The selection of this highly respected Islamic holiday by Ode-lay groups pointed to a change in the religious configuration of Freetown. Before the turn of this century, the Creoles were the majority of the population and Christianity was the common religion. To be a Muslim was, in the eyes of the Creole Christian, to be inferior. With the later migrations, however, Islam surfaced as a dominant force. Neighborhoods representing a variety of ethnic groups took great pride in building their own mosques, and the mosques became a focal point for political activity.

The three Ode-lay societies, Paddle, Firestone, and Bloody Mary, selected the Islamic holiday to gain popularity with the Muslim community. Their choice was also influenced by the lantern processions that appear at the end of Ramadan or Eid-ul-Fitry. In the lantern celebrations, music, drama, dance, and art were already being used in a competitive context on an Islamic holiday. The Ode-lay societies, also, intended to win public favor by displaying their masquerades in praise of Allah.

The Bid for Unity

Several weeks before the planned celebration in 1977, each society commissioned an artist to carve the headpieces for its costumes. Remnants of devil costumes of previous years were reused in the new constructions. Contributions and taxes were allocated by each group for food, music, and uniform dress. The three societies determined to show the public and the government that they could stage peaceful presentations. The words *brotherhood* and *unity* were spoken repeatedly during the preparations. To demonstrate its constructive intentions and to convince the government that the Ode-lay associations could cooperate, Firestone sent a letter to Paddle and Bloody Mary. This was the idea of one of Firestone's political sponsors. The letter read:

> Dear Polish Friends,
> Dear Comrades,
> My Young Friends,
>
> Permit me first of all to convey to your society our club's warm greetings and sincere congratulations from the committee of the people's Republic of FIRESTONE SOCIETY. On behalf of the Society, I am directed to inform you that the Society has a special and grand charity, which will take place on Sunday 6th November 1977 at 11 A.M. Lastly I am also directed through the Society to invite five (5) of your society members to make this venture a success.
>
> God bless you all and free our hearts from disunity.
>
> Time: 11 A.M.
>
> Place: 101 Red Pump Road, Foulah Town, Freetown.
>
> Thanks. See you.

The revolutionary tone of the letter, typical of Ode-lay correspondence, betrays the influence of APC rhetoric. Leading the groups in the spirit of unity, Firestone invited representatives from other societies to the devil sacrifice held before their annual celebration.

This first attempt to unify the Ode-lay groups in ritual was followed by a meeting of historical significance. The meeting, it was hoped, would raise the political consciousness of the Ode-lay general membership. The minutes of the meeting, which was held at a community center on 17 November 1977, read:

> The Chairman spoke about the difficulties which have plagued the three groups as a result of the wide-scale thuggery and violence demonstrated by some unscrupulous members of similar societies during processions on Public Holidays. The Chairman appealed for cooperation from all angles with a view to the promotion of a successful masquerade procession on the day of the feast of Eid-ul-Adha. He went on further to admonish members that masquerading in the form of mask devils should not be regarded as a foolish affair and that all seriousness and devotion should be invested in it. The Chairman appealed for unity and cooperation and to show our restraint in avoiding open confrontation between different groups but instead to dance in between ourselves whenever two groups come in contact with each other during processions.[5]

The chairman's plea that dancers buffer their societies' processions underscored the problem of devil confrontation. The strong identification with the spiritual symbols of masquerades effected violent behavior on the part of rival groups that often exceeded leadership control. It was hoped that dancing and mailo jazz music would express these rivalries peacefully.

A Paddle leader asserted that the time was at hand for one society's concern to be that of the others. He suggested that a method for obtaining permits be instituted and that future joint meetings be convened to solve this problem. He advised the Ode-lay representatives to inform the president of Sierra Leone of the "transition they were in." These overtures of unity and brotherhood were strong indicators of a developing collective consciousness among the Ode-lay members. Additional suggestions for intergroup football matches and picnics reveal the sincerity with which members wished to avoid confrontation. The meeting was held specifically to obtain permits, but it significantly marked the first time the Ode-lays had cooperated in an effort to find a solution to a common problem. Despite these efforts, however, the government refused to grant the desired permits. Its refusal characterized a change in the relationship between the Ode-lay societies and the national leadership.

On 18 November 1977 Paddle put together the last pieces of a devil costume at the south end of Hagan Street. The leaders made arrangements to have the costume photographed. On the same day Firestone members had their costume assembled on a small table at a location below 101 Red Pump. The four-foot-high assemblage consisted of wooden face-masks, snakes, animal skins, mirrors, porcupine quills, and cowrie-shell decorations. The pants and undershirts were tailored of a popular cloth pattern. The costume combined elements of the fancy and fierce aesthetics. Both Paddle and Firestone were confident the desired permits would be granted.

On the eve of Eid-ul-Adha, Monday, 21 November 1977, the requested permits still had not been issued to any of the three groups. At Firestone the youths were drinking quietly and becoming frustrated over their dilemma; they had spent all their funds in preparation for a celebration that might be canceled. That evening members of Paddle met at the north end of Hagan Street, where their mask had been taken. Traditionally the devil made this trip on Hagan Street before the play. Here everyone was confident that the permits would be given. Two prominent political sponsors asked the president to grant the permits. At Pike Street the members of Bloody Mary smoked marijuana and claimed that their devil would parade regardless of the government's decision. Later that night Firestone displayed two clown masqueraders, yamamah and gaboi, who paraded down Adelaide Street on the way to the Bloody Mary residence, where they took refuge from the police. Soon afterward, the Bloody Mary devil was arrested.

The following morning permits were still withheld. Throughout the city Muslims attended Eid-ul-Adha services at various parade grounds and parks. The sound of drums and the processions of imams marked the way for the faithful. The poor were nearby to accept alms from their more fortunate brothers. At each of the gathering points, women sat behind men who knelt on prayer rugs close to the speakers. When the services ended at noon, the people returned home for the traditional meal and further celebrations.

Contrary to tradition, however, the police cleared the streets, and patrols of Internal Security Unit troops were stationed at key positions. At Hagan Street police officers shot tear gas into a crowd gathering in anticipation of the Paddle Society procession. Scores of state and private cars of government officials patrolled the area. By 2:00 P.M. Mountain Cut Road was filled with spectators who were anxious to see the Firestone masquerade. Members of Paddle, who had given up hope of obtaining a permit, were also on hand. Here, too, police used tear gas and the threat of arms to disperse the crowd. Firestone members questioned the government's right to take away the people's culture. At Kissi Street, a main procession thoroughfare, spectators waiting for the devils were also dispersed by the police. Word spread that some of the Ode-lay societies in the communities outside Freetown would masquerade, but at Wellington (see map 2), about five miles from the city, the police had also broken up the devil procession of a group called Moscow. The promise of masked celebrations for the Eid-ul-Adha was unfulfilled, and the city was quiet for the remainder of the day.

Reactions to Permit Suppression

Reactions of the Ode-lay associations to the failure of Eid-ul-Adha varied. Some felt the permits were not given because of violence and street muggings that had characterized the lantern parades held earlier, on 16 September 1977. Others felt the government's refusal was designed to embarrass certain officials who had sponsored the societies. Their inability to obtain permits on behalf of the Ode-lay, it was believed, would diminish their influence among Ode-lay members.

Yet another rationale implicated party politics. It was pointed out that the opposition to the APC might use the disruptive results of such an event against the party, and the government refused to grant the permits out of fear that the violence would become a political issue. However, with the army, ISU, and Sierra Leone police under government control at the time, it is difficult to imagine how the processions of Eid-ul-Adha could have threatened political stability.

Another explanation for the failure of the Ode-lays came from a member of Paddle. He believed that the efforts of a certain high-ranking member of Paddle to back a candidate who represented an opposition party had influenced the government's decision not to issue permits. Instead of singling out Paddle by refusing a permit to that group, the reprisal was covered by withholding permits from all groups.

The majority opinion about the withheld permits focused, however, on the violence and general hooliganism that usually results from Ode-lay celebrations; but this was only part of the explanation. The three Ode-lay groups expressed desire to join together into an amalgamated society, as the Free Masons and Hunting societies had done, that threatened a kind of cohesion the government feared. It therefore asserted its authority against the masquerades to prevent what might have become a strong, independent political force. With the right leadership, the sharing of group activities could have brought about a class consciousness that might have fostered an independent party and might even have led someday to a new form of government.

The failure of Wallace Johnson's political programs after 1939, particularly those that centered on the labor movement and sought to unite the peoples of the city with those of the province, was due to a lack of class awareness that could cut across rural and urban regional interests. Such a political alliance, based on the common cause of labor and farmers, would have posed a serious threat to those in power. Siaka Stevens, who was once a friend of Johnson's and also a labor organizer, had used some of his friend's organizational techniques, especially in the formation of the West African Youth League. Stevens had conceived the APC Youth League, which, unlike Johnson's organization, succeeded in uniting the young people of the cities and of the rural areas.

The Bloody Mary poster for the cancelled celebration best expressed that group's excitement about the anticipated masquerade. The line "Bloody Mary Festac 77 gonna be like it never used to be before" signifies the hopes of all individuals connected with the society. (See figure 21.) But when the government refused to issue the desired permit to parade, a major confrontation ensued. (See figure 74.) After the Bloody Mary devil was arrested and taken to the Central Street Station for parading without a permit, the group claimed that they did not intend to masquerade in public and that they only wanted to proceed with their devil to Pike Street, where it would be safely guarded. They accused the police of having entered their settlement illegally to confiscate the costume. They were discouraged and humiliated, for they believed their devil would not be returned. Each day for a week, a delegation from the group went to the police to retrieve the costume. Although the costume was eventually returned, Bloody Mary did not perform again in 1977.[6]

Members of Paddle objected to the government's position on permits,

Police in big clash with masqueraders

BLOODY MARY ARRESTED

AS the feast of Eid-Ul-Adha was celebrated yesterday, Freetown was not without its incidents of drama.

It was a test of strength and will power between the police and masqueraders who went out to defy the ban on street performing.

As the defiance continued, police pounced.

Scores of arrests were made and heavily armed policemen patrolled the streets the whole of the day.

The mask of the popular 'Bloody Mary' devil was seized by police at Fergusson Street as the group masqueraded in the street.

As the devil was grabbed, the followers fled.

Along Mountain Cut and Kroo Town Road, Siaka Stevens Street and Campbell Street, dancers were out as early as Monday night, the eve of the holiday.

Much alcohol flowed as the night progressed and in the morning the streets were a sea of broken bottles.

The police were put on the alert and the war of Wills began.

And yesterday, by midday, teargass was used at a number of points

FIGURE 74   Source: *Sierra Leone Daily Mail*, 23 November 1977.

but they refused to see the larger implications of such a stand. The majority of the group blamed the problem on the uncivilized conduct of their "lesser" brothers. One faction of Paddle, however, moved to select representatives from the three societies to go before the president to show that they could work together. Others objected to the idea, stating that "if you lead a horse to the water you might get kicked." They felt that the higher level of education of their membership separated them from the other groups.[7]

Paddle and Bloody Mary refused to select another occasion during 1977 for a celebration. They objected because Eid-ul-Adha was the traditional day for their masquerades. They also claimed that, as a public celebration, their masquerades should be held in the streets and not at the settlements as the government stipulated. Only Firestone decided to hold a celebration on another day in compliance with an ordinance passed, which precluded street or public processions.[8]

Control of Devil Processions

The problem of maintaining order during public celebrations touches upon several issues of government, as well as upon concerns of artistic display. On 22 March 1978 the commissioner of police held a meeting with representatives of the Egungun, Hunting, and Ode-lay societies to inform them of the regulation of masked processions. The societies welcomed the meeting because, since the previous cancellation of masquerades, they were uncertain about the government's position on permits. Aside from the political motivation behind the granting of permits, the police appeared to be genuinely concerned about public order.

At the meeting the commissioner distributed forms entitled "Permission for Masked Devil Procession" (see appendix 2). The form asserted the commissioner's power to regulate masked celebrations and specifically forbade societies from the east side of the city to enter the west side and vice versa. Specific streets were designated for masquerading, while others were designated off limits. The central part of the city was designated off limits to all masking groups. With this central area as a buffer, the authorities believed contact between the groups could be avoided.

The form set forth other requirements as well. An important requirement was that all members of celebrating societies wear uniform dress or ashoebi. The purpose of the uniforms from the point of view of the police was to make it possible to distinguish members from nonmembers in Ode-lay crowds. This regulation, it was hoped, would make it possible to report to what extent members themselves participated in street crimes. The permit also forbade groups to carry sticks, bottles, or other offensive weapons; and songs of a provocative, inflammatory, or rude nature were disallowed.[9]

The elders in attendance at the meeting with the commissioners put the responsibility for street disorders on Ode-lay members, who were in sparse attendance. The prestigious Hunting and Egungun representatives used the occasion to denounce youths and to laud their own efforts to maintain peace during the masquerades. The commissioner, for the most part, ignored this attack on youth and argued that the permits applied to all secret societies. Despite his statements, the meeting maintained an anti-Ode-lay spirit. Several police were themselves members of the older Yoruba-based societies. They apparently had forgotten their own inter-group rivalries. Their negative attitude stemmed from their social and political biases. The Egungun and Hunting associations of which they were members had denied membership to migrants, who were considered to be of a lower educational and economic status. To make matters worse, these new arrivals had then established Hunting and Egungun organizations of their own, thus exacerbating the feelings between the old and new societies.

A new application-for-permit form for holidays issued in 1978 dropped the restrictions on the movements of groups from one side of the city to the other (see appendix 3). The new guidelines were designed to keep the devils from confronting each other while allowing them to compete aesthetically with their crosstown rivals. The form stated, "Masked 'Dev-ils' and their supporters will be permitted to parade from East to West and West to East respectively in a clockwise direction along the following route. . . ." The route constituted a large, double loop, in all about ten miles long, that circumscribed the city. Devil societies could join the main route at any point, provided they moved in a clockwise direction. Civilian Rule and Rainbow performed under the guidance of the new permit in the spring of 1978, and except for the incident involving a Civilian Rule mailo jazz musician and a driver representing Rainbow, the celebrations were relatively peaceful.[10] Bloody Mary planned a presen-tation for later that year. (See figure 75.)

The elaborate procedures regarding the regulation of masquerades stemmed from police recognition that the spirited tensions of masquer-ading could develop into physical violence. Traditional medicines and the spiritual aspect of the celebrations added to this effect. The power of juweni men could cause injury to participants, and the devils could raise the anxiety level of participants. Members of one society were constantly aware of the potential for spiritual interference by another society. This spiritual aspect raised some tough legal questions for the law enforcers. If, for example, a devil was to parade without a permit, could it be arrested? The permit stated that any person who broke the rules was subject to a fine of two hundred leones or six months in prison.[11] Yet a devil was a spirit and as such fell outside the jurisdiction of men.

Potential Potential Potential
Heavy Heavy Heavy
Na We Yes

We say life is a mission, and we are after that mission.
The Super Heavy

Mission Bloody Mary

will be OUT again in Full Festac swing

On the 11th November 1978

We have been lying low in the Wilderness for-a-long
long time and now we are Coming Back on the scene with

our *Tondo Tondo Dancing*

WHAT HAS BEEN IS WHAT WILL BE, AND WHAT HAS BEEN DONE IS WHAT WILL BE DONE !
SO BROTHERS AND SISTERS LET THE IRONY OF ALL THAT HAS PASSED BE A LESSON TO ONE
AND ALL.
LET ALL GRIEVANCES SUBSIDE AND PEACE ABIDE
LET ILL FEELINGS BE ERASED, AND POSITIVE VIBRATION REIGN.

Mission Mary: Say any good Hustler must some how try
to keep on his Guard and realize that real is ofen.

*So hustle with every mustle and make the show funky. We gonna
portray the cultural heritage of our papa's land, so lets join hands
together and make the Carnival Hectic.*

Remember we say to you Goodness is a Benediction,

Padlock all the Bad Mouth so Peace must Prevail.

Mission Mary   Mission Mary   Mission Mary

AGBA   Sec Gen.   PUBLICITY MAN
WONTI (Jr.)   MOMOH "C"   MR. T

FIGURE 75   Bloody Mary poster for its 1978 masquerade. Courtesy of Bloody Mary
Ode-lay Society.

This problem surfaced when Bloody Mary "pulled" its devil without a permit for Eid-ul-Adha in 1977. They performed on the eve of the holiday, proceeding to the central part of the city on Mountain Cut Road, where they celebrated near Firestone. Later they returned home, escaping pursuit of the police. The devil was stored at the Fergeson Street settlement, but that night the police confiscated it. Members were outraged by the act; they claimed the police could not technically arrest a devil. Tensions remained high, and for several days the devil was moved from one station to another to avoid a possible attack. Finally it was returned to the society.

This incident underscores the strong cultural need for masquerades. From a Western perspective the masquerade constitutes an event, a panoply of related arts in time and space. From an African perspective this aesthetic experience also has a spiritual dimension that gives the devil its attractive power. The masquerade, as a symbol at the ancestral level and a symbol of a particular society, was an effective instrument of social expression and of control. If the government could restrict movements of the devil, it could as well maintain political hegemony over the Ode-lay societies.

The restrictions placed on masquerade societies by the government have characterized the relationship between government and secret societies from the founding of the colony. Today, as in the early days, these masking associations pose a threat to institutionalized authority. The labile nature of masquerading, its violence, and its ability to bring its participants to ecstatic states are difficult to control. In the past, legislation to suppress these groups has not been popular. Currently the All Peoples Congress party is faced with the dilemma of needing the Ode-lay societies for political support and demonstration while recognizing that their potential for organizing and pressuring the government for change is great.

The issue of masquerade permits was critical in 1977 and 1978. Behind this issue was the bid for control. If the All Peoples Congress party could control the masqueraders, it could control the secret societies.[12] That Paddle, Firestone, and Bloody Mary were denied masking permits in 1977 was a dramatic gesture on the part of the party that demonstrated its political strength. While this move did affirm APC hegemony, it also showed the ability of the young men's societies to join forces, as described in the above letter addressed to dear "Polish" friends, and must have impressed party officials, who ordered Internal Security Unit troops armed with guns and tear gas to keep the groups from masquerading.

A report written by the commissioner of police in 1978 revealed the government's willingness to reconsider masking in the streets—a sign of respect for the Ode-lay's strength and their genuine concern that events remain peaceful. The report specified which streets and directions the masquerade processions could take. If its guidelines were obeyed, the secret societies would avoid contact and the possibility of conflict.

Leaders of the Ode-lay, like those of the Hunting and, as of 1978, the Egungun societies, have made an attempt at amalgamation to strengthen their position in the patronage system. Their success in this pursuit will determine the kind of vision of reality to which they will eventually aspire. That vision, which forms around an African aesthetic religious and political sensibility, will be tempered or torn apart by an adapted vision of a life-style presented by the media in a country where economic conditions are in a state of decline.

12

Tea Kettles and
the Cooling Effects of Art

My first fieldwork in Africa was conducted from 1972 to 1973 among the Sisala people of northern Ghana. I vividly recall my small compound room in the town of Tumu. I was a tenant there and paid rent to Isaka Bujan, a local farmer from a town of four hundred. With the help of Islam and the belief in capital investment, Bujan bought yams from local farmers and sold them retail to government institutions throughout the north. On either side of my quarters were a mosque and some unfinished apartments owned by my landlord. He was visibly on the way up. His model of a successful man was a former minister of education who like himself was raised a farm boy in a small Sisala hamlet and occasionally returned to visit with his old friends in the north. He arrived in a Mercedes-Benz and slept at his large Western-style house. He had clearly made it.

A few yards from the largest mosque in town stood the main latrine, which Muslims, Christians, and traditional Sisala were all legally bound to use. Men entered and left this building with tea kettles full of water to use for cleaning. They carried the kettles everywhere. Upon entering the latrine I realized the source of their cleaning compulsion and the reason why they carried kettles wherever they went—on buses, lorries, trains, and on foot. The latrine holes had not been cleaned for weeks, because the local government could not pay the custodians for their labor. As a result, the waste had crested above the surface of the floor. The kettles, I understood, were part of a body ritual that was inspired by the town's deep-seated fear of the breakdown of the old social and moral order and the physical and spiritual contamination of a new order.

Young Sisala males left their natal villages in search of a new lifestyle, part of which they envisioned through exposure to the media. Their migration to the city destroyed the continuity between generations and, as a result, much knowledge about the visual arts of masquerading has been lost. Wherever I researched the *sikilen* masquerade or the great funerary stools once so elaborately carved, I discovered that the only remains were fragments of masks, which were no longer used in the dance, and bits and pieces of the stools, which had been propped up and tied together for the second burial rites of the deceased. No one could remember how to make these objects.[1] This visual arts tradition of Ghana had practically disappeared.

Technology could not escape the general atrophy of life in Sisalaland. North of my compound, on a hill opposite an earthen dam, were hundreds of bodies and parts of tractors long abandoned. Their rusty surfaces and cracked, rolled-steel parts, oddly enough, resembled the broken artifacts I had been researching. Even the architecture did not escape this de-plorable state. Compounds were in constant need of repair. Walls often collapsed in the rainy season to the detriment of building occupants. It was easy to see why Sisala males were eager to find a new life in the city.

Whereas the Sisala who remained in their homeland coped with ac-celerated change and cultural decline with the compulsive cleansing rite of the tea kettle, their migrant counterparts, like other Freetown migrants, strove to find a place in the city with the cooling effects of art based on traditional sources.

The preface of this book was written partly in impressionistic terms, in awe of the seething creativity in Freetown. Those opening remarks established the presence of a moral edge in urban Africa tempered by traditional African art and aesthetic sensibility. Furthermore, it was main-tained that the arts and secret societies in the nation-state fostered an African ipseity and beyond, a Pan-African identity.

I wonder now if it is too late for Africa, if a set of forces is at play that will eventually destroy anything of traditional value in its arts and culture. William Butler Yeats's prophetic words in *The Second Coming* may well apply to Africa's future: "That twenty centuries of stoney sleep / Were vexed to nightmare by a rocking cradle, / And what rough beast, its hour come round at last, / Slouches toward Bethlehem to be born?"[2] Conditions that were favorable to the arrival of a new rough beast had developed in northern Ghana when I was doing fieldwork there. Yeats's creature seemed close at hand, with the talismanic kettles as its only opposition.

My Sisala experience echoes the scatological imagery employed by Aye Kwei Armah in *The Beautyful Ones Are Not Yet Born*, a novel about life in urban Ghana in which the characters must live out their existence in what the author calls *shit*. The postcolonial order, Armah writes, caused the breakdown of African moral and ethical institutions. This resulted in a general putrefaction of society and culture. In northern Ghana waste quite literally spilled onto community space in the latrines, at once both contaminating and challenging the old social and moral order. In another book, *Why Are We So Blest?* Armah concludes that the former white colonial slaver simply had been replaced by the corrupt black politician, the only difference between the two being that the former was candid and direct in his exploitation of people.[3]

The strong-arm governments that come and go in Africa are, of course, the subject of many Neo-African literary artists. A few, like Achebe, have traced their roots to the breakdown of traditional art and culture. The stripping of an Egungun masquerader in *Things Fall Apart* has reminded many Africans, including a Sierra Leone newspaper reporter, how quickly African culture could be stripped from the landscape in the colonial era.

Without African art and ritual and without the balance, control, and individuality in community it has provided and still provides, Africa is headed for destruction. William Cook, who believed in the healing effects of art and ritual, however, has referred to Robert Thompson's remarks about the therapeutic effects of art: "Art cools the earth and makes life viable. If entertainment is cool and the nature of the act is generosity, a sharing of time and money by artist and patrons, then artistic act is profoundly moral."[4]

What is this cooling effect of art of which Thompson speaks so eloquently? The term *cool* must be a paradoxical one, for certainly the cool of the Shango dancers of Nigeria, who balance hot coals on their heads while dancing, is anything but a temperature-moderating experience. *Cool* must mean the ability to remain in control under the most heated circumstances. The potential for spilling hot coals on the body is exciting. It represents a kind of potential energy—a boulder resting at the edge of a cliff. The potential for destruction and risk is the hot side of *cool* in the Freetown masquerades. Occasionally the metaphor of fierceness becomes real, with the result that violence erupts. For Thompson this represents a cessation of the *cool,* an end to the cooling and moral effect of art.

The Nigerian Yoruba are probably different from those who are descended from the expatriated slaves of Sierra Leone. Comparative studies of these differences have not been conducted, and they remain outside the scope of this text. On firsthand observation it seems that the notion of *cool* in Freetown masquerades *is* different from that of its Nigerian-Yoruba parent culture. How does the offspring differ from its parent? What is its temperament: hot-blooded, easily upset, well organized, calculating, quiet?

The Creolized sons of the liberated slaves observe rites and rituals during their masquerades. Such observances do represent control; they frame, segment, and sequence the masquerade scenario. Yet the urban environment in Freetown and the modern nation-state have created conditions in which control is occasionally lost and violence breaks out. This may be uncool, but the Ode-lay societies in Freetown consider this a sign of their toughness. Ogun, iron, guns, hunters, and soldiers all add to the fierce aesthetic.

The secrets of Freetown masking societies are rooted in each group's concept of purity, danger, and medicine; they are also based on a common belief in the brotherhood of the group members. If a member should reveal the secret of his group, thus exposing the group's medicine, he may expect to die after his belly reacts to the destructive effects of exposure; exposure pollutes the medicine. That Freetown masquerade societies employ Ogun (god of hunting), weapons, and medicine to protect the sanctity of their brotherhood demonstrates the ingenious means they employ to protect themselves from the pollution that stems from the outside force of colonialism. Their written constitutions, guns, patronage system, and masquerades may prove to be stronger deterrents to cultural pollution than the tea kettles of northern Ghana.

Political scientists have been reluctant to include cultural systems in their analyses of African nation-states. Typically, they fail to recognize the role of culture in the formation, stabilization, and destabilization of these state systems. Regarding politics in Sierra Leone, Walter Barrows concludes:

> The most pressing challenge to political creativity in Sierra Leone is the problem of devising a set of symbols and ideas which can accommodate yet overcome its distinctive style of politics by tempering materialism with morality and utilitarianism with utopia. Development and integration depend ultimately upon the inventiveness of political elites.[5]

Where diverse ethnic and cultural systems exist, Barrows argues, there is a need for a set of symbols that can facilitate the process of national integration. He calls upon the elite to develop the means by which this integration can be achieved. He has placed this burden squarely on the shoulders of the government while underestimating or perhaps overlooking what the urban secret societies and their branches throughout the country have done to provide a national cultural and social base.

Drawing from traditions of the repatriated slaves and the dance companies of the 1930s, the Ode-lay societies have provided an association that meets the needs of the younger population irrespective of ethnicity. These persons have left their rural lifestyles and have entered the national urban mainstream. That Ode-lay groups hold celebrations on Islamic holidays, Christian holidays, and political occasions both in Freetown and in what were once called the provinces is important for the creation of a stable government and national integration. Only a stable government can deal with the problems of development. But Ode-lay societies are only part of the picture, for the rural Poro societies and other groups of Yoruba descent have also played an integrative role. With respect to the future, however, the increase in unemployment and continued migration of the young to Freetown and secondary cities means that the

Ode-lay societies might well play a larger role in meeting the expressive needs of the people and might in turn exert greater pressure on the government.

It came as no surprise in 1981 that William Q. Tolbert, Jr., the president of Liberia, was assassinated by a 28-year-old sergeant. The assassin's age, rank, and background are similar to those of most Ode-lay members. Although Ode-lay groups have personal contacts in Monrovia, the capital of Liberia, it remains to be seen how broad the network of young men's societies is in that country—if it exists there at all—and what role, if any, it might have played in the assassination. Another interesting point of speculation is whether the assassination would have occurred at all if that country had had such a broadly based young men's society.

The development of Ode-lay culture in the urban environment is a fait accompli, and strong ties have been established with the rest of the country. Within Ode-lay art, music, and celebrations, a large part of the population has identified a common ground. One must give credit to the All Peoples Congress party for acknowledging this phenomenon and for its ability to fit it within a patronage system. Successful celebrations of the Ode-lay societies in Freetown and of its sister societies in Kenema, Kono, Mekene, and Port Loko have furthered the cause of the APC. The masquerade held in Kenema by Back to Power is just one example that illustrates the close relations between the government and these urban groups. The forces that have brought the Ode-lay and the APC together are dynamic, and one might question how long the two groups can continue in a working relationship. This depends upon the wisdom of the government elite. The events in Liberia have served the APC with notice of the grave consequences that may arise when culture and government are alienated from one another.

Beyond the realm of national politics, Ode-lay art represents the essence of an African aesthetic sensibility. The impetus for the development of the elaborate Ode-lay costumes and mailo jazz is found, not in the desire to imitate outside cultures, but rather in the desire of young people to adapt traditional culture to the urban environment. Moreover, the excitement of the emphatic visual presence of the costumes and the mailo jazz sound mark a persistent African penchant for interrelating the arts, drama, and ritual on occasions of celebration. Spectators and actors alike take part in this comprehensive experience. With all the senses tuned to the celebration, participants become one with the performance. This is why Ode-lay art is so powerful. The objectivity of the analytical perspective, which organizes artistic phenomena into discrete categories, has little application to this oneness of experience. Indeed, the whole is greater than the sum of its parts. With what we have called the gestalt perception, Ode-lay art reaches beyond ethnicity and religion. Thus Temne, Mende, Krio, and Limba of traditional Christian or Islamic background can all share in an intense expressive experience.

From the early years of the Great Experiment through confrontation with missionaries and government, Freetown secret societies have been treated ambivalently by men of authority. Recall, for example, the murders committed before World War II,[6] which the government blamed on secret societies. Despite the condemnation of these crimes, the public supported the rights of masquerade societies to meet and celebrate in public places and thus opposed a government campaign to ban masquerades. In Western terms the right to masquerade might be compared to the right of freedom of assembly.

The government's ambivalence toward masquerades stems from a contradiction between African and Western concepts of governance and arts in the social-cultural matrix. Freetown secret societies, in the words of Boyce, do constitute a government within a government.[7] Their arts, constitutions, religion, and concepts of medicine infringe upon unique, separate Western institutions that have been adopted from colonial times. The masquerade societies do not function within well-defined lines; and, as such, their labile borders are a cause for concern to those who rule under cleanly defined and separately derived Western institutions.

The first years of the Great Experiment demonstrated the modus operandi of colonization. The British believed the medium of monumental architecture would effect the European-style outpost they desired and felt was necessary to feed its industry at home. Schools, warehouses, jails, courthouses, government facilities, and churches were the primary forms of building. To convince the Africans that God was, indeed, on the side of British and Western society, churches were at first hastily built of mud and wattle construction. These proved ineffective, however, to quote the Reverend G. Lane:

> This is killing work! Our country-built chapels require great exertion of the lungs . . . to make the words distinctly to be heard. . . . There is nothing in [them] to act as a conductor. Nay, [they are as unapt to sound as the African's mind (generally) is to comprehend.[8]

The African "temple" described by Lane was not suited for analytical rationalist discourse concerning the Word of God and, concomitantly, the word of Western society. African architecture may distinguish between ritual and profane space, yet it does not confine ritual and religious activities. Masquerades, for example, which are a primary tool of enculturation, define open, closed, and fluid space by movement, whereas fixed Western architecture defines the motion of its occupants. In the African tradition, motion defines space; in the Western tradition, space defines motion.

The predisposition of masquerades to move on and off a "stage" frustrated European attempts to abolish these indigenous cultural-political institutions. Masqueraders appeared and disappeared before the white man, as in guerilla warfare, interrupting sermons *inside* from *outside*. It occurred to missionaries that the only recourse was to take the masqueraders house by house, visiting individual compounds and confiscating masking accoutrements.

In Freetown, worship, debate, role-playing, and expressive behavior during masquerades all define the space they require. The introduction of European architecture may be seen as an attempt by the colonial powers to contain specialized behaviors inside separate and discrete spaces. Justice was to be exercised in the court, religious sentiment in the church, family concerns in the home, education in the school, and the arts in the theater or museum. The masquerade, on the other hand, provided the context for all these behaviors. In so doing, it lessened the hardship of sweeping discontinuities introduced by specialized Western societies. African arts, in their ritual context, carried the weight of a civilization opposed to the very spirit of its colonial subjugators.

Western architectural space and space determined by traditional African masquerades coexist in Freetown. Ironically the postcolonial leadership, including the All Peoples Congress party and the Sierra Leone Peoples party, has taken the position of the former British leadership with regard to imposing architecture, such as the new city hall and the parliament, which overlooks Freetown from a distant hill. Like the early missionaries, contemporary government recognizes that architecture controls behavior and provides a set of visual symbols representing its authority.

Linked to architecture was and is the concern for a Western style of education, with its emphasis on the written word. Both the courts and the Church depend upon literacy to further their cause. Opposed to this manner of wielding authority, traditional Yoruba-descended Africans stress the importance of dance, music, song, and the visual elements of the masquerade to organize society and provide models of behavior that are based upon traditional values.

The bid for control of masquerade groups is symbolic of the two different approaches to organizing society. The resolution of the conflict between society membership and the government elite will provide a basis for a post-neocolonial African society. What its character will be and whether or not it can be accomplished in Sierra Leone remains to be seen. Conflict of this order has occurred and is occurring elsewhere in West Africa and, indeed, in the Caribbean, where other Creole societies were also born of the black diaspora. Currently it is an issue where Caribbean migrants stage masquerades in London, Toronto, Miami, and Brooklyn. As this conflict continues, questions of the relationship between art and politics will become increasingly important in the study of Third World societies.

Appendix 1

Freetown Masking Societies in 1978 by Ward

WEST I

Type	Name	Address	Head
Ode-lay	Civilian Rule	Kroo Bay	Banki
	Red Indians	Barne Street	Abdul
	Bantus	Main Road, Ascension Town	Matamboy
	Nongowha	Main Road, Congo Town	Kanehka
	"E" Lef Pan Yu	Main Road, Ascension Town	Johny Banko
Hunting	Congo Town	Main Road, Ascension Town	Vincent
	Urban	Brookfields	?
	Urban I	Hennesy Street	King
	Brookfields	Brookfields	?
Egungun	Old Rising Oje	Hennesy Street	Campbell

WEST II

Type	Name	Address	Head
Ode-lay	Bloody Mary	Phillip Street	Wonti George
	Black Stone	?	?
Hunting	Egba I.H.S.	Jones Street	?
	Egba II	Fergusson Street	Sabalu Decker
	Egba III	Fergusson Street	Charlie King
	Decker	Elizabeth Street	Decker
	Grassfield II	Sankee Street	Mr. Jones
	Grassfield I	John Street	Olohun Ojeh
Egungun	Limba Oje II	Peter Lane	Kabba
	Logoo W. Awodie	Fergusson Street	Johny Sawyerr
	Sabanoh	Thomas Street	?
Other	Black Star Jolly	?	?
	Egunugu	Campbell Street	Taylor
	Enshor	Peter Lane	Kabba
	Ehyoh	?	?
	Masianday Jolly	Peter Lane	Bruma ?

WEST III

Type	Name	Address	Head
Ode-lay	Dortington	Freetown Road	Momodu Dumbuya
Hunting	Arthur Lewis H.S.	Sumerset Street	Arthur Lewis
	Cole Farm	?	?
	Lumley	Freetown Road	Goldstone
	Wilberforce	Regent Road	Mr. Keitell
Egungun	Murray Town Oje	Milton Street	Dosuma
	Egba I	Sumerset Street	Noah
	Aberdeen	Cape Road	?
Other	Sunshine Jolly	Irelauney Street	Oduntor
	Arishola	?	Tamu
	Aberdeen Rd. Ehyoh	Macauley Street	?
	Aree Shola	Sharp Street	Alusine Koonta
	Bonically	Sharp Street	Mornoh
	Lumley Ehyoh	Main Road, Lumley	Kabba

EAST I

Type	Name	Address	Head
Ode-lay	Education	Upper Savage Square	Okone (leading officer)
	Maju Mao National	Canton Street	Boy Maneh
	Gladiators	Humphrey Lane	Bamie
	Tagbota	Cline Town	Leweh
Egungun	Hastings Descendant	Oldfield Street	York
	Kossoh Town Oje	Lucas Street	Rashidu Thomas
	Aric Adaba	Malta Street	Mansaray
	Tourist Oje	Savage Square	Abdul Mahk
	Ari Elephant	Lucas Street	Fijabi
	Biafra	Fly Street	Ashim
	Awodie	Fly Street	Sherifu Carew
	Kolleh	Green Street	Sumoila
	Kanikay	Cline Town	Amadu Lelleh
Hunting	Omo Jessah	Ingham Street	Aruna Wilson
	"E" Jessah	Easton Street	?
	Midlands	Savage Square	Abudun Robinson

EAST II

Type	Name	Address	Head
Ode-lay	Firestone	Owen Street	Amadu Kanu
	Paddle Society	Hagan Street	Abdul Banta Sesay
	Kalabush	Guard Street	Sanpha
Egungun	Navy	Mill Street	Ansumana Bangura
	Marampa Oje	Upper Patton Street	Man Na Hose
	Ayeba	Mountain Cut	?
	Limba I	Owen Street	?
	Young Rising I (Kolleh Oje)	?	?
	Young Rising II	Montague Street	Bruma Bataline
Hunting	Odileh Hunters	Garber Lane	Pa Walker
Other	High Way Jolly	Owen Street	Pa Lokosi
	Upper Regent Rd. Egunugu	Upper Regent	Abibafu Martin
	Aree Orba	Rocklyn Street	Jalleh
	"E" Lainshu	Mountain Cut	?
	Owo Lankeh	Upper Patton Street	Maruf Rahman
	Unity (BoniKalli)	Moa Wharf	Hasan Bangurah

EAST III

Type	Name	Address	Head
Ode-lay	Liner	?	William George
	Mexico	New Castle Street	Baraylor ?
	Apollo	Kissy Brook	Aruna
Egungun	Adelekun	Thompson Street, Kissy	Adebi King
	Sabanoh	New Castle Street	Sanah Bailey
	Upsie Limba	William Street	Sunny John
	Eboe Town	Davies Street	"EW" Gray
Hunting	Eboe Town Hunting	Winter Street	P. J. C. Thompson
	Konsho	Arch Street	Sanah Bailey
	Luna St. Hunting	Winter Street	Balogun Lewis
	Okormor	Lunar Street	Frank Vincent
	Back St.	Back Street	William Davies
Other	Bonikalli	Leaden Hall Street	Assana ?
	Low Cost Jolly	Low Cost Housing	Roger

CENTRAL I

Type	Name	Address	Head
Ode-lay	Japan	Fisher Street	?
	Rainbow	East Brook Lane	Okin
	Sangai Joe	Lumley Street	Aruna Tokora
	Kaibara City	Circular Road	Morgan
	Tetina Boys	Mends Street	?
	Sukuma Boys	Mends Street	Ensly Dwdas
Egungun	Obasie	Frederick Street	Alie Kundoh
	Seaside	East Brook Street	Sidi Body
	O. K. Mori	Circular Road	Hara Gibril
Hunting	Oke Mori	Allen Street	Pa Thompson
	Lord Have Marcy	Soldier Street	Brah Foday
Other	Arishola	Sackville Street	Dauda Bangura

Appendix 2

Permission for Masked Devil Procession

To: ....
   ....
   ....

[1.]   In exercise of the powers conferred upon me by Sub-Section (2) of Section 17 of the Public Order Act No. 46 of 1965, permission is hereby granted to your society members to process along certain areas of FREETOWN on Monday, 27th March 1978, subject to the following conditions:

(i) The procession shall NOT start before 0800 hrs. (8 a.m.) and shall finish NOT later than 1900 hrs. (7 p.m.)

(ii) If your group is at the East End of Freetown your members will NOT process past the following places:
   (a) Top of Circular Road at its junction with Macauley Street
   (b) Garrison Street

(iii) If your group is at the West End of Freetown your members will NOT process past the following places:
   (a) Circular Road at its junction with Model School and Tower Hill Road
   (b) Pademba Road and Siaka Stevens Street at their junction at the Cotton Tree
   (c) The whole of State Avenue
   (d) The whole of Walpole Street

(iv) Your members are banned from processing into the centre of Freetown bounded by:
   (a) Walpole Street (Top and Bottom)
   (b) Lightfoot-Boston Street
   (c) Wallace-Johnson Street at its junction with Walpole Street up to Little East Street
   (d) East Street and Little East Street
   (e) Wilberforce Street, Howe Street, Charlotte Street, Gloucester Street
   (f) State Avenue and Independence Avenue.

(v) You should as far as practicable let all your members wear a uniform dress (ashoebi) to facilitate identification

(vi) You should by all means avoid unruly gangs joining your own group and you should limit the size of the procession

(vii) You should appoint several *marshals* with distinctive identification to control your group

(viii) No members of your group will carry sticks, bottles, or any other implement or offensive weapons

(ix) No provocative, inflammatory, or rude songs should be sung

(x) Members of your group should refrain from molesting other groups
    or other members of the public
(xi) Your group should NOT unduly obstruct vehicular traffic
(xii) All members of your group will comply with all lawful instructions
     given by Police personnel on duty.

2.   For your guidance, copy of sections 6, 16, 17, 18, 19, and 20 relating to
processions etc. under the Public Order Act No. 46 of 1965 is attached hereto.
3.   This permit must be carried by the leader of your procession and must
be produced to the Police for inspection.
4.   Breach of any of the conditions of this permit will result to its withdrawal
and all members of your group will be required to disperse immediately; refused
of which may result to the relevant law being invoked.

                                                (E. A. Coker)
                                        for Ag. Commissioner of Police.

Appendix 3

POLICE PUBLIC NOTICE
MASKED DEVILS

As already announced, in view of the co-operation obtained from all the masked "devils" and their supporters who were permitted to parade Freetown on Easter Monday last, the Police now intend to relax the restriction placed on the movement of masked "Devils" and their supporters for the Republican Day Anniversary celebrations April, 1978.

Masked "Devils" and their supporters will be permitted to parade from East to West and West to East respectively in a Clockwise direction along the following route:

(a) Fourah Bay Road Eastwards to
(b) Ross Road then to
(c) Kissy Road
(d) Up Mountain Cut
(e) Macauley Street
(f) then left into Circular Road
(g)   ″   ″   ″   Pademba Road
(h) then to Campbell Street
(i)   ″   ″   Sanders Street
(j) Siaka Stevens Street
(k) Wilberforce Street
(l) Kissy Street
(m) Fourah Bay Road

Masked "Devils" and their supporters from Streets which adjoin the main route already mentioned will join the main route at any point but the direction of movement should be in the same clockwise direction already listed. No devils and their supporters will be permitted to travel in the opposite direction to that already prescribed.

Appendix 4

Minutes of Meeting between Representatives of Eastern Paddle Society, Firestone Hunting Society and Bloody Mary Hunting Society Held at the Community Centre on Thursday 17th November 1977.

The meeting started at 6.05 hrs with the offering of Silent Prayers followed by an introductory speech by the Chairman, Mr. Abdul Sesay, outlining the objective for which the meeting was convened. The Chairman spoke about the difficulties which have plagued the three groups as a result of the wide scale thuggery and violence demonstrated by some unscrupulous members of similar societies during processions on Public Holidays. The Chairman appealed for cooperation from all angles with a view to the promotion of a successful masquerade procession on the day of the feast of Eid ul-Adha. He went on further to admonish members that masquerading in the form of mask devils should not be regarded as a foolish affair and that all seriousness and devotion should be invested in it. To buttress his point, the Chairman informed the meeting that a gentleman from the University of Illinois has come all the way from America for the purpose of witnessing the masquerade procession of the Eastern Paddle Society this year with a view to the preparation of a comprehensive report as part of his thesis, which he is presently writing up. The Chairman appealed for unity and cooperation and to show more restraint in avoiding open confrontation between different groups but instead to dance in between ourselves whenever two groups come in contact with each other during processions.

The Chairman suggested that football matches and picnics could be arranged, as these could be effective weapons for the promotion of unity and cooperation among the members of the different groups. The suggestion was acclaimed by members. Satti Sesay of the Bloody Mary group supported all what the Chairman had said and also reiterated the appeal for unity and cooperation. He went on further to appeal to members to keep a watchful interest to the advantage of other groups as a whole. He appealed for togetherness and a fusion of all groups if possible during processions.

Prince Nicol was the next speaker. He said that Sierra Leone is just one unit incorporating various groups, which in effect meant that every body belong to the same family. He implored the meeting that every thing should be done within the limit of possibility in order to create surprises in the minds of those who have already started cherishing the belief that there will be a lot of fighting on the day of the forth-coming procession.

He ended up his speech by advising members to keep a watchful eye on those whom we have always regarded as trouble-makers.

Mr. Alusine Kamara of the Eastern Paddle Society informed the meeting that the Paddle society is already in possession of identity cards. He went on further to inform the society that his society have [sic] always provided between 20 and 30 marshals on the day of its processions, whose duty it is to aid the Police in their work. He further remarked that the results at the end have been very satisfactory.

Mr. Prince Nicol of the Bloody Mary group moved that the three groups of Eastern Paddle Society, Firestone Hunting Society, and Bloody Mary Hunting Society should provide three bottles of champaigne each for the purpose of sealing the bond of friendship when the groups come into contact on the day of the procession.

The motion was passed. Mr. Jokosene of the Bloody Mary group suggested a similar arrangement on the eve of the procession, but it was decided to concentrate on the purchasing of the three bottles for the day of the procession.

Mr. Lasisi of the Fire Stone Hunting group moved that on the day of the procession, no one should be allowed to be in possession of offensive weapons such as sticks, broken bottles, knives, and swords. This met with tremendous applause from members and the motion was passed.

Mr. Harouna Conteh of the Eastern Paddle society then addressed the meeting. In his speech he said that the time has now come when one society's affair should be the concern of other societies. He suggested that in relation to the application for permit, all applications should come from a common source and with the inception of the present meeting similar ones should be convened where members could submit for discussion whatever complaints or grievances they had. He ended up by saying that with this kind of approach a carnival could be staged by the different societies and visits made to the State House to apprise the President of the transition which we are now trying to build.

The   *Chairman*   *Secretary*

The following motion was put to the meeting and passed:

The motion reads: On behalf of our jointed societies—

> Eastern Paddle Society,
> Firestone Hunting Society, and
> Bloody Mary Hunting Society,

We, the undersigned hereby move that as of today 17 November 1977 we will live in peace, harmony, and brotherliness in the history of Sierra Leone and its people not only to feed our own selfish ends but to entertain the people of Sierra Leone at all times for the socio-economic progress of our New Republic.

We also affirm that in our process of entertaining we will refrain from violence, petty jealousies, and self-aggrandisement for the good of all who listen and watch the peaceful progress of our societies.

We do solemnly declare:

Abdul Bunta Sesay
G. T. Coker   } Eastern Paddle Society.

Amadu Kanu
Abdul Mustar   } Firestone Hunting Society.

Wonthi George
Prince Nicol   } Bloody Mary Hunting Society.

Notes

Preface

1. John Nunley, "Implications of the African Aesthetic Impulse for Pan African Art," *New Art Examiner* 6 (1975): 5, 9.
2. Carl Jung, *The Spirit of Man in Art and Literature* (New York: Pantheon, 1966), p. 133.
3. Jean Rouch, *Les Maîtres Fous* (Ghana, West Africa, 1953). See the film review by Jean Claude Muller in *American Anthropologist* 73:6 (1971): 1471–73.
4. Research by the author among the Sisala of northern Ghana was carried out from December 1972 through August 1973. The focus of the project was on the problems of specialized artistry in a nonspecialized society. See John Nunley, "Sisala Sculpture of Northern Ghana" (Ph.D. diss., University of Washington, 1977).
5. See P. Ben-Amos, *The Art of Benin* (New York: Thames & Hudson, 1980); D. Fraser and H. Cole, eds., *African Art and Leadership* (Madison: University of Wisconsin Press, 1972); R. F. Thompson, *Black Gods and Kings: Yoruba Art at UCLA* (Los Angeles: University of California Press, 1971).
6. The author witnessed the spring 1978 referendum, which was accompanied by mass Ode-lay demonstrations. From November 1977 to the following spring, a major theme of masking associations was the coming of the one-party state.
7. Graham Greene, *The Heart of the Matter* (London: Heinemann, 1959), pp. 35–36.

Chapter 1

1. John Peterson, *Province of Freedom: A History of Sierra Leone, 1787–1870* (London: Faber & Faber, 1969), p. 17.
2. Ibid., p. 19.
3. Ibid., p. 20.
4. Ibid.
5. Ibid., p. 28.
6. Ibid., p. 31.
7. Ibid., p. 34.
8. Ibid., p. 13.
9. Lt.-Col. Dixon Denham to R. W. Hays, 21 January 1827, Public Record Office, Kew Gardens, London (hereafter cited as PRO), CO/323/148, pp. 536–37.
10. Ibid., p. 592.
11. G. Lane, Journal, Methodist Missionary Society Papers (hereafter MMS), box 279, file 2, no. 28,

School of Oriental and African Studies, London.

12. Mr. McCaulay, private correspondence, PRO, CO/323/151, p. 214.

13. MMS, box 279, file 3, no. 48.

14. Rev. R. Amos to Fathers, 3 May 1842, MMS, box 281, file 2, no. 13.

15. Ibid.

16. The *Missionary Register* (London: Church Missionary Society, 1828), pp. 274–76.

17. PRO, FO/84/38, p. 186.

18. Gov. Sir Neil Campbell to Bathurst, Report of 20 January 1827, PRO, CO/267/81.

19. The full text has been published as "Joseph Wright of the Egba," in *Africa Remembered: Narratives by West Africans from the Era of the Slave Trade*, ed. Philip Curtin (Madison: University of Wisconsin Press, 1967), pp. 317–33. For the original text, see Joseph Wright, "Life of Joseph Wright, A Native Ackoo," 26 June 1839, MMS, box 280, file 3, no. 13.

20. Wright, "Life of Joseph Wright," p. 1.

21. Ibid., p. 14.

22. Ibid.

23. Ibid., p. 21.

24. Ibid., p. 26.

25. General Census of the Colony, MMS, box 279, file 2, no. 3.

26. Blue Book, Sierra Leone, 1824, PRO, CO/272/1.

27. D. M. Hamilton to Foreign Office, Report of January 1825, PRO, FO/84/38, no. 5, p. 12.

28. MMS, box 281, file 5, no. 47.

29. Wright, "Life of Joseph Wright," p. 29.

30. T. Edwards, Report, MMS, box 28, file 3, no. 21.

31. R. Dillon, Report, MMS, box 286, file 1, no. 53.

32. *Missionary Register* (1837): 180.

33. Ibid., p. 423.

34. Ibid.

35. R. Dillon to [————], 18 August 1857, MMS, box 282, file 7, no. 34.

36. E. Mark to [————], 19 March 1858, MMS, box 286, file 7, no. 22.

37. *Gleaner Pictorial Album* (London: Church Missionary Society, 1887), vol. 1, plate 13.

38. Mr. Kissling, Report of 25 March 1838, *Missionary Register* (1839), p. 117.

39. Mr. Kissling, "Idolatrous Practices of the Unconverted Natives," ibid. (1840).

40. Ibid.

41. See also n. 19 above.

42. Mr. Schön, "Instance of Continuance of Idol Worship," *Missionary Register* (1833), p. 359.

43. J. G. Macauley, Report, *Proceedings of the Church Missionary Record* (1863), p. 10.

44. For a discussion of role reversals as symbols of death, see John Nunley, "Sisala Sculpture of Northern Ghana" (Ph.D. diss., University of Washington [Seattle], 1977); see also Jack Goody, *Death, Property, and the Ancestors: A Study of the Mortuary Customs of the Lodagaa of West Africa* (Stanford: Stanford University Press, 1962).

45. Rev. T. Edwards to his father, 3 May 1839, MMS, box 28, file 3, no. 21.

46. Peterson, *Province of Freedom*, p. 212.

47. Abraham Potts to Mr. Metlings, 18 June 1827, PRO, CO/267/82.

48. Ibid., 19 June.

49. Ibid., 18 June.

50. Chief Supt. Denham, Report of 30 July 1827, PRO, CO/267/82.

51. Ibid.

52. Ibid.

53. Peterson, *Province of Freedom*, pp. 211–12.

54. This complaint was heard frequently by Rev. Fletcher, who conducted weekly idol purges in various parts of Freetown. See MMS, box 282, file 3, no. 14.

55. E. Dannatt, Report, MMS, box 283, file 1872–73, no. 24.

56. Ibid. Dannatt's use of the term *tribe* refers to those repatriated Africans

who settled in the colony villages and were descendants of Yoruba, Ibibio, Ibo, and other ethnic groups of Nigeria.

57. Rev. Thorpe to MMS, ibid., 14 June 1872.

58. *Sierra Leone Weekly News* (hereafter *SLWN*), 19 January 1889. Many early Sierra Leone newspaper records are found at the British Newspaper Library, London (Colindale). Their microfilm deposit number is M.C. 1812.

Chapter 2

1. For an excellent discussion of settlement planning of the colony, see Peter K. Mitchell, "Eighteenth and Nineteenth Century Printed Maps of Sierra Leone: A Preliminary Listing," *Sierra Leone Studies* 22 (1968): 60.

2. For several essays covering all aspects of urban planning and the problems of a developing city, see Christopher Frye and Eldred Jones, eds., *Freetown: A Symposium* (Freetown: Sierra Leone University Press, 1968).

3. For a map showing the population density, see ibid., p. 182.

4. Robert Wellesley Cole, *Kossoh Town Boy* (Cambridge: Cambridge University Press, 1960), p. 21.

5. Ibid., p. 22.

6. Ibid., p. 64.

7. Ibid., p. 126.

8. Michael Banton, *West African City: A Study of Tribal Life in Freetown* (London: Oxford University Press, 1957), pp. 186–95.

9. Cole, *Kossoh Town Boy*, p. 128.

10. "Heathenizing Christian Officers," *SLWN*, 11 October 1919, p. 4.

11. J.B.C., "Gang of Young Hooligans, A Grave Peril," ibid., 10 March 1917, p. 9.

12. Ibid., p. 13.

13. "High Handed Robbery," ibid., 22 November 1919, pp. 8–9.

14. "Native Customs," *Sierra Leone Guardian* (hereafter *SLG*), 28 February 1913, p. 4.

15. "Would It Pay for Sierra Leone to Become Pagan," ibid., 25 July 1913.

16. "Better Knowledge of Oku Languages," ibid., 28 February 1919.

17. Ibid., 4 April 1919.

18. *SLWN*, 17 May 1919.

19. *Colony and Provincial Reporter*, 6 December 1913, p. 4.

20. "The Native Comedy Co.," ibid., 30 May 1914, p. 4.

21. Abdul Haqq, "Islamism and the Muslim People," ibid., 20 October 1917.

22. "African Comedy Co.," *SLG*, 21 May 1915, p. 5.

23. "Nicol's Electric Cinema," *SLWN*, 4 September 1915, p. 4.

24. "Announcement," *Sierra Leone Daily Mail* (hereafter *SLDM*), 24 June 1939.

25. Sierra Leone Legislative Council, Minutes, 1933–39, PRO, CO/270/75, 1937–38, p. 16.

26. Banton, *West African City*, p. 176.

27. "The Christmas of 1939," *SLWN*, 25 December 1939.

28. "The Unlawful Societies Ordinance, 1942," ibid., 9 May 1942.

29. Sierra Leone Legislative Council, Minutes, 1940–45, 12 May 1942, PRO, CO/270/79.

30. "Wastrels in the Community," *SLWN*, 26 October 1940, p. 6.

31. "Caution—All Is Not Well," ibid., 14 June 1941.

32. "The Crime Wave," ibid., 5 May 1945, p. 7.

33. "Gangs Come to Town," ibid., 22 September 1945, p. 7.

34. "Members of Alikali Society Fined 3 Pounds for Unlawful Assault," *SLDM*, 3 May 1947.

35. "The Dancing Craze in the City of Freetown," *SLWN*, 14 March 1942, p. 6.

36. "At the Pictures," ibid., 6 November 1943.

37. "Empire Cinema," *SLDM*, 8 December 1942.

38. "Sackville Saloon Bar," ibid., 3 October 1941.

39. "The Happy Eight Youth Songo Club," ibid., 10 April 1943.

40. "Empire Cinema," ibid., 28 April 1944.

41. Ibid., 6, 24 September, 16 November 1946.

42. "The Cinema and Its Influence on African Life," ibid., 9 September 1944.

43. "Cinema House in Building," *SLWN*, 1 December 1945, p. 1.

44. Crito, "The Challenge of the Agoo-goo Society," *SLDM*, 24 March 1950.

45. "What Is This Bundo?" ibid., 7 April 1955.

46. "Xmas Festivities in Pictures," ibid., 28 December 1955.

47. *The Report of the Commission of Inquiry into Disturbances in the Provinces in November 1955 and March 1956* (London: Crown Agents, 1956), p. 77.

48. Kenneth Little, "The Political Function of the Poro," *Africa* 15 (1965), 16 (1966).

49. *SLDM*, 16 January 1959.

50. "Ban All Useless and Aimless Clubs," ibid., 4 January 1958.

51. "Headline," ibid., 18, 19 March 1961.

52. "Roxy Theatre," ibid., 2, 5 January 1961.

53. Ibid., 27 May 1961.

54. "Boxing Day—They Celebrated with Masks and Dancing," ibid., 28 December 1962.

55. Ibid., 26 December 1961.

56. "Alikali Boys in Court," ibid., 30 April 1963.

57. Ibid.

58. "Police State Rules for Lantern Parade," ibid., 30 December 1967.

59. See chap. 12 below.

60. "Today Is Lantern Day," *SLDM*, 1 January 1968.

61. "200 Masqueraders Rounded Up," ibid., 31 December 1968.

62. "Clash at East End," ibid., 2 January 1969.

63. "Youths Held at Ministerial Building," ibid., 1 January 1969.

64. "Masqueraders Treated for Stab Wounds," ibid., 30 April 1969.

65. "Masked Devils Stripped Naked," ibid., 29 April 1969.

66. "Independence Day Tragedy," ibid., 29 April 1970.

67. "Police Beaten," ibid., 28 December 1970.

68. "First Vice President and Prime Minister," ibid., 26 April 1971.

69. Ibid., 1 January 1973.

70. "Appeal to Masqueraders, Mask Devils," ibid., 24 December 1973.

Chapter 3

1. See chap. 8 below.

2. Several authors have noted that Egungun and Gelede female officers in Nigeria play an important role in society presentations. The name for the Yoruba officers is phonetically similar to the Freetown word. Drewal and Drewal have diagrammed an Egungun social structure calling the head female *Iyaagan*. See Drewal and Drewal, "More Powerful Than Each Other: An Egbado Classification of Egungun," *African Arts* 3 (1978): 98.

3. Banton, *West African City*, p. 171.

4. Ibid., p. 172.

5. Announcements like this issued by Civilian Rule in 1978 were routinely circulated by all secret societies.

6. Drewal and Drewal, "More Powerful Than Each Other," p. 33, state that the *onidan* possess an almost unlimited number of miracles. These acts of magic are commonly performed by masqueraders who undergo several transformations in costume and spirit to prove their abilities. See also Marilyn Houlberg, "Egungun Masquerades of the Remo Yoruba," *African Arts* 3 (1978): 26.

7. For this account I am indebted to Ajagunsi of Hastings, who is considered to be the most powerful living medicine man of the Yoruba-descended societies. Ajagunsi's Christian name is David Nelson Brown.

8. Peterson, *Province of Freedom*, p. 266.

9. Ibid., p. 253.

10. Ibid., p. 255.

11. Johnny Shaft (a society alias) to author, interview, 1978, Freetown.

12. Emile Durkheim, *Division of Labor in Society,* trans. George Simpson (New York: Macmillan Co., 1933), pp. 109–16.

13. Ibid., pp. 246–47.

14. Banton, *West African City,* pp. 181–83.

15. See chap. 9 below for a more detailed discussion of this point.

Chapter 4

1. Graham Greene, *The Heart of the Matter,* p. xiv.

2. Eid ul-Adha is a major Islamic holiday, during which followers who cannot make the trip to Mecca instead offer sacrifices to show their humility.

3. Banton, *West African City,* pp. 172–73.

4. The term *taingaise* refers to elders, whose out-of-date fashion and general manner are sources of amusement to the younger generation. See chap. 5 below for more on this event.

5. See William Siegmann and Judith Perani, "Men's Masquerades of Sierra Leone and Liberia," *African Arts* 9 (1976): 42–47, for further discussion of the role of masquerading at the Kenema Fair.

6. Many documents concerning Paddle and its members were held by one of the society's leading officers. The author was fortunate to have read some of these papers.

7. Anonymous member of Paddle to author, interview, 12 January 1978.

8. Ibid.

9. Peterson, *Province of Freedom,* p. 87.

10. *Sierra Leone Gazette,* 29 August 1968. On the same page of the *Gazette* the Tourist Egungun Society was listed, some thirty years after the society was founded. The year

1968 stands out as the time when secret societies sought official recognition; the same year marked the rise of the APC party. Like the Ode-lay societies, Tourist stated that its objectives were to give financial and moral assistance to members in time of stress.

11. See chap. 1 above.

12. I am fortunate to have had an opportunity to read some of the Paddle Society minutes. Minutes pertaining to its customs are presented here; others concerning its political nature are discussed in chap. 11 below. See also appendix 4.

13. That artist may well have been Eku Williams, who, it was claimed, had introduced carved headpieces to the Hunting societies.

14. See chap. 9 below for further discussion of this event.

15. The Jolly circular headpieces with conical caps were known as pumpkin heads.

16. T. O. Ranger, *Dance and Society in Eastern Africa, 1890–1970: The Beningoma* (Berkeley: University of California Press, 1975), p. 78. Ranger noted that a dominant Western theme in the Beni dance associations of East Africa was the American cowboy, probably stimulated by Wild West films. The films' impact seemed to have reached both sides of the African continent simultaneously.

17. John Nunley, "Sisala Sculpture of Northern Ghana," pp. 111–12.

18. Johnny Shaft to author, interview, 9 January 1978.

19. S. Benedict-Sam, in "What Meaneth This Rasta Faying?" (*Sunday We Yone,* 18 December 1977), wrote: "Slowly, but in-exorably the Rastafarian breeze is creeping over Freetown, with its accompanying far-reaching implication." Citing the popular recorded music of Jamaican singers Peter Tosh, Jimmy Cliff, and the late Bob Marley, the article focused on the ideals of the move-

ment, questioning how Creoles and other peoples of Freetown could embrace the smoking of marijuana, the dirty dreadlock hairstyle, and the negative attitude toward work when the work ethic and desire for material wealth were so prevalent in the city. Though Benedict-Sam doubted the sincerity of the youth in their adaptation of rasta doctrines, he praised the movement: "Boosting the African image and the world Black Community at large, the Jamaican Reggae-Rasta artists are doing to the Black man what freedom-fighters in Biko's line did."

20. Shaft to author, interview.

21. S. Benedict-Sam, "We must Bridge This Generation Gap" (*Sunday We Yone,* 14 June 1978), reported that this gap reminded him of Okonkwo in Chinua Achebe, *Things Fall Apart* (New York: Astor-Honor, 1959), a classic African novel about the collapse of Ibo culture in the colonial period. Okonkwo, who represents the old order, despises his son for joining the Church. Their opposing views on religion make the father-son relationship irreconcilable.

22. At the time of my departure from Freetown in 1978, a load of timber for boat construction had been delivered to the settlement.

23. An account of this event appears in chap. 5.

24. See preface, n. 7.

25. Since many members of Rainbow are Temne, it is not inconceivable that the coffin may have been associated with a Temne ordeal called an-binto, in which, in an effort to locate a guilty party or a source of illness, two persons would carry an empty coffin containing hair and nail clippings wrapped in white satin. The coffin would direct them to the guilty party. See Vernon R. Dorjahn, "Some Aspects of Temne Divination," *Sierra Leone Bulletin of Religion* 1 (1962): 6.

26. Anonymous member of Rainbow to

author, interview, 16 February 1978.

27. Ibid.

28. Ibid.

29. *Sierra Leone Weekly News,* 22 November 1919, pp. 8–9.

30. Kaka devils conform to neither the fancy nor the fierce aesthetic. They are at odds with the Freetown aesthetic sensibility regarding masquerades and for this reason are free to do as they please.

31. This is the only occasion on which I observed a masquerade from an apartment.

32. See chap. 5.

Chapter 5

1. Banton, *West African City,* p. 173. For further discussion of this subject, see also John Nunley, "The Fancy and the Fierce: Yoruba Masking Traditions of Sierra Leone," *African Arts* 2 (1981): 53–59.

2. Banton, *West African City,* p. 173.

3. R. F. Thompson, *Black Gods and Kings: Yoruba Art at UCLA* (Los Angeles: University of California Press, 1971), chap. 3, p. 2.

4. For a complete discussion of witchcraft among the Temne, see Vernon R. Dorjahn, "Some Aspects of Temne Divination," *Sierra Leone Bulletin of Religion* 4, no. 1, pp. 1–9.

5. J. Warburton, *Missionary Register,* 28 February 1837, p. 423. The elaborately carved masks with bird motifs worn by male masqueraders impersonating females described by Warburton are strong evidence of an early introduction of Gelede into Sierra Leone.

6. John Nunley, "African Art, Sexuality, and Adrogeny," *New Art Examiner* 6 (Summer 1979): 8.

7. The classification of mask costumes by Freetown society members is far from rigid. Mask costumes of one style appear in Hunting, Egungun, and Ode-lay, while certain Gelede costumes appear in other associa-

tions with different functions. The presence of the same type of costume in many societies suggests that another taxonomic principle is at work. See Nunley, "The Fancy and the Fierce," p. 52.

8. Dennis Duerden, *The Invisible Present: African Art and Literature* (New York: Harper & Row, 1975), p. 53.

9. Jack Goody speculated that this hostility toward the ancestors stemmed from ambivalence, and he credited this notion to Freud. See Goody, *Death Property and the Ancestors,* p. 24. Freud explained that "in almost every case where there is an intensive emotional attachment to a particular person we find that behind the tender love there is a concealed hostility in the unconscious." Sigmund Freud, *Totem and Taboo* (New York: W. W. Norton, 1950), p. 60. Thus, he concluded, the closer one is related to the deceased, the greater one's love and also one's hostility. Freud believed that a person who struggled over his mixed feelings for a deceased person was condemned to punish himself ritually for his latent hostile feelings and hidden satisfaction at the person's death. For protection and defense in this emotional tug-of-war, the survivor displaces his own hostility and projects it upon the deceased's spirit. Ibid., p. 61. If we accept a priori Freud's assumption of ambivalence in close human relations, the association with the ancestors of the Egungun, Hunting, and Ode-lay costumes may explain the projected hostile character, namely the fierceness, of these entities. See Nunley, "The Fancy and the Fierce," p. 58.

10. Thompson, *Black Gods and Kings,* chap. 3, p. 5.

11. Peterson, *Province of Freedom,* p. 255.

12. Since the ritual center of the Freetown Hunting societies is Allen Street, it is my speculation that *alan-*

koba is Krio for *Allen cover* or *Allen-style headpiece.*

13. Mike Reed of the Field Museum of Natural History in Chicago has further identified the materials used for Hunting costumes. The skins are from *Viverra civetta* (African civet), *Cercocebus torquatus atys* (Smokey mangabey), and *Tragelaphus scriptus* (bushbuck); the shells from *Achatina achatina* (African land snail) and *Monaria moneta* (money cowrie); and the horns from *Tragelaphus scriptus* and the duiker.

14. Margaret Drewal, "Projections from the Top in Yoruba Art," *African Arts* 1 (1977): 46.

15. Ibid., p. 44.

16. John Pemberton III to John Nunley, 16 April 1980. Pemberton has replaced the term *ancestor* in his teaching with the expression *living dead.* The latter expression describes more accurately the dynamic relationship between the living and the dead.

17. For this description I am indebted to one of Freetown's best lantern builders, an active Egungun and Ode-lay member, who wished to remain anonymous.

18. M. Drewal, "Projections from the Top In Yoruba Art," p. 44.

19. J. L. Dawson, also, notes that the ayogbo devils appear in the Egungun societies of the Temne, their assigned task being to find witches. See J. L. Dawson, "Temne Witchcraft Vocabulary," *Sierra Leone Language Review* 2 (1963): 21.

20. Although the term *ojé* is used synonymously with *Egungun,* it literally means *branch.* Navy Ojé, for example, means Navy branch of Egungun.

21. Ajanioke (The Dog That Flies) to author, interview, spring 1978, Freetown.

22. Duerden, *The Invisible Present,* p. 119.

23. The sea porcupine is also known as the puffer fish. It is used, incidentally, to make a toxic mixture in

Haitian vodun. This medicine causes the victim to take on the likeness of death, whereupon he or she becomes a zombie.

24. Ogun has obtained great popularity in Haiti at the expense of Shango. According to Maya Derin, Shango appeals to the higher-status groups and Ogun to the oppressed. For this reason Ogun is more likely to fulfill a political function in contemporary urban society. Furthermore, Derin's conclusion explains Shango rather than Ogun's popularity in Trinidad, which is considerably wealthier than Haiti. Maya Derin, *Divine Horsemen: The Living Gods of Haiti* (New York: McPherson & Co., 1953), p. 131.

Chapter 6

1. John Nunley, "The Fancy and the Fierce," p. 52.
2. George Mills, "Art: An Introduction to Qualitative Anthropology," in *Art and Aesthetics in Primitive Societies*, ed. C. Jopling (New York: E. P. Dutton, 1971), pp. 76–78.
3. John Nunley, "Ntowie: First Sisala Carver," *African Arts* 13 (1979): 70. The surviving kin of Ntowie made yearly sacrifices to the artist's personal shrine. They consisted of a hoe blade and a carved *kantomung* (fairy or bush spirit), as though farming and carving (taught by the bush spirits) were prudently brought together in the shrine for all Sisala to witness and approve.
4. Peterson, *Province of Freedom*, p. 254.
5. See also chap. 9 below. *Maringa*, which is a transliteration of *meringue*, is discussed by John Chernoff, who noted its popularity among the Dagomba of northern Ghana. See John M. Chernoff, *African Rhythm and African Sensibility* (Chicago: University of Chicago Press, 1980).
6. With an employee of the Sierra

Leone National Museum, Kargbo once established a craft shop oriented to the tourist trade, but the business failed.

7. Like his French counterpart, the bricouleur, Ajani is involved in many semispecialized occupations, and he uses his basic tool kit for all of these pursuits. His reliance on a particular set of tools to solve all building problems brings him, according to Levi-Strauss, to the position of bricouleur. See Claude Levi-Strauss, "The Science of the Concrete," in *Art and Aesthetics in Primitive Societies*, ed. Jopling, pp. 225–49.
8. Ajani to author, interview, spring 1978, Freetown.
9. Marilyn Houlberg, "Ibeji Images of the Yoruba," *African Arts* 7 (1973): 20–27.
10. Ajani to author, letter, 1978. Note the artist's spelling alternative for *igbale* is *egballeh*. Orthography with respect to the secret societies in Freetown is far from systematic.
11. Mammy Wata has become a mainstream icon in African art and ritual. The spirit of this half human, half fish figure often torments men with her overpowering beauty. She occasionally appears to them in dreams. See Jill Salmons, "Mammy Wata," *African Arts* 11 (1977): 8–15. See figure 64 below.
12. Hans Schaal, with a grant from the University of Illinois, worked with Freetown artists during the summer of 1979.
13. See chap. 6 above.
14. See n. 11 above.
15. See plate 4 for an example of this type of Goba's work.
16. Edmund Coker had a collection of illustrations of African sculpture that he cut from selected books on the subject. These prints enabled him to create costumes in a variety of styles and forms.
17. This costume highlighted the Juju Wata masquerade discussed in chap. 8 below.

18. The popularity of film in Freetown has only been hinted at in these pages. The presence of three film posters on the walls of Ajani's studio suggests such an influence. Of intriguing interest is the nature of one of the posters. One film represented, *Terminal Island,* explodes with violence and double standards: purported good guys turn out to be bad guys, and purported bad guys turn out to be good. Its plot is that good overcomes evil, and the ultimate goal sought and achieved lies in the utopian society that emerges in the end. This film corresponds with the Ode-lay acceptance of violence in the fierce aesthetic and suggests a justification of violence in the pursuit of a just society and a better world.

Chapter 7

1. Banton, *West African City,* pp. 165, 166.
2. Ibid.
3. Ibid.
4. Ibid.
5. Ibid., p. 165.
6. Ibid., pp. 166, 167.
7. Judith Bettelheim to author, 19 May 1982. Bettelheim has researched festival arts in West Africa and the Caribbean. On both sides of the Atlantic she has found parallels in artistic motifs, in methods of presentation, and in violence associated with festival arts. Judith Bettelheim, "The Lantern Festival in Senegambia," *African Arts* 18, no. 2 (1985): 50–53, 95–97, 101. John W. Nunley, "The Lantern Festival in Sierra Leone," *African Arts* 18, no. 2 (1985): 45–49, 97, 101.
8. See chap. 3 above.
9. Olufumbe Cole to author, interview, February 1978, Freetown.
10. These song texts were translated from recordings of Egungun and Hunting societies in Freetown by persons who wish to remain anonymous.

11. Matembe to author, interview, 23 May 1978.
12. *A* here may be translated as the personal pronoun I.

Chapter 8

1. See chap. 5 above.
2. See figure 45 for a photograph of this devil created by John Goba.
3. For a description of the preparation of this costume, see the section on Coker and Silla in chap. 6 above.
4. William Siegmann and Judith Perani, "Men's Masquerades of Sierra Leone and Liberia," *African Arts* 9 (1976): 42–47, for further discussion of the role of masquerading at the Kenema fair.
5. See chap. 6, n. 10.
6. See also fig. 62 above.
7. Roger Abrahams, "Toward an Enactment-Centered Theory of Folklore," in *Frontiers of Folklore,* ed. W. Bascom (Boulder, Colo.: Westview Press, 1977), p. 80.
8. Ibid., p. 98.
9. See Mary Douglas, *Purity and Danger* (London: Routledge & Kegan Paul, 1966); Gregory Bateson, *Steps to an Ecology of Mind* (San Francisco: Chandler Publishing Co., 1972).
10. Douglas, *Purity and Danger,* p. 128.
11. Ibid., p. 122.
12. See chap. 6 above for the belief that artist Eku Williams died of a similar malady.
13. The author observed one Egungun performance which on signal of the head drummer came abruptly to an end. The problem was a small opening in the asho of one of the dancers, which made the masquerader vulnerable to fangay poisoning.
14. Abrahams, "Toward an Enactment-Centered Theory of Folklore," p. 105.
15. Bateson, *Steps to an Ecology of Mind,* pp. 178–81.
16. Ibid., p. 182.
17. Ibid., p. 189.

18. Ibid., p. 191.
19. Ibid., p. 183.
20. See chap. 4 above.

Chapter 9

1. John Thompson was a head of Gelede as well as an active Hunting member. In 1978 he served as an elderman on the city council. As herbalist he wore a *lappa* (a calf-length cloth resembling a skirt that wrapped around the waist) and a T-shirt; as councilman he wore a three-piece suit.
2. See chap. 8 above for a discussion of this event.
3. *Sierra Leone Daily Mail*, 28 February 1978.
4. See also chap. 6 above.
5. Jina-musa (spirit of Moses), according to Dorjahn, is a technique employed by diviners to contact spirits, who help them with questions. The diviner invokes the spirits by reciting the Koran while peering into a basin of water and medicine. See Vernon R. Dorjahn, "Temne Divination," p. 7.
6. This is one of many articles written during 1978 about witchcraft as a cause of illness.
7. Johnny Shaft to author, interview, 6 January 1978, Freetown.

Chapter 10

1. Banton, *West African City*, pp. 165, 166.
2. Ibid., p. 176.
3. Ibid., p. 177.
4. Frederick Lamp to author, 1 November 1980. Lamp noted in his fieldwork with the Temne that many of the young men preferred to join the urban Yoruba-based societies that had spread to their area rather than the traditional indigenous organizations.
5. The author was invited to attend this event by a grand patron of the society, the Honorable Alfred Akibo

Betts, special parliamentary assistant to the Ministry of Social Welfare.
6. Walter Barrows, *Grassroots Politics in an African State: Integration and Development in Sierra Leone* (New York: Africana Publishing Co., 1976), p. 170.
7. Ibid., p. 172.

Chapter 11

1. James Fernandez, "African Religious Movements: The Worst or Best of All Possible Microcosms," *Issue* 4 (1978): 50-53. Fernandez discusses the various positions ruling elites may take in regard to the expressive and instrumental African ritual associations. He points out that a large number of governments have exploited such groups to solidify their rule. The Ode-lay societies meet both the expressive and instrumental needs of their members and, as such, constitute a potentially powerful force in national politics. They are needed currently by the APC, yet the party fears them. What one might term a tiger-by-the-tail relationship prevails between the Ode-lay societies and the government.
2. Ranger, *Dance and Society in Eastern Africa*, pp. 164-66.
3. Ibid., p. 164.
4. For a detailed discussion of this aspect of Islamic doctrine, see René A. Bravmann, *Islam and Tribal Art in West Africa* (London: Cambridge University Press, 1974); Joseph Greenberg, *The Religion of Sudanese Culture as Influenced by Islam* (Ph.D. diss., Northwestern University, 1941).
5. G. T. Coker, Minutes submitted 17 November 1977, Freetown, S.L., mimeographed and distributed to members of Paddle, Firestone, and Bloody Mary societies. See app. 4 for complete document.
6. "Bloody Mary Arrested," *Sierra Leone Daily Mail*, 23 November 1977.

7. Several executive committeemen expressed this elitist point of view during Paddle meetings attended by the author.

8. See chap. 9 above for a discussion of this event.

9. Public Order Act 46, Freetown, S.L., 1965, sec. 17(2).

10. See chap. 9 above for a discussion of this incident.

11. See n. 9 above.

12. The APC again refused to issue masking permits in Freetown during 1980; however, Ode-lay performances were held in secondary towns. John Goba and other Freetown artists were kept busy with commissions from these outlying areas. John Goba to John Nunley, October 1980.

Chapter 12

1. John W. Nunley, "Sikilen: Transformation of a Sisala Masquerade," *African Arts* 11, no. 1 (1977): 62.

2. William Butler Yeats, *The Second Coming*, in *The Collected Poems of William Butler Yeats* (New York: Macmillan Publishing Co., 1924).

3. For an excellent discussion of the writing of Armah and the new African literature, see William Cook, "What Rough Beast: Neo-African Literature and the Force of Social Change," *Issue: A Quarterly Journal of Africanist Opinion* 8 (1978): 53–59.

4. Ibid., p. 54.

5. Walter Barrows, *Grassroots Politics in an African State: Integration and Development in Sierra Leone* (New York: Africana Publishing Co., 1976), p. 262.

6. See chap. 2, p. 49.

7. See chap. 1, p. 35.

8. See chap. 1, n. 11.

Glossary

agbaru agbadu According to some informants, the phrase means *black snake*. An Egungun masker whose fierce costume is similar to that of the Hunting society maskers.

agbo The Yoruba word for *ram*, the preferred sacrificial animal in the Egungun cult. The name of the area designated for Egungun masquerade dancing.

agoogoo A double-gong instrument used by mailo jazz bands; it is attached at the waist of the performer.

ahada or àrá The axe or hammer carried by the Egungun masquerader agbaru agbadu.

aja The Yoruba word for *dog*; it is used to describe the iron hand-rattles played by Gelede masqueraders.

ajade A Hunting society officer.

ajo or ejò The word for *snake*.

Aku The term that describes the early Yoruba settlers of Muslim faith in Freetown; it also means *dead man*.

alabukun An elaborately dressed fancy Egungun masquerader.

alé or alay A medicine referred to as *skin poiler* (skin spoiler); it is used by Hunting and Egungun masqueraders to destroy the skin of competitors.

Alikali A word used to describe Muslim leaders and counselors of Freetown who in the 1930s formed dance groups that evolved into masquerades called by the same name.

Ambas Geda A phrase meaning *we are together*; it became the name of associations composed of Temne and other local ethnic groups that appeared in Freetown in the 1930s.

Arishola	A secret society known for its fancy masquerade costumes.
ashigba	The leader of the Hunting society.
ashoebi or ashorbi	A term that in Yoruba means *we of one dress;* a Krio expression denoting uniform dress of masquerade society members.
asusu	A small banking institution whose members contribute to a rotating fund; it appeared in Sierra Leone after 1808 with the arrival of the first Yoruba expatriots.
Awodie	The Yoruba word for *hawk (Elanus caeruleus)*; it is the name of one of the oldest and most prestigious Egungun societies in Freetown, which is composed mainly of Muslims of Yoruba descent.
awoko	The leader of the Egungun chorus.
ayogbo	The Yoruba word *arugbo* means *old woman* and may be the source of the Krio term *ayogbo,* which is the name of an antiwitchcraft mask used in some Egungun societies especially among the Temne; old women are frequently charged with witchcraft.
babalowu	The term used by Creoles to describe a diviner.
bass box	An instrument modeled after the hi-fi baffle box and used in mailo jazz ensembles.
bila man	The Hunting and Ode-lay masquerader's escort who carries a carved gun to protect the performers.
campin	The term derives from the French word for *company;*[1] it denoted urban associations established in Freetown after World War I.
caroling	The early morning masquerades that announce the main day celebrations of the Egungun, Hunting, and Ode-lay societies.
dada	Long tightly coiled curls displayed by some males who are said to have spiritual powers.
devil or debil	The word adopted by the early black settlers of Sierra Leone, where it is still in current use.
digba	An officer of the women's Bundu or Bondo society most commonly found among the Mende of Sierra Leone.
djiamba or diamba	The term widely used to denot marijuana (*Cannabis sativa*).

egun or eégũ	A term that is interchangeable with *egungun* or *egugu;* it is the general name for Egungun masquerade types.
Egungun society	A masquerade society that originated with the Yoruba of Nigeria and is dedicated to the ancestors.
e ya aga	The female head of the Gelede society in Sierra Leone.
fangay	A type of bad medicine that afflicts the skin of its victims.
freethinkers	Individuals who borrow from African, Islamic, and Christian traditions to form their own world views and philosophies.
Gbagbani	The Limba men's initiation society.
gongoli	A Mende clown masquerader who is identified by a large and often grotesquely carved face mask.
Hunting society	The Freetown association dedicated to the Yoruba god of iron, Ogun, who is the patron saint of hunters.
igbale	The Hunting shrine house in which the head of a dog or ram is buried in honor of Ogun.
Jinna musa	A divination ritual in which a diviner employs reflective sources, such as mirrors or water, to find a guilty party.
juju	The Krio term for secret society medicine.
juweni man	A diviner who is well versed in malevalent medicines.
kaka devil	In Krio literally *shit devil;* a clown who, dressed in rags and wearing an ugly face mask, usually appears before Ode-lay masquerades accompanied by an attendant who gathers money from his performance.
kola nut	Cola acuminata, a white or red nut with high caffeine content that is chewed to curb the appetite while supplying quick energy; it is a common sacrifice to the ancestors and to Ogun and is also given to visitors as a token of hospitality. Kola nuts may symbolize Shango, whose colors are red and white.
Lanterns	The name of the festival marking the end of Ramadan in which floatlike constructions called lanterns are paraded on the streets.
mailo jazz	A contemporary urban musical ensemble apparently indigenous to Sierra Leone.
mammy queen	A female officer of the Ode-lay society.
Maroon	A free man of African descent recruited by the British from Jamaica to help maintain order in Sierra Leone in the early days of the colony.

Ode-lay or Odé-lay society	The term *odé* among Nigerian Yorubas means *hunter*—literally *animal or fish catcher;* hence Ode-lay may be translated as hunter's lay society, although this interpretation was not common in Freetown. Ode-lay is the term currently used to describe the young men's masquerade societies that are based on the original Yoruba associations.
Ogboni	A secret society of a highly political order in Yorubaland, Nigeria; to the Creole of Sierra Leone it denotes simply a big or important man.
ojofoembo	In Krio literally *a white man;* it denotes a particular Egungun masquerader who wears a red and white cloth cover.
okosha	A clown devil appearing in Egungun societies of Freetown.
oku or òkú	A dead man or corpse; also a man's ghost.
olukortu	An officer in the Egungun and Ode-lay societies whose Western homologue might be described as the secretary.
omoli	Distilled gin made in the Freetown area.
onifakun	The Yoruba word *onifegu,* to which this term may be related, means *one making medicine.*[2] *Onifakun* denotes the person who dances in a masquerade costume; such persons have strong medicinal powers and great athletic abilities.
oogun or oogu	A general term that describes secret-society medicine.
orbeh or obe	A term meaning *knife;* it was the original name of the Rainbow Ode-lay Society.
Oru	A society of a highly secretive order said to be ancestral and to have originated with the Yoruba of Nigeria. Women, children, and foreigners are sequestered in their rooms when this society performs in the King Tom area of Freetown; any such witnesses may be stoned to death.
oywa	A medicine used in the Gelede antiwitchcraft society.
pan-bodi ose	A Krio term for houses made of sheet metal and flattened metal scraps nailed over balanced wooden frames; these structures provide housing for migrants in Freetown.
Poro	This term denotes the rural men's societies of various ethnic groups in Sierra Leone and Liberia.
ronko or uronko[3]	A type of sleeveless smock made of strips of cloth woven on a vertical loom and sewn together; among the Limba it is printed with designs that give it magical powers and protect the wearer from witchguns. Egungun and Hunting masqueraders often wear this garment under their dance costumes for protection.

saddaka   A sacrifice to the ancestors performed in Egungun, Hunting, and Ode-lay societies.

Shango   The Yoruba god of thunder and reportedly the fourth king of the Yoruba people. Well known in nineteenth-century Freetown, Shango is no longer recognized there; but evidence suggests that this deity may have been subsumed by Ogun.

shegita   A Krio term meaning *scattered nuts;* it refers to complex dance steps of Egungun masqueraders, which are likened to the random patterns formed by nuts thrown on the ground.

soweh or sawéh   Medicines made of herbs and water used by secret-society members to protect themselves and their masqueraders from witches, diviners, and others in control of magical forces.

Wende   An alternative name for women's Bundo or Bondo society.

witchgun   A weapon purportedly used by witches to kill adversaries and victims of a client's choice. In Freetown it is usually described as a peanut or coconut that shoots a needle from within, the projectile entering the victim's stomach, causing it to swell, killing him. The Limba describe it as a horn that shoots rice. This is the most frequently cited cause of death in cases where medicine or foul play is suspected.

Glossary Notes

1. Michael Banton.
2. Robert G. Armstrong, "Comparative Word Lists of Two Dialects of Yoruba and Ingala," *Journal of West African Languages* 11, no. 2 (1965): 51–78, at 60.

3. Uronko is the term used by Joseph A. Opala (personal communication, Apr. 1983).

Bibliography

Unpublished Sources

Cannizzo, Jeanne. "Alikali Devils: Children's Masquerades in a West African Town." Ph.D. dissertation, University of Washington, Seattle.

E. O. J. Untitled history of Hastings, Sierra Leone, pages 3–30, dated December 1948. Manuscript.

Freetown Police. Permits and regulations for masked devil processions and masked demonstrations. Police headquarters, Freetown.

Methodist Missionary Society. Correspondence arranged chronologically. Boxes 279–86. School of Oriental and African Studies, London.

Public Record Office. Correspondence. Boxes CO 267, CO 270-71, CO 275, CO 279, and CO 323. Kew Gardens, London.

Turay, H., and Abraham, A. "Catalog of Sierra Leone—Arts and Crafts." Museum of African Art, Washington, D.C. Typescript.

Wright, Joseph. "Life of Joseph Wright: A Native Ackoo," 26 June 1839. Manuscript. See Methodist Missionary Society above. Box 280, file 3, no. 13.

Books

Achebe, Chinua. *Things Fall Apart*. New York: Astor-Honor, 1959.

Amin, Samir. *Neo-Colonialism in West Africa*. New York: Monthly Review Press, 1974.

Armah, Ayi Kwei. *The Beautyful Ones Are Not Yet Born*. New York: Collier Books, 1969.

Banbury, G. A. L. *Sierra Leone; or, The White Man's Grave*. London, 1881.

Banton, Michael. *West African City: A Study of Tribal Life in Freetown*. London: Oxford University Press, 1957.

Barrows, Walter. *Grassroots Politics in an African State: Integration and Development in Sierra Leone*. New York and London: Africana Publishing Co., 1976.

Bascom, William. *Shango in the New World.* Austin: African and Afro-American Research Institute, University of Texas, 1972.

————. *The Yoruba of Southwest Nigeria: A Study in Cultural Anthropology.* New York: Holt, Rinehart & Winston, 1969.

Bateson, Gregory. *Steps to an Ecology of Mind.* San Francisco: Chandler Publishing Co., 1972.

Biebuyck, Daniel P. *Tradition and Creativity in Tribal Art.* Berkeley: University of California Press, 1969.

Blier, Susan P. *Beauty and the Beast.* New York: Tribal Arts Gallery, 1976.

Booth, Richard. *The Armed Forces of African States, 1970.* Adelphi Papers, no. 67. London: Institute for Strategic Studies, 1970.

Bravmann, René A. *Islam and Tribal Art in West Africa.* London: Cambridge University Press, 1974.

Cartwright, John R. *Political Leadership in Sierra Leone.* Toronto: University of Toronto Press, 1978.

————. *Politics in Sierra Leone, 1947–67.* Toronto: University of Toronto Press, 1970.

Chernoff, John M. *African Rhythm and African Sensibility.* Chicago: University of Chicago Press, 1980.

Cohen, Abner. *The Politics of Elite Culture: Explorations in the Dramaturgy of Power in a Modern African Society.* Berkeley: University of California Press, 1981.

Cole, Robert Wellesley. *Kossoh Town Boy.* Cambridge: Macmillan, 1960.

Cox, S. Thomas. *Civil-military Relations in Sierra Leone.* Cambridge: Harvard University Press, 1976.

Curtin, Philip. *Africa Remembered: Narratives by West Africans from the Era of the Slave Trade.* Madison: University of Wisconsin Press, 1967.

Deren, Maya. *Divine Horsemen: The Living Gods of Haiti.* New York: McPherson & Company, 1953.

Douglas, Mary. *Purity and Danger.* London: Routledge & Kegan Paul, 1966.

Duerden, Dennis. *The Invisible Present: African Art and Literature.* New York: Harper & Row, 1975.

Durkheim, Emile. *Division of Labor in Society.* New York: Macmillan Co., 1933.

————. *The Elementary Forms of Religious Life: A Study in Religious Society.* Glencoe, Ill.: Free Press, 1947.

duToit, Brian M. *Ethnicity in Modern Africa.* Boulder, Colo.: Westview Press, 1978.

Ellis, A. B. *The Yoruba-speaking Peoples of the Slave Coast of West Africa.* London: Chapman & Hall, 1894.

Fanon, Frantz. *The Wretched of the Earth.* New York: Grove Press, 1965.

Feit, Edward. *The Armed Bureaucrats: Military-administrative Regimes and Political Development.* Boston: Houghton Mifflin Co., 1973.

Finnegan, Ruth. *Survey of the Limba People of Northern Sierra Leone.* London: Her Majesty's Stationery Office, 1965.

First, Ruth. *The Barrel of a Gun: Political Power in Africa and the Coup d'Etat.* London: Allen Lane, Penguin Press, 1970.

Fowler-Lunn, Katharine. *The Gold Missus: A Woman Prospector in Sierra Leone.* New York: W. W. Norton & Co., 1938.

Freud, Sigmund. *Totem and Taboo.* New York: W. W. Norton & Co., 1950.

Fyfe, Christopher. *A Short History of Sierra Leone.* London: Longman, 1962.

————, and Jones, Eldred, eds. *Freetown: A Symposium.* Freetown: Sierra Leone University Press, 1968.

Goody, Jack. *Death, Property, and the Ancestors: A Study of the Mortuary Customs of the Lodagaa of West Africa.* Stanford: Stanford University Press, 1962.

Greenberg, Joseph Harold. *The Influence of Islam on a Sudanese Religion.* New York: J. J. Augustin, 1946.

Greene, Graham. *The Heart of the Matter.* New York: Viking Press, 1948.

————. *Journey without Maps.* Garden City, N.Y.: Doubleday, Doran, & Co., 1936.

Gutteridge, William F. *Armed Forces in New States.* London and New York: Oxford University Press, for the Institute of Race Relations, 1962.

Herskovits, Melville J. *Dahomey: An Ancient West African Kingdom.* Vols. 1 and 2. New York: J. J. August, 1938.

Hommel, William L. *Art of the Mende.* College Park: University of Maryland, 1974.

Kilson, M. *Political Change in a West African State.* Cambridge: Harvard University Press, 1966.

Kopytoff, Jean Herskovits. *A Preface to Modern Nigeria: The "Sierra Leonians" in Yoruba, 1830–1890.* Madison: University of Wisconsin Press, 1965.

Lamp, Frederick. *African Art of the West Atlantic Coast.* New York: L. Kahan Gallery, 1979.

Little, Kenneth. *West African Urbanization: A Study of Voluntary Associations in Social Change.* Cambridge: Cambridge University Press, 1965.

Naipaul, V. S. *A Bend in the River.* New York: Knopf, 1979.

Newland, H. Osman. *Sierra Leone: Its People, Products, and Secret Societies.* Westport, Conn.: Negro Universities Press, 1969.

Nunley, John. *Sisala Sculpture of Northern Ghana.* Ann Arbor: University Microfilms, 1977.

————, and Schaal, Hans. *Reflections of African Artistry.* Chicago: University of Illinois, 1981.

Ojo, G. *Yoruba Culture.* Ife: University of Ife and University of London Press, 1966.

Ottenberg, Simon. *Masked Rituals of Afikpo: The Context of an African Art.* Seattle: University of Washington Press, 1975.

Peterson, John. *Province of Freedom: A History of Sierra Leone, 1787–1870.* London: Faber & Faber, 1969.

Ranger, T. O. *Dance and Society in Eastern Africa, 1890–1970: The Beningoma.* Berkeley: University of California Press, 1975.

Sandoval, Mercedes C., and Poyner, Robin. *Thunder over Miami: Ritual Objects of Nigerian and AfroCuban Religion.* Miami: University of Florida, 1982.

Schuler, Monica. *"Alas, Alas, Kongo": A Social History of Indentured African Immigration into Jamaica, 1841–1865.* Baltimore: Johns Hopkins University Press, 1980.

Spencer, Sue. *African Creeks I Have Been Up.* New York: David McKay Co., n.d.

Spitzer, Leo. *The Creoles of Sierra Leone: Responses to Colonialism, 1870–1945.* Madison: University of Wisconsin Press, 1974.

Thompson, Robert F. *African Art in Motion.* Berkeley: University of California Press, 1974.

————. *Black Gods and Kings: Yoruba Art at UCLA.* Los Angeles: University of California Press, 1971.

Articles

Abrahams, Roger. "Toward an Enactment-centered Theory of Folklore." In *Frontiers of Folklore,* edited by W. Bascom, 79–120. Boulder, Colo.: Westview Press, 1977.

Allen, Christopher. "Sierra Leone." In *West African States: Failure and Promise,* edited by John Dunn, 189–210. London: Cambridge University Press, 1978.

————. "Sierra Leone Politics since Independence." *African Affairs* 67 (October 1968): 305–29.

Bettelheim, Judith. "The Lantern Festival in Senegambia." *African Arts* 18, no. 2 (1985): 50–53.

Borgatti, Jean M. "Dead Mothers of Okpella." *African Arts* 12, no. 4 (1979): 48–57, 91–92.

Cannizzo, Jeanne. "Alikali Devils of Sierra Leone." *African Arts* 12, no. 4 (1979): 64–70, 92.

Carpenter, Edmund. "Comments." In *Tradition and Creativity in Tribal Art,* edited by Biebuyck, 203–13. See Biebuyck under Books above.

Church, Mary (pseud.). "Liberated Africans." *In a Series of Letters from a Young Lady to Her Sister in 1832–1834.* London, 1835.

Clifford, James. "On Ethnographic Surrealism." *Comparative Studies in Society and History* 23, no. 1 (1981): 539–64.

Cook, William. "What Rough Beast: Neo-African Literature and the Force of Social Change." *Issue* 8, no. 4 (1978): 53–59.

Curtin, Philip. "Joseph Wright of the Egba." in *Africa Remembered: Narratives by West Africans from the Era of the Slave Trade,* edited by Philip Curtin, 317–33. Madison: University of Wisconsin Press, 1967.

Dalby, David. "The Military Takeover in Sierra Leone, 1967." *World Today* 23 (August 1967): 354–60.

Dawson, F. L. "Temne Witchcraft Vocabulary." *Sierra Leone Language Review* 2 (1963): 16–22.

Devereux, George. "Art and Mythology: A General Theory." In *Art and Aesthetics in Primitive Societies,* edited by C. Jopling, 183–224. New York: E. P. Dutton, 1971.

Dorjahn, Vernon R. "Some Aspects of Temne Divination." *Sierra Leone Bulletin of Religion* 4, no. 1: 1–9.

Drewal, Margaret. "Projections from the Top in Yoruba Art." *African Arts* 11, no. 1 (1977): 43–49, 91–92.

————, and Drewal, Henry. "More Powerful Than Each Other: An Egbado Classification of Egungun." *African Arts* 11, no. 3 (1978): 28–39, 98–99.

Easmon, M. C. F. "Madam Yoko, Ruler of the Mende Confederacy." *Sierra Leone Studies* 11 (December 1958): 165–68.

Fernandez, James. "African Religious Movements: The Worst or the Best of All Possible Microcosms." *Issues* 8, no. 4 (1978): 50–53.

Fyfe, C. H. "The Sierra Leone Press in the Nineteenth Century." *Sierra Leone Studies* 1 (June 1957): 226–36.

————. "European and Creole Influence in the Hinterland of Sierra Leone before 1896." *Sierra Leone Studies* 6 (June 1956): 10–23.

Ghazali, A. K. "Sierra Leone Muslims and Sacrificial Rituals." *Sierra Leone Bulletin of Religion* 2, no. 1 (1960): 27–32.

Glickman, Harvey. "The Military in African Politics: A Bibliographic Essay," *African Forum* 2, no. 1 (1966): 68–75.

Harvey, Milton. "Planning Problems in Freetown." In *Freetown: A Symposium*, 179–95. See Fyfe and Jones under Books above.

Houlberg, Marilyn, "Egungun Masquerades of the Remo Yoruba." *African Arts* 11, no. 3 (1978): 20–27, 100.

————. "Ibeji Images of the Yoruba." *African Arts* 7, no. 1 (1973): 20–27.

Iris, Kay. "FESTAC 1977." *African Arts* 11, no. 1 (1977): 50–51.

Kirk-Greene, Anthony. "David George: The Nova Scotian Experience." *Sierra Leone Studies* 14 (December 1960): 93–120.

Kreutzinger, H. "The Eri Devil in Freetown, Sierra Leone." *ACTA Ethnologica* 9 (1966).

Levi-Strauss, Claude. "The Science of the Concrete." In *Art and Aesthetics in Primitive Societies*, edited by C. Jopling, 225–49. See Devereux, George, above.

Little, K. "The Political Function of the Poro." *Africa* 35 (1965): 349–65; 36 (1966): 62–71.

————. "The Significance of the West African Creole for Africanists and Afro-American Studies." *African Affairs* 49 (October 1950): 308–19.

Mills, George. "Art: An Introduction to Qualitative Anthropology, Art, and Aesthetics in Primitive Societies." In *Art and Aesthetics in Primitive Societies*, edited by C. Jopling, 76–78. See Devereux, George, above.

Mitchell, Peter K. "Eighteenth and Nineteenth Century Printed Maps of Sierra Leone: A Preliminary Listing," *Sierra Leone Studies* 22 (January 1968): 60–83.

Morton-Williams, Peter. "The Egungun Society in South-western Yoruba Kingdoms." In *Proceedings of the Third Annual Conference of the West African Institute of Social and Economic Research*, 90–103. Ibadan: University College, 1956.

Nicol, Abioseh. "West Indians in West Africa." *Sierra Leone Studies* 13 (June 1960): 14–23.

Nunley, John. "The Lantern Festival in Sierra Leone." *African Arts* 18, no. 2 (1985): 45–49.

————. "Images and Printed Words in Freetown Masquerades." *African Arts* 15, no. 4 (1982): 42–46, 92.

————. "The Fancy and the Fierce: Yoruba Masking Tradition of Sierra Leone." *African Arts* 14, no. 2 (1981): 52–59, 87.

————. "Ntowie: First Sisala Carver." *African Arts* 13, no. 1 (1979): 68–73, 98.

————. "African Art, Sexuality, and Androgeny." *New Art Examiner* 6, no. 10 (1979): 8.

————. "Implications of the African Aesthetic Impulse for Pan-African Art." *New Art Examiner* 6, no. 7 (1979): 4, 9.

Ogunlusi, Jola. "Igunnuko Festival." *African Arts* 4, no. 4 (1971): 60–61.

Olu-Wright, R. J. "The Physical Growth of Freetown." In *Freetown: A Symposium,* 24–37. See Fyfe and Jones under Books above.

Ottenberg, Simon. "Illusion, Communication, and Psychology in West African Masquerades." *ETHOS* 10, no. 2 (1982): 149–85.

Porter, Arthur T. "Religious Affiliation in Freetown, Sierra Leone." *Africa* 23, no. 1 (1953): 3–14.

Proudfoot, L. "Towards Muslim Solidarity in Freetown." *Africa* 31 (1961): 147–57.

————. "Mosque-building and Tribal Separatism in Freetown East." *Africa* 29 (1959): 405–16.

Richards, J. V. Olufemi. "The Sande: A Socio-cultural Organization in the Mende Community of Sierra Leone." *Braessler Archive* 22 (1971): 65–281.

Salmons, Jill. "Mammy Wata." *African Arts* 11, no. 3 (1977): 8–15, 87.

Sawyer, Harry. "Traditional Sacrificial Rituals and Christian Worship." *Sierra Leone Bulletin of Religion* 2, no. 1 (1960): 18–27.

Schiltz, Marc. "Egungun Masquerades in Iganna." *African Arts* 11, no. 3 (1978): 48–55, 100.

Siegmann, William, and Perani, Judith. "Men's Masquerades of Sierra Leone and Liberia." *African Arts* 9, no. 3 (1976): 42–47, 92.

Sprague, Stephen F. "Yoruba Photography: How the Yoruba See Themselves." *African Arts* 12, no. 1 (1978): 52–59, 107.

Swindell, Kenneth. "Mining Workers in Sierra Leone: Their Stability and Marital Status." *African Affairs* 74 (1975): 180–90.

Van Oven, Cootje. "Music of Sierra Leone." *African Arts* 3, no. 4 (1970): 20–27, 71.

Warren, Harold G. "Secret Societies." *Sierra Leone Studies* 3 (1919): 8–12.

Wiseberg, Laurie. "Human Rights in Africa: Toward a Definition of the Problem of a Double Standard." *Issue* 6, no. 4 (1976): 3–13.

Miscellaneous

The Church Missionary Gleaner. Annual bound volumes. Church Missionary Society, London.

The Church Missionary Register. 1828–53. Church Missionary Society, London.

The Gleaner Pictorial Album. Vol. 1. London: Church Missionary House, 1887.

Film Facts 16, no. 2. New York: Association for the Center for Understanding Media, 1973.

Media Review Digest. Part 1. Ann Arbor: Pierian Press, 1975–76.

Report of Commission of Inquiry into Disturbances in the Provinces, November 1955, March 1956. London: Crown Agents, for the Sierra Leone Government, n.d.

Phonograph Records

Cliff, Jimmy. *The Harder They Come.* Hollywood: Mango Records, Irving Music Co., 1972. SMAS 7400.

Marley, Bob. *Burnin'*. Los Angeles: Island Records, Caymon Music Co., 1973. ILPS 9256.

Newspapers

The Daily Mail (Sierra Leone), in the 1950s renamed *Sierra Leone Daily Mail*.
Sierra Leone Weekly News.
We Yone and *Sunday We Yone* (Sierra Leone).

Index

About the Author

John Nunley first studied the art of traditional West African cultures in 1972–73 among the Sisala people in rural Ghana. He found that colonization and slave raids had had a devastating effect on Sisala sculpture and that few sculptors were left. He then researched the role of traditional arts in the modern urban setting, primarily in Freetown. This work disclosed that much of the base of the traditional masquerade societies and their urban offshoots derived from the Yoruba of Nigeria who had settled Freetown in 1807.

His interest in the spread of Yoruba culture continues with his organization of Caribbean Festival Arts, a major traveling exhibit scheduled to open at the Saint Louis Art Museum in 1988. For this project Nunley lived and studied in Trinidad, a community with a strong Yoruba base; in Nassau, the Bahamas, and Jamaica; as well as in North American cities. This work has taken him to the masquerade festivals of Miami, Toronto, and Brooklyn, and his coresearchers to London, New Orleans, and Cuba.

Nunley is currently curator of the arts of Africa, Oceania, and the Americas at the Saint Louis Art Museum. He has taught these subjects at the University of Illinois at Chicago, the Field Museum of Natural History, and Washington University in St. Louis.